Shopping For a Shrink: Finding the Right Psychotherapist For You or Your Child

Sound Advice and Stories to Change Your Life

Also by Stanley Goldstein

Nonfiction

Troubled Children/Troubled Parents
2nd Edition

Fiction

Lies In Progress

Park West:
A Novel of Love and Murder and Redemption

Ghosts And Angels: A Memoir
How, During An Epoch Of Terror,
Goodness Vanquished Evil And Restored Faith

STANLEY GOLDSTEIN

Shopping For a Shrink: Finding the Right Psychotherapist For You or Your Child

Sound Advice and Stories to Change Your Life

WYSTON BOOKS, INC.

WYSTON BOOKS, INC.
P. O. Box 1280
Warwick, NY 10990-1280

Tel.: (845) 986-6888
E-mail: askus@wystonbooks.com
Please visit our website: www.wystonbooks.com

Identifying characteristics not essential to understanding the condition and course of treatment of patients described in this work have been changed to assure their anonymity.

Goldstein, Stanley
Shopping For A Shrink: Finding the Right
Psychotherapist For You Or Your Child
Sound Advice And Stories To Change Your Life
First Edition
Includes bibliographical references

Library of Congress Subject Headings
1. Psychotherapy
2. Psychotherapist and Patient
3. Child Psychotherapy
4. Adolescent Psychotherapy
5. Adult Psychotherapy
6. Marriage Counseling
7. Consumer Education

Library of Congress Control Number: 2010941595
ISBN 978-0-9717705-5-3 (print)
ISBN 978-0-9717705-0-8 (E-book)

Cover photograph by Adam Gault/Digital Vision/ Licensed from Getty Images.

What men have seen they know;
But what shall come hereafter
No man before the event can see,
Nor what end waits for him.
—Sophocles, *Ajax*

Contents

Introduction

"How do you tell a good therapist from the bad?"

P<small>AT WAS MY LAST PATIENT</small> and arrived late. She was thirty-two, worked as a computer systems analyst, and began crying as soon as I closed the door. Her marriage was crumbling, her boss and young daughter were impossible, and she got a ticket while driving to my office. It hadn't been a good day or week or year for her.

She consulted another therapist* before me, fleeing after twenty-three sessions in his antique filled office. "It shattered me," she said. "What he did was anti-therapy. He made me worse." "Why did you wait so long before leaving?" I asked. Pat thought for a moment before answering. "I don't know anything about therapy. How do you tell a good therapist from the bad?"

I treated Pat, then her and her husband together. Later I treated their five year old daughter, who was a delight. Long afterward, Pat's question lingered in my mind: With all the intimidating jargon, how can the ordinary person choose an effective therapist?

*Throughout this book the term "therapist" refers to "psychotherapist" though other professionals also use this noun (physical therapist, occupational therapist, respiratory therapist, etc.)

Not by going with the largest, most impressive Yellow Pages ad for marketing skill and expense have nothing to do with competence in therapy. Nor does being widely known or belonging to a professional organization. Reputation is based on the research published or job title, not skill as a therapist which no group measures.

What every buyer of therapy wants is for their problem to be quickly explained, in ordinary language so it makes sense; and then to be helped with changing their life or that of their child. This therapy—effective therapy—is priceless. Though costing less than the exorbitant fees charged by some.

This book enables you to gain value for your money. More expensive is not necessarily better, as readers of *Consumer Reports* know and Pat discovered. But even knowledgeable therapists can have difficulty gaining effective treatment. One psychoanalyst, after being warned of the dire consequences were she to discontinue her treatment, wrote, "In retrospect, fleeing that analysis was one of the healthiest steps I took in my life." Another psychoanalyst described his treatment experience: "Luckily, in later therapies...I was able or enabled to break out of these deathlike hours on the couch."*

*Berman, Emanuel, Others' Failures—And One's Own. In Reppen, Joseph and Schulman, Martin A., *Failures in Psychoanalytic Treatment*, International Universities Press, Madison, CT, 2002, p. 265. This is a valuable book; the paper by Ann-Louise S. Silver, M.D., Thorns in the Rose Garden: Failures at Chestnut Lodge, is particularly moving (pp. 37-62).

Though simply written, the information in this book is sophisticated. And, because people tend to forget facts but remember stories, many anecdotes are included. Some you may find unforgettable. Like those of the abused American wife who, along with her children, was forced to hide in a deserted apartment in Iraqi occupied Kuwait; and the reformed ex-member of the Witness Protection Program who again hungered for his pistol.

Here, there is drama. But no greater than is present in any life were it to be closely studied. As psychotherapists have the privilege of doing.

Read how the lives of these women, men, and children were changed. And yours will be too.

Chapter One

When Psychotherapists Are Toxic:
Melanie and Hugh, In Crisis

Melanie

MELANIE FELT DEPRESSED. So would anyone living her life, she thought. She had been forty for three days. As a Budding Senior Citizen, she wondered if the AARP had a special membership category for her. She knew this was a crazy thought but it was how she felt. Unmarried and childless, living in a small Manhattan apartment, she had always feared this would be her fate.

On her thirty-fifth birthday, Melanie vowed to kill herself if she wasn't married within five years. Now, this Friday evening in early November, it was time to act.

Leaving her office, Melanie carried her black Cross briefcase and laptop case, the common accessories of tax lawyers. Her firm was the first to move from downtown Wall Street to Madison Avenue, so she could avoid the subway and walk to work. Drifting slowly along the eight blocks to her apartment, her final trip she told herself, she watched children beside their mothers. Eavesdropping, and wishing that they were her's. "Hold my hand when we cross the street." "Right after you do your homework, dear."

And, what hurt most, the declaration from a man to his companion: "I adore you." Yet I'm so much prettier, Melanie thought. She puzzled over her lonely life and remembered the opening line from a trashy novel, *Peyton Place*, which she found in the back of a closet and devoured when she was twelve: "Indian summer is like a woman, ripe and passionate." Not anymore—it's over, she thought.

Melanie returned the doorman's greeting with a tight smile and rode the empty elevator to her apartment. There, she flung her briefcase into a corner and barely kept herself from doing the same with her laptop. Though what does it matter now, she told herself as she undressed, consumed by the thought that she would soon be dead without ever having loved.

Even her hot shower, an after-work ritual, couldn't dissolve this obsession. Fearing that she might change her mind, Melanie quickly grabbed the vial of Xanax from the night table and the unopened bottle of limited edition malt Scotch from a kitchen cabinet. The bottle she was saving for her engagement party which never arrived.

Melanie's parents were dead and she hadn't spoken with her brother in four years. No one would mourn her. As she considered this, tears began flowing. First singly, then in rivers. Her body convulsed with emotion as she threw herself onto the bed before falling into a deep sleep.

Melanie was less depressed when she awoke seven hours later, to begin another of her lonely weekends. Hours filled with Yoga classes, rented movies, and unneeded shopping. During the 11PM news on Sunday, while Melanie congratulated herself on having survived another weekend, she again began thinking that her life was meaningless and she would be better off dead. Rousing herself, Melanie flushed the Xanax down the toilet and grabbed the Yellow

Pages, remembering that several co-workers had credited psychotherapy for their happiness and marriage.

As Melanie scanned the ads for a therapist her depression lifted—as it always did when she became involved in a project. One ad caught her attention: "Specializing in Love Relationships. Trained at Ivy League Universities. Evening Appointments Available." The words "love" and "Ivy League" seemed to speak directly to Melanie, who graduated from Harvard.

Melanie dialed the doctor's number. She was impressed that he was automatically paged and returned her phone message quickly though it was Sunday night. He scheduled her appointment for Monday evening.

. The doctor's hushed waiting room was a welcome retreat from the noise of the city. He was in his fifties, gray haired and of average height. His black suit and striped Guardsman tie bespoke solemnity. He greeted Melanie with a warm handshake. When she described being lonely, the doctor smilingly responded, "I can help you with that."

Leaving his office, Melanie felt hopeful. Probably because I spoke so openly, she told herself.

Hugh

Unlike Melanie, Hugh was married and had children. He was one of the few workers with a college degree at the auto plant he worked. Because of his education and seriousness he was repeatedly offered promotion to a foreman's job. But he always turned it down, not wanting to have to judge his co-workers. Particularly those who made his role as union shop steward nearly impossible. "Goof-off" was the least colorful adjective he applied to them.

He tried ignoring them but they wouldn't let up and harassed him by sabotaging his work. Once they stole equipment and placed suspicion for the theft on him. Which the plant manager refused to believe. Were Hugh less resolute he would have quit his job. Instead, at his wife's suggestion, he told their family doctor about the stress on his job. But the doctor said little and wrote a prescription for a tranquilizer.

Neither Hugh's doctor or his tormentors knew how dangerous Hugh had been.

Hugh grew up in a series of foster homes, each worse than the other. On his good days he was ignored; more frequently, he was beaten. When he was fifteen he ran away and lived on the streets, supporting himself through low-level drug selling activity.

Because of his intelligence and great size, Hugh advanced quickly in the gang. One day, as he lay drunk on a sofa, his doorbell rang. Two young women asked if they could discuss the Mormon religion with him. "They were so pretty I would have listened to anything they said," he told me.

Hugh did more than just listen. He stopped drinking and moved a thousand miles away to attend a Mormon college. There he married another student, Kristine. By the time his sixth child was born he had nearly forgotten his earlier life: the crimes he committed and the murders he narrowly missed being involved in. He avoided prison by informing, and then entered the Witness Protection Program. Now his best friend was the county sheriff.

Hugh's youngest daughter was turning six. To surprise her, he hid her birthday present in his locker at work: the American Girl doll she so wanted. Even the gruffest of his co-workers admired it. At quitting time, Hugh immediately identified the pungent odor from his locker. Kerosene had been sprayed through the vents onto the doll. Hugh's face tightened as rage poured through him. That feeling which, decades before, he had prayed to lose forever. "They didn't know who they were dealing with," he told me. "Years before I would have killed them without a second thought."

Hugh didn't remember leaving the plant. He thought only of getting his pistol which lay hidden in the basement, wrapped in plastic under a loose cement block beside the washer. While driving home he passed a familiar billboard which he seemed to notice for the first time: "Stress Getting You Down? See Our Therapist Before Your Divorce Attorney." Though Kristine would be the only woman in his life, the ad made sense to him. Hugh stopped his car by the side of the road and dialed the clinic's number. When the receptionist answered he told her that he wanted to make an appointment. She put him through to the doctor on call.

The doctor's voice was soothing. Hugh said he was suffering from work stress and an appointment was scheduled for later that evening.

Hugh was calmer when he arrived home. He played with his children, complimented Kristine on her cooking, and then drove to the clinic. Hugh felt that by calling this clinic he had made the right decision.

But he and Melanie could not have been more wrong. By choosing their particular therapists both had made one of the biggest mistakes of their lives.

Before describing their experiences and those of others you will meet on these pages, I should perhaps declare my position: *I believe in psychotherapy!* When effective it can transform lives and, by reducing stress, even forestall the development of physical illness. But some therapists cause unnecessary anxiety, depression, and wasted years. They provide treatment which is as destructive as botched heart surgery—even while being warm and friendly. Just like lawyers, auto salespeople, and others who successfully market their wares. A skillful psychotherapist would be a far better choice. As Melanie and Hugh wished they had initially made.

But what they did had seemed so correct. Each recognized their unhappiness and sought treatment from a well-credentialed, licensed professional. Doing just what troubled people are always advised. Yet before getting the right help, they endured unnecessary suffering. That pain which you might experience—or be experiencing— too.

Chapter Two

The "Magic" of Psychotherapy

A DICTIONARY DEFINES "MAGIC" AS being "the art of producing a desired result through the use of various techniques that presumably assure human control of supernatural agencies or the forces of nature." While there is nothing supernatural about therapy it does have powerful effects. Some, which include gaining better control over one's behavior, may indeed seem magical.

And therapy and magic do share similarities. They involve a suspension of belief with both the therapist and the magician being viewed as practitioners of great power. Psychotropic (mental health) medications may even be considered magical potions. Particularly since the research on the effectiveness of many of these drugs is wanting, with most studies lasting less than two months.*

What is Psychotherapy?

So if psychotherapy is not magic, what is it? All psychotherapy, no matter what marketing term is used to describe it, have common elements. Talk and interaction are central to the experience and there is only one—identical—goal: to effect behavior.

---

*The noted physician, Andrew Weil, has stated of medication in general that "the efficacy of these drugs are greatly exaggerated." (PBS radio, September 15, 2009).

Laurie, at Eleven

Eleven year old Laurie did not want to be in my office. But her parents dragged her there since they and the school found her behavior impossible. She upset even the usually unflappable teacher of her religion class by repeatedly insisting that she was an atheist. Besides failing all of her classes. "At least she's consistent," her mother remarked, after describing how Laurie had failed gym for refusing to change into uniform. At home, her room was a disaster, with food being left strewn about for days.

Her only interests were: her hair and clothes; her friends; her cell phone on which she spoke almost continuously; and her desire to leave my office as quickly as possible and never return.

"I have homework to do. You're interfering with my life," she informed me at our first meeting. Though I learned earlier from her mother that Laurie never did homework, I didn't argue with her. As I always tell parents, to argue with an illogical child just invites madness.

What was most striking about Laurie was not her behavior, which was subdued in my office, but her appearance. Though only eleven she looked sixteen and, I soon learned, considered herself an adult. She would advise me how to dress and when I needed a haircut. Yet at home, when not given what she wanted, she screamed like a three year old.

Despite the disgust for therapy which Laurie expressed, she freely answered my questions during our first meeting. She must sense that she needs help, I concluded, noting this cooperation and her very good question: "Why am I here?" Which allowed me to provide her with that information which would make her life more understandable.

"Because you have many things going on inside you. This makes it hard for you to pay attention in school and explains why your grades have gone down. But you don't have problems in all areas of your life—just a few. So our job is to change only those things which will keep you from getting what you want in life."

While relating is part of every business interaction, the relationship in psychotherapy is of crucial importance. A doctor, lawyer, or carpenter can be unfriendly or even obnoxious but still do a skillful job. Not so for a therapist who must relate in a warm, friendly fashion. Which is not to say that a patient must like everything about their therapist, They may consider that the pictures on the wall are too conventional or that there are too many family mementos in the office. One patient, a physician, felt this way after laying on her psychoanalyst's couch for nine years. Each year she faced a newer photo of her therapist's aging grandchildren—even as the patient's life remained the same. While not unfriendly, this therapist lacked sensitivity in the opinion of her patient.

Friendly concern can be expressed in different ways. By offering water or soda at the beginning of a session or asking if the room is too warm or cold. An effective therapist is receptive to their patients' needs when making appointments and will not be late in keeping them though emergencies can occasionally interfere. Nor should their staff be discourteous: conduct personal conversations while a patient waits for service or addressing them inappropriately by their first name.

A therapist's clothing should also indicate respect. I have heard of therapists who dress in jeans and sandals and sit on the floor on pillows but never of an attorney or physician who did so. Nor would I feel confident consulting one or, if I did, paying more than five cents for advice as in the celebrated Peanuts cartoon. A person charging a considerable sum should at least dress as if they deserved it.

How Psychotherapy Differs From Friendships

1. *Physical contact is forbidden in therapy but permitted in friendships*

Six year old Veronica had never met her father. Before her birth he was jailed for a series of bank robberies. During her first therapy session, after we played games and she listened to my tales of the stuffed animals in the office, she ran to hug me goodbye. I quickly put out my hands and said, "Nope. There can't be touching here. But you can hug Benjamin Bear if you want," and she did.

Though hugging while greeting is commonplace between friends, it would send the wrong message in therapy. Make it seem like ordinary friendship or one where communication—and healing—can be through other than verbal means. Moreover, people who enter therapy have compelling conflicts they are trying to resolve and physical reassurance through hugs can be easily misinterpreted. Thus this rule against physical contact serves to protect both the patient *and* the therapist.

2. *The duration of psychotherapy and friendships*

Meetings with friends can last as long as both value it but therapy has a time limit, usually between thirty and sixty minutes though longer or shorter sessions are possible. Setting a time limit is necessary both because therapy is a business and to provide a structure within which healing–which is the job of therapy–can proceed. The stability provided by the expected predictable structure of the therapy session facilitates this healing.

3. *Talk in psychotherapy is more controlled than in friendships*

Harry was a tall beefy man in his fifties who owned a business in New York City's garment district. Though only a high school graduate he was shrewd, or lucky enough, to win six figure sums in bets on sporting events—only to lose it and more over the following days. His therapy sessions always began with his conversation about casual events: my office's decor or that of the building's lobby. This lasted until he felt comfortable enough to speak of his personal concerns. It was as if he had to reconnoiter the territory before risking painful disclosure.

4. *The presence of authority*

Friends ordinarily share authority with each being more knowledgeable about particular areas or interests. But a therapist is consulted precisely because they better understand what most worries the patient. And, possessing this knowledge, *they* are the authority on what is discussed. Which is not to say that the patient must always follow the advice of their therapist, or even that therapy is mostly the giving of advice.

Marianne was an unmarried thirty one year old woman. She held a graduate degree and mid-level management position in a huge multinational corporation. But despite these career achievements she had no social life or friends. Moreover, both of her parents were dead and there were no relatives for her to confide in.

At 2AM one morning, Marianne called me from Bucharest, the site of her temporary assignment. She had a personality dispute with her boss and was afraid of being fired. He offered her a transfer to another job which included more money and promotion, though she would have to relocate to a suburban facility in America. Should she take the new job or leave the company and risk looking for another in the present poor job market?

We discussed her alternatives and she decided to take the job. Four years later, depressed by her continued lack of intimacy and failure to gain a promised promotion, she returned to therapy and blamed *me* for taking this job. "You should have insisted that I look for work in New York City," she complained. "I would have been happier there."

A therapist *cannot* make a decision for a patient for it is they who must live with the consequences.

5. *The presence of commitment*

Even long-term friendships can end because of changed circumstances: marriage, children, or the development of new, differing interests. But commitment is essential in the practice of therapy. For the most part, so long as the patient abides by such common business rules as keeping appointments, paying fees, and not being threatening or otherwise improper, the therapy will continue.

But this is a very general rule. Patients with pervasive emotional difficulties may severely try a therapist's patience and still be treated. A woman in her twenties set a fire in each woman's bathroom on the twelve floors of the medical building in which her therapist had an office. He tolerated this and similar difficult behaviors and the patient was eventually healed. But the treatment was unusually stressful for him since he narrowly avoided being thrown out of his office.*

This commitment exists despite the problems which some patients arouse and can lead to therapist burnout and deficiencies in treatment: trying to avoid the patient by shortening sessions or lengthening the interval between them; prescribing unneeded medication; or labeling them with inaccurate, too severe diagnoses.**

*Lindon, John A. Does Technique Require Theory, *Bulletin of the Menninger Clinic,* Winter, 1991, 55:1, p. 6.
**Wise, T.N., & Berlin, R.M. 1981. Burnout: Stresses in Consultation-liason Psychiatry. *Psychosomatics* 22 (9).

This dedication to the patient's healing is why a social relationship between the therapist and the patient are not permitted even after the therapy ends. For apart from the lingering therapeutic influence, becoming intimate ends any possibility of future therapy with the same clinician—who may be that therapist most able to foster healing. Thus therapy usually continues until the patient ends it or the therapist feels that no further progress can be made.

Chapter Three

Early Days in Psychotherapy

WHY DO PEOPLE CONSULT PSYCHOTHERAPISTS? This question may seem obvious but it is not. Many who enter therapy do not understand exactly what therapy is despite the popularity of the term. This is why the most frequent number of therapy sessions is just one—when the patient realizes that therapy is not what they expected, or concludes that the therapist cannot help them to fulfill their needs.

Becoming A Patient

Neither Melanie or Hugh wanted to consult a therapist. No one does. Sharing private thoughts and feelings is never easy, even with a person you trust. Now consider how you would feel speaking of these matters to a complete stranger.

While therapy isn't universal, everyone has been in the patient role at some point in their life. Like when they are in a doctor's office and susceptible to being greatly influenced by their opinion, though these doctors do not delve into the mysterious and frightening, unconscious portion of their mind.

One can be a doctor without having patients, but being in the patient role requires the presence of a doctor or other authority figure. Part of their job is to explain and thereby, hopefully, reduce the distress which the patient feels. Similarly, psychotherapy is a business relationship between two people who have come together for a particular purpose. One, the therapist, possesses training which allows them to understand and heal mental health difficulties. For which purpose the patient must reveal personal aspects of their life, though the facts which are first presented will not be complete since honesty derives from trust which takes time to develop.

For this reason the diagnostic conclusions which the therapist initially constructs may change over time as more facts become revealed. But this modification will not be great with skillful practitioners, leading to a tinkering about the edges and not a radical change if it does occur.

Melanie Begins Psychotherapy

Melanie was excited before her first therapy session. Though having spent all day thinking about it, she still wasn't sure what she would say. But she was sure that she wanted the doctor to know how really unhappy she was. She felt that so much depended on her therapy: marriage, children, everything.

Even though she was responsible for planning many meetings at work, she had no idea of how her first therapy session would go. The doctor, not me, is the one setting the agenda, she reminded herself, feeling more relaxed. She was tired of always being in charge. Let someone else make the decisions for her, someone trustworthy, an expert.

The doctor's waiting room was unlike any which she had been in for it resembled a living room. Instead of the metal chairs which are typical of medical offices, there were three sofas patterned in gray/while squares with throw pillows to make them inviting. Pale blue plastic end tables held white table lamps with black shades. The colored drawings on the wall were of flowers but the plants in the room were real: Jade and Jerusalem cherry.

The receptionist's desk was of blond wood, in the Scandinavian style. No file cabinets were visible. They were probably in a file room, Melanie thought.

Melanie told her name to the receptionist and was given a questionnaire. Before completing it she filled a cup with coffee from an urn on a table in the corner of the room, noting the bittersweet chocolate laced cookies on the tray. These aren't cheap, she told herself after her second bite. I guess that's why I'm paying so much, she added, with a small smile.

A few minutes later a man of medium height entered the room through a door behind the secretary's desk. He was dressed in an obviously expensive black suit with light gray pinstripes. He greeted Melanie, who was the only patient in the room, and invited her into his office.

Though there was a coat rack in the waiting room, Melanie brought her coat, briefcase, and laptop with her into the doctor's office. Her years in Manhattan had taught her, through painful experience, not to leave possessions unwatched. She learned that people steal from doctor's offices too.

Melanie thought that her first comment sounded dumb: "Where should I sit?" The doctor indicated the deep sofa against the wall and seated himself in the black Eames chair. Melanie dropped her possessions onto the sofa beside her and sat, crossing her legs and carefully smoothing her skirt.

The doctor went over her answers on the questionnaire. He asked her to expand on some of her responses, particularly her recent thought about killing herself. "That would be selfish," he joked, "I can't bill dead patients."

Melanie smiled approvingly: at least he's not dead, she thought. She liked people with a sense of humor and optimistically awaited his next comment—which never came. In fact the doctor said nothing else until the end of the session. Which was when he smiled again and murmured, "We'll have to stop now." Melanie returned his smile, rose, and gathered her things. The doctor smiled again. "Next Monday at the same time?" Melanie nodded.

That night Melanie felt depressed, though not suicidal as on the previous weekend. Just "down." She had expected the therapy experience to explosively transform her life, not leave it with a dull thud. She had so anticipated it.

The following week the doctor's broader smile met her strained look. Sensing her distress, he spoke a little more and alluded to the first session's prolonged silence.

"How did you feel when you left last Monday?"

"Not as well as I hoped."

"You haven't had therapy before. Maybe you feel like you have nothing to say. But one's life is like a large lake, filled with unspoken thoughts and feelings waiting to be revealed."

Melanie nodded as if she understood and tried to think of something to say.

"I want to be married."

"Yes," the doctor purred.

"And have children," she added.

The doctor nodded, and turned his attention to the flower vase which lay on the end table beside the sofa on which Melanie sat.

Each of Melanie's weekly sessions over the next three months was similar. The doctor would smile and, occasionally, offer encouraging words. Melanie would describe stressful events at work and bemoan her non-existent social life. Once a co-worker asked her, "How is your therapy going?" "Fine," she answered brightly, even as she wondered what, if anything, was happening.

One Saturday, Melanie did more than just wonder as her depression returned with a vengeance. Enough of this pain, she screamed to herself, gobbling down a bottle of Tylenol. Then, staring at the empty bottle, she realized the horror of what she just did and called 911. Later that day she was sure that the embarrassment of being paraded on a stretcher before shocked neighbors and the discomfort of having her stomach pumped had permanently removed any intention of killing herself.

But as surprising as this experience had been was her therapist's response to it. For, after she promised that she would never again attempt suicide, he dropped this subject with an understanding smile.

This smile, and his continuing silence about her most recent crisis, drained whatever remaining confidence she had in him. Both convinced Melanie that her choice of therapist was a mistake. Ivy League trained or not, this doctor could not help her change her life though she didn't yet know why.

Melanie returned his smile at the end of the session and knew that she would never return.

Making an Accurate Diagnosis: What is Causing Your Unhappiness?

To my life-long regret, I know little about cars. Just enough to buy gas, check the tires, and get the oil changed every three months. I can also add to the engine's coolant and replace the air filter. But all other maintenance and repairs I leave to the dealer who sold me the car. Which, for me, is being smart.

Once, a month after changing a tire, I was asked by the mechanic, "Who changed this tire?" "I did," I answered. "You put the wheel lug on backwards," I was informed. It was then that I decided to leave all mechanical work on my car to those who know how to do it.

Could I become a knowledgeable mechanic? Probably—if I were willing to take the training which would be needed for me to be able to make an accurate diagnosis, or determination, of what is wrong with the car when it breaks down, and then to know how to fix it.

Psychotherapy is a method of treatment for mental health conditions. Thus, just as with a malfunctioning car, an accurate diagnosis must first be made before the repair begins.

Though sounding complex, a diagnosis is simply a scientific description, or classification, of a problem. For mental health conditions this is made through questions, observations, and, occasionally, psychological tests. Why did you come? How are things going in your marriage?

What was your mother/father like when you were growing up? How much do you drink? And many others.

The questions asked of children and adolescents are different but have the same purpose. Do you have scary dreams? Do you ever get angry with your mother or father? What do they do that makes you angry? Do you have a best friend? What do you like about them? What type of work would you like to do when you are older?

Unpredictable, Five Year Old Josiah

Though he was only five years old, Josiah terrified his teacher for she could never predict what he would do. She was sure that, if he wasn't already crazy, he was very close to it—which is how she considered herself too.

Josiah was the youngest of four boys in his family. Over the years I had treated each child very briefly: their parents believed that therapy was needed only during a crisis. When each was over, so was their therapy. Now it was Josiah's turn to see me. I was nervous for I didn't want him to repeat in my office what his mother told me he was doing in school: peeing on the floor when he got angry. Would he soil my floor too?

Josiah entered my office, sat on the sofa, and calmly answered my questions. Then we played the Chutes and Ladders board game. Despite my concern, he was courteous and well-behaved. A delight. Why had he behaved so terribly in school? Because he felt that his teacher was trying to boss him around and he was showing her that he should not be treated discourteously.

I came to this conclusion by combining the information I gained from Josiah and his mother with my professional knowledge and clinical experience. This is how all therapists make their diagnoses. But because the knowledge, experience, and talent of each therapist is different, so will the accuracy of their conclusions and their ability to use this information in a helpful manner.

Why An Accurate Diagnosis Is Essential Before Treatment Begins

A diagnosis in psychotherapy is a brief description of a problem using terms which can be readily understood by mental health professionals. Thus when a therapist describes their patient as being "phobic" they are saying, very quickly in shorthand, that the major presenting problem, the *symptom* or *sign that something is wrong,* derives from a high level of anxiety.

But a diagnosis is more than just a rapid way of communicating. It provides the essential framework from which treatment follows and within which it is conducted. Without an accurate diagnosis, meaningful collaboration between the therapist and the patient is impossible*. To return to my example of auto repair, if, when asked what was wrong with a car, a mechanic responded, "Beats me but I'll fix it immediately," he would have few repeat customers and fewer new one.

Insurance plans require that a condition which is being treated fit within a particular category so that they can determine whether it is covered by the issued policy. Which is why a general description, as that a person is "unhappy," is unacceptable to them. But, though they are essential for insurance reimbursement purposes, mental health diagnostic terms reveal little about the aspects of life with which most people are concerned: their capacities to fully use their abilities, and to achieve intimacy. Nor is our government concerned with these matters or anything other than that a person is an adequate student, worker, or parent and breaks no laws. There is, unfortunately, no insurance coverage for treating important problems like "wanting joy in life."

Though formulating a diagnosis is essential before therapy begins, it is usually little considered thereafter. Unless something puzzling or unexpected happens, like the patient attempting suicide. Then the therapist must, perhaps, reconsider their original diagnosis.

Because therapy is an interpersonal experience, the framework for treatment which a diagnosis provides also advises the therapist how to relate. Can the patient tolerate silence or should the therapist be more active: ask questions and tell instructive, supportive anecdotes.

*Dr. Lisa Sanders emphasizes the importance of the diagnosis in her book, *Every Patient Tells a Story: Medical Mysteries and the Art of Diagnosis* (New York: Broadway Books, 2009)

Why People Begin Psychotherapy—or Don't

The first choice of unhappy people is not to call a therapist. Instead, they hope their painful mood will soon pass, or seek advice and support from a friend or relative. Therapy is a last resort. Having to reveal personal matters to a stranger is so uncomfortable that a person seeks therapy only when they feel they absolutely must. Or if they are being pressured to do so, this most frequently happening when they are referred by their employer, a court, or an angry spouse.

Eric Arrives Home and Finds His Family Gone

Thirty-four year old Eric was puzzled for he had thought that things were going very well in his life. His promotion to Senior Account Manager at the ad agency where he worked came through, and there were no rumors of any of the accounts he was working on being shifted to another agency. So as far as his job was concerned, things were now as stable as they ever got in the advertising business, where accounts were always in flux and intermittent unemployment was a way of life.

Moreover, the mortgage payment on the family's Westchester house was current like all of their other bills. And though the children's grades, eleven year old Amanda's and nine year old Phil's, were down from their usual "A's" into the "B" range, these were still better than his had ever been. Even the fights with his wife had ended.

So it was a huge surprise when, upon arriving home on the 5:16PM Harlem Line express from New York's

Grand Central Station, he found his usually well-lit, noisy house to be dark. There, instead of the hugs and dinner he expected, a letter awaited him on the kitchen table. Simple and to the point it read: "We're staying at my parents. If you're interested in saving our marriage, call me. But only after you start therapy!"

Where did this idea of therapy come from, Eric asked himself. He could see nothing wrong with his marriage. Here, "could see" were the significant words, for an important task of therapy is to enable a person to view matters differently and to understand them.

Joanne, the Distracted Police Officer

Nor was Joanne a completely voluntary patient. She had been a police officer for several years. A job which, despite the potential danger, she loved and which she performed well. Then she suddenly became afraid of driving across bridges. Even just thinking about it would cause her blood pressure to skyrocket and odd feelings to pervade her, first of warmth and then chill. This made getting to work nearly impossible for her office lay past two long bridges. She couldn't afford this distraction considering the normal stress of her job duties.

Adding to this worry were the recent problems caused by her twelve year old daughter. Joanne considered psychotherapy but hesitated. She wondered how confidential the information on her health insurance forms really was and was afraid that her boss would learn of her treatment. Maybe he would force her to go for a psychological screening and her gun would be taken away. She knew of officers who were forced onto desk duty for more than a year before the department's skittish bureaucracy finally cleared them. So Joanne waited for several months before calling me. And this was only after her boss noted her tension, asked if anything was wrong, and suggested counseling.

Contrary to popular thinking, people do not seek therapy for superficial reasons: because their best friend has a therapist and they *must* imitate them, or wanting a buddy to discuss fun activities with. Nor would an ethical therapist engage such a patient for psychotherapy is one of the most serious of all activities. It is the business of healing.

Chapter Four
What Psychotherapy Is, and Is Not

THE WORDS "THERAPY" AND "therapeutic" are heard and read daily. The purchase of a car or dress will be described as "therapeutic" rather than a good decision, and a week long beach vacation may be termed "therapy" instead of relaxation. But *therapy* and *therapeutic* were originally professional terms and have very different meanings to clinicians.

Psychotherapy is a treatment for emotional or behavioral difficulties. Which can vary widely from wanting to stop smoking to being unable to behave appropriately in even the most conventional interaction, like buying a newspaper.

Important problems in living are caused by unproductive habits, psychological limitations, or self-defeating fears.

Janet – A Single Parent Limited by Habit

Janet was a newly divorced parent of three teenage boys and a younger girl. Her ex-husband, Tom, though once a devoted father, began using cocaine to cope with the stress of his Wall Street career. As his company's problems increased, so did Tom's drug use, leading to his family's financial ruin. Which became worse when Tom, an Irish citizen, returned to Ireland to avoid paying child support. At thirty-nine, Janet found herself the sole support of their four children.

The ownership of the family's house had been registered in Tom's name. Without her knowledge, he took out loans against it to maintain their life style which, because of his expensive drug habit, they could no longer afford. Thus, soon after Tom abruptly fled the marriage, Janet was shocked to find herself not only impoverished but verging on homelessness. How would she pay the bills which were arriving daily?

Her parents helped a little, her younger brother more, and Janet cut the family's expenses drastically. She found another single mother to live with and they shared the rent, utilities, and the cost of one phone line. Cable TV, eating out, movies, and ballet and guitar lessons for the children were ended.

Food stamps, which she barely heard of previously, helped greatly, and the family now made an adventure of shopping for clothes at their local Salvation Army and Goodwill thrift stores. "None of their friends can see the difference," Janet remarked, holding back tears."Some of the children they meet there have never shopped in real stores."

Janet had a B.A. in art which prepared her "for unemployment." A state she hoped to exit as quickly as possible by accepting virtually any work she could find which fit within the hours she had available. Her first was being the assistant manager of a strippers bar which promised patrons the most beautiful women in the world. She left after two weeks, exhausted by her duties which included paying the bills, handling the payroll, *and* getting the dancers on stage on time while she made popcorn, "As unsexy a job as you could imagine," she concluded.

Her next job required her to be proficient on Quickbooks, a computer program she had no experience with. Feeling desperate, she assured her interviewer that she regularly used this program on a past volunteer job. After being hired, she quickly learned it through early morning practice with the manual.

Her boss was pleased with her performance and wanted to promote her. "There's just one problem. You seem cold and disinterested with new customers. They've remarked on it. Smile—it costs nothing and means a lot."

Janet took this friendly advice seriously and puzzled over her behavior. As a child she remembered being told by her mother not to smile at strangers. Doing so had apparently become a habit and persisted across these decades. That evening, Janet practiced smiling before a mirror. At first, relating so differently to customers felt strange. But this feeling soon disappeared and she won her promotion.

Daniel – A Lawyer Paralyzed by His Psychological Limitations

As a teenager, Daniel's favorite TV program was *Law & Order*. It was also his mother's and she often praised his speaking ability. So it surprised no one when, upon beginning college, Daniel declared his intention to become a lawyer.

Daniel graduated from college with a little above a "B" average. This was a surprise since he had graduated from high school with an "A" average and his SAT scores were nearly perfect. But, his parents told themselves, he deserved to relax for awhile. This "relaxation" came at a price, and Daniel failed to be admitted to any of the top three law schools he wanted. Instead, he attended and graduated from a less prestigious school—which is a problem for no profession is as status conscious as law.

Unable to find employment, Daniel spent the months after graduation studying for his state's bar exam, which he passed by three points. "Three points is as good as thirty," his mother reassured him, as Daniel relaxed before re-starting his job search. Which never seriously began.

On Sundays, Daniel scanned the want ads, considered some and circled them. Then he would drop the newspaper onto the floor and turn his attention to the TV in his room, which he kept on even while sleeping. Reruns of old series, *Law & Order* or *Hawaii Five O,* and movies, the titles of which didn't seem to matter so long as there was noise from this or the computer games he frequently played.

Daniel's father described his son's life best: "It seemed like when his school was over so was his life." The explanation for why this occurred is not simple.

All people have basic psychological abilities. These enable them to control their thinking and behavior; to modulate their mood; to express and cope with feelings; and to develop a sense of who they are or, as it is professionally described, to develop a *sense of self.* But these crucial capacities are not present at birth. Instead, they develop within the first three years of life through the child's complex moment-to-moment interplay with their parents or other parenting figures.

Because this interaction between the child and their parents is never perfect, weakness of one or more of these psychological abilities may develop. Thus a child may have an inadequate ability to tolerate feelings or to control their behavior, leading to difficulties with intimacy or with job supervisors after they reach adulthood.

Daniel's problems were caused by his difficulty with feelings and that he lacked a clear sense of who he was. When he was provided direction and structure by his college and earlier by his parents, Daniel functioned well and seemed no different from his peers. But after graduating from law school, he was unable to make the personal decisions required of all adults, and to gain intimacy.

Thus, lacking a sense of who he really was and fearing his feelings, Daniel remained at home. Playing video games and watching TV like a child. Trying to avoid the adult experiences which would arouse anxiety and his life-long depression caused by the sensing of his great emotional difficulties.

Anna, A Frightened Teenager

Anna ran as quickly as she could but the man kept gaining on her. When she first noticed him she had a hundred foot lead. Now he was closing the distance and barely thirty feet separated them. She fled her friend's house just after midnight when what she had believed to be a sleepover turned into something very different.

Daphne told her that it would be just she and some friends who were coming over while Daphne's parents were away. Girls hanging out: watching movies, snacking, sharing rumors about the latest teen relationships. Anna didn't know that boys were invited too. Though not (she believed) the only virgin there, she was probably the girl who was most uncomfortable about sexual matters.

Daphne's boy friend groped over Daphne's thigh as they huddled on the couch. Anna felt she had to leave. If this was happening at midnight, what pressures would she face by 2AM? Anna touched her forehead, said that she had a headache, and left with just a wave to the others. Who didn't seem as if they would miss her, she thought.

Anna's house was less than a mile away, a fifteen minute walk during the day, more quickly at night. Anna didn't like walking alone at night. The streets in her small town were deserted after 7PM and there were alleys with frightening shadows to pass.

Anna trembled slightly at this thought and walked faster. To calm herself, she began counting seconds. Each brought her closer to the door of her home. One, one hundred. Two, one hundred. At sixty, one hundred, only ten minutes remained until she reached safety.

Then she heard the sound of footsteps matching hers. When she stopped for a moment, so did the sound. Anna ran the remaining distance, holding the house key in her hand so she could open the door quickly. She tripped over the outside steps but a moment later was inside and safe. She double locked the door, fastened the chain, and turned on all of the downstairs lights before fleeing to her room and locking that door too.

Anna forced her breathing to slow and smiled. There was no one, she told herself. The man following her was her imagination acting up. Her backpack went onto a chair and she began undressing. It had been a long day. Her parents and younger brother would return in the morning. They were unable to get an evening flight home from her mother's combination brief business trip and family vacation. One which Anna couldn't join because it involved flying.

Anna had read about people who were so afraid of flying that they would never enter an airport. She flew just once, a year before, and vividly remembered the experience. The feeling of being enclosed in a small space and unable to leave. The pounding heart rate and clammy hands. The odd feeling in her throat and fear that she was unable to swallow. She never told her parents that she was afraid to fly but always found some excuse not to. Daphne's sleepover was the latest.

Though it is terrifying, a fear, or as it is professionally termed, a *phobia*, is helpful. For it reduces the large, troubling, unconscious concern to the smaller size of an avoidable activity. This enables a person to function better than were they to try to cope with the underlying worry. Thus by avoiding flying, an event which Anna rarely confronted, she could ignore the pressing *unconscious* concerns which she wasn't yet ready to face.

How Does Psychotherapy Work?

Psychotherapy is a special, highly controlled relationship through which positive change can occur. If a person has habits they wish to change (for example, a self-defeating way of relating to others, or smoking, or over-eating) these may be eliminated. If ego or psychological limitations are present (as, having difficulty experiencing feelings or controlling behavior), these may be healed by replacing them with more maturely developed ones. And fears can be reduced by dealing with the underlying issues which motivated the unconscious mind to construct them.

Why Children are More Receptive to Psychotherapy Than Adults

This statement isn't exactly true for some children do object upon hearing that they will be seeing "a therapist," for they inaccurately associate this experience with their pediatrician's painful procedures. But after the first session even these children anticipate therapy with delight. One three year old found therapy so enjoyable that she insisted on bringing her younger sister with her. After the older child's therapy session ended, they would play in the waiting room while I spoke with their mother.

Most children respond receptively to new experiences for they lack the heavy baggage of past fears and humiliations which can burden adults.

Why therapy frightens

1. Psychotherapy can be frightening because it looks different

People have consulted physicians since childhood and know what to expect when they enter their offices. But therapy is a new and different experience. There are no machines to observe or tasks to perform and the office may seem like someone's home. Children sometimes ask whether I live in my office for, though it is in a commercial area, it looks like a two bedroom apartment and the bathroom has a shower. To satisfy their curiosity and evidence my truthfulness, I offer a tour of the office which includes peeking into all of the closets.

2. Psychotherapy can be frightening because it feels different

People consult physicians for a definite reason. Apart from the annual check-up, they see them only when there is some discomfort like persisting pain or dizziness. The doctor then performs their investigation, which may include a medical scan or blood test, pronounces their judgment, and the interaction ends. But in the therapy office there are no instruments to impress and what is most startling is also the most frightening: becoming aware of the power of the mind.

Clark: The FBI Agent Who Always Forgot My Name

I never learned exactly what Clark did for a living apart from that he worked for the FBI. Periodically he would leave the city "on business" for several months, then return to resume his therapy and deal with issues relating to his marriage and children. His job was the only satisfactory part of his life.

What I most remember about Clark was that he was a prolific dreamer. Each session he would bring a loose-leaf binder holding his notes of the previous week's dreams. Our interpretation of them told us much about how he viewed his life. Despite which, he continued to insist that he didn't believe in unconscious processes. But one continuing event eventually changed his mind

At that time I had an office in an apartment house and my name was written in a brass plate affixed to the door. Each week, Clark would look at the small sign before entering my office—and then promptly forget my last name. Eventually he made a comment which most therapists and many therapy patients would endorse: "You have to respect the power of the unconscious."

Not only respect it but fear it, in the view of many. Does anyone really feel comfortable with the idea that an invisible power, without their knowledge, can mold their behavior?

3. Psychotherapy can frighten from the fear that it will inhibit behavior

While all people hold opinions about religion, sex, politics, medical treatments, and the like, therapists are expected to avoid imposing theirs on patients. Which is not to say that they must avoid discussing them. I encourage patients to get second opinions about serious medical conditions though my comments usually just support their existing tendency to do so. And I would not feel comfortable treating people whose income derived from burglary or muggings; nor are they likely to seek mental health treatment.

But sharing one's life with a therapist often arouses the fantasy that, though an adult, the patient is now gaining a parenting figure: one who will judge what they say and will reduce their freedom to behave as they choose. This is not true for experienced therapists have heard just about everything and are rarely shocked or deliver advice. Still, some people feel freer after terminating their therapy or by not beginning it, though what really constrains people are their unconscious conflicts and not mental health treatment.

With so many natural resistances to therapy it is a wonder that people ever seek it. Doing so after asking themselves that same question as before they make any expensive purchase: Do I really need it?

Do I Really Need a Therapist?

While engaging in formal therapy is a relatively new activity in human history, its purpose—to seek comfort and change behavior—is as old as the human species. Even elephants and other animals have been seen to comfort each other after the death of a familiar figure.

Carla, *Twice* a Victim

It was the wine which saved Carla's life. A childhood friend from Indiana was visiting and they spent an evening drinking and sharing remembrances of earlier romances. So it was nearly 2AM when Carla got to sleep. This, and the effect of the wine, made her a half-hour late to work that September 11th. The morning of the terrorist attack on the World Trade Center where she worked.

This wasn't her first narrow escape. Eight years before she had experienced the World Trade Center's first attack. "That's enough bombings for one lifetime. I'm already the poster girl," she remarked.

Carla had felt nervous when she re-entered the World Trade Center building after its first bombing. After her second such experience, things were worse and she tried to avoid using the elevators. She was afraid of being caught in it in a future attack. Several friends suggested that she seek counseling but Carla refused, saying that she had friends to talk to and their sympathy was enough. She believed that her fear was normal. Anyone would be afraid after such a frightening experience, and she expected that her fear would eventually disappear on its own, just as it had eight years before. And, over time, it did.

People encounter stressful experiences throughout life and cope with them on their own with varying degrees of success. A worrisome medical diagnosis, an unhelpful teacher, a troubled relationship. These are part of the fabric of human existence. Only sometimes is therapy necessary: when a symptom persists and becomes bothersome.

When a stress persists a *symptom*, or the sign that something is wrong, develops. This can be anything out of the ordinary: nightmares; over-concern with cleanliness or germs; depression; anxiety or panic attacks. Temporary symptoms are termed *reactive,* for they derive from, *are reactive to*, a recent stress. When the stress disappears, so will the symptom.

But when stress persists, it affects the structure of the mind. Then these symptoms continue because they now reflect an *internalized* psychological change, one which will not go away even when the stress is no longer present.

While it is not necessary, therapy can be helpful in coping with reactive symptoms. But therapy is essential to reduce the symptoms which derive from internalized psychological changes, for with these, the therapist must work *inside of the patient's mind.*

Doing Treatment Inside the Mind

The concept of "treatment inside the mind" is not as familiar a notion as when one speaks of matters effecting the body. Most people have experienced some type of surgery: the common stitches to help a small wound heal or the unfortunate need for major surgery. Scalpel and strange frightening contraptions are then seen. Some have tried using these to change the mind too. Medical history is filled with such unsuccessful attempts using water, electricity, and even ice picks. But psychotherapy uses none of these, only words. Which is not as radical as it sounds.

More than thirty years ago it was scientifically established that the mind can change the body's autonomic functioning once this is made visible. This procedure, biofeedback, measures a bodily operation like blood pressure and shows this magnitude on a screen, making it possible for the person to know when their thought or subtle awareness is having an effect. This is necessary because change in blood pressure cannot be felt.

Since it took so long to consider that a person might be able to control their biological processes, consider how difficult it is to believe that one can transform their *mind.* Something which, though we use the term daily, is wholly theoretical and incapable of being touched. But this happens all of the time and not only by therapists but with others too, for the transforming power of love has been long recognized.

But just as not every relationship involves love, not all therapy fosters psychological change and leads to healing. That which does, *effective therapy*, has particular characteristics and is useful, but only under certain circumstances.

The notion of engaging in therapy "to change," if this is the only reason, makes as little sense as would undergoing weight reduction surgery to lose five pounds.

Altering the diet would be far safer and cheaper. Likewise, one should seek therapy only when gaining aid through personal relationships, from friends and relatives, hasn't worked.

Chapter Five
When Your Personal Relationships Can't Help

PSYCHOTHERAPY IS REQUIRED TO solve a problem when support or advice from a friend or a relative cannot help.

1. *Psychotherapy is required when there is a need for secrecy*

Lanny's Military Secret

Lanny was the youngest of six children and the only boy in his family. His parents were in their late forties when he was born and, because of the age difference, his older sisters related to him more as aunts than siblings. Lanny was bright and perceptive. He was also so handsome that it was often recommended to his parents that they seek modeling work for him, a suggestion which couldn't be followed because of the family's life style.

Lanny's father was a career military officer, an army physician who helped train members of the special forces in emergency medical techniques. Thus Lanny grew up on many military bases and was educated in the military's school facilities. He was an excellent student and eventually studied engineering on an Air Force ROTC scholarship at an Ivy League university. His commission as a second lieutenant began a fruitful military career, marred only by the continuing stress of having to cope with his forbidding secret: that he was homosexual.

Though being in his late thirties, Lanny had never married. Some gay men do, for business reasons, children, or because their sense of who they are sexually occurred late in life. Though being older and unmarried in the military was unusual, it isn't unknown. Douglas MacArthur, one of the most famous American generals, lived with his mother for much of his life. He married when he was in his fifties, to a woman he met while traveling by ship to his assignment in the Philippines.

But the stress of being gay while in the military is great. Discovery means the end of their chosen career, which is crucially important to a person's identity. While therapy can reduce this stress, it contains its own risk. Not that of gaining counseling because this stigma has diminished in the military, which now encourages it.* But because of the limited privacy which medical communication has within the armed forces. Only with civilian therapists do the traditional rules of confidentiality apply.

*In February and April of 2009, three American army generals discussed with troops and reporters their wartime trauma experiences and the treatment they received. The military's anti-stigma campaign, "Real Warriors, Real Battles, Real Strength," includes a Web site, _www.realwarriors.net_, which contains information on psychological difficulties and treatment.

Thus Lanny endured his pain, being unable to gain support from within his military "family," finally gaining it within a legally protected private practice setting. The issue of confidentiality in therapy and mental health treatment in the military are explored in Chapter Twenty One.

2. Psychotherapy is required when a third party is needed

Harriet's Unknown Husband

Harriet was forty seven when she married for the first time, an event which surprised her and shocked her family. She was the oldest of four children, the others having married decades before, with two being married twice.

Harriet never could figure out why it took her so long to marry. She wasn't, relatively speaking, less attractive than others and didn't consider herself unusually picky. Certainly not as much as the New York women she read about who would reject a man if they disliked fish or for another nonsensical excuse. The drinkers and addicts she passed on; also those who were married or, if divorced, ignored their children. Not that she objected to help parent another person's child but she felt that their father should.

While Harriet dated and considered, the years flew by; her career as political lobbyist for a large bank advanced; and she didn't feel seriously unhappy. But, deep down, she knew that she was. A big Fidelity account can't keep you warm in bed, she increasingly told herself.

Then she met Clinton at a noisy bar. He worked as sales manager for an auto dealer. They spoke briefly, and left to drink coffee at a nearby Starbucks. They spent two hours together that night and had dinner every evening that week. Clinton moved in with her the following week and they married two months later. Neither saw any sense in a long engagement at their ages (he was fifty-one) or in having a large wedding.

The guest list totaled twenty six, all being her relatives, and their honeymoon was a weekend at a suburban Bed and Breakfast. Both considered silly the "Just Married" banner which her youngest brother affixed to their car, but Harriet was secretly pleased and they kept it on until reaching the B&B.

"It was the scar on his arm which got me thinking," Harriet told me eight months later. "I noticed it before but didn't question him about it. Why would I? It would be like asking someone about their acne scar. But this time, while lying in bed, I ran my finger along it and asked how he got it. It looked like it was from a knife and I expected him to say that it was caused by a nail or some such thing. Instead, he froze and his eyes grew cold. Just for an instant. Then he turned the question back to me. It was because he couldn't think of a quick answer to satisfy me. I know. I've done the same thing when giving a talk and am asked a question which I can't answer. I return it to the audience and someone always has a reasonable opinion. That's what I felt Clint was doing.

Instead of questioning him further, I went along. It seemed a big issue to him and I wanted to calm things down. So I suggested, "a nail scratch?" and he replied, "Exactly."

Harriet paused. I didn't know what to say. Her story was starting to sound like a Woman in Peril movie.

"Then there was the locked drawer and private e-mail account."

"Wanting a sense of privacy is normal," I suggested. "Maybe they were for business."

"Just what I first thought," she said. "But I couldn't explain away the other things. We're both Catholic—he said he was brought up Catholic—but when we went to church he didn't know the prayers or routine. And he's obsessed with guns. He keeps three loaded ones around as if he expects a break-in at any moment. And it's not like we live in a high-crime area."

Harriet desperately needed a third party, one with whom she could share her concern about her husband. An objective outsider who wouldn't gossip, for her worry might simply reflect errors in marital communication. Or was her fear justified? Perhaps Clinton wasn't the man she thought him to be when they married.

3. Psychotherapy is needed when a problem persists

Joel's Fear

Joel avoided learning to drive for as long as he could and this wasn't a problem for most of his life. Comparatively few people in New York City own cars. Parking in a garage is expensive and the daily need to follow the City's alternate parking rules is a major headache. But when Joel's job forced him to moved to Connecticut, taking a bus or subway to work was no longer an option for there weren't any.

Joel briefly, though not seriously, considered getting a bike—until he remembered that he never learned to operate that either. Besides, only a car was feasible in the suburbs, and a BMW or Lexus would improve his business image more than the best two wheeler. He smiled at this thought but the idea of driving had always frightened him. Was this a personal quirk, something which everyone has, or a real problem for which he needed professional help?

Joel knew that he would benefit from having a driver's license long before he moved to Greenwich. He sold industrial chemicals and there were good accounts he could have solicited in New Jersey if he drove. What fear or feeling of inadequacy had kept him from learning what every suburban teenager could? Why did he so doubt his ability to learn to drive? It must be a real problem—and one for which he needed help.

4. *Psychotherapy is needed when a symptom*
   seems bizarre

Karin's Monster

Karin wanted to be a cheerleader ever since she could remember. Choosing this was her and not her parents' decision, one she made because of her enjoyment of gymnastics and her father long calling her "Ms. Supercute." Being small, she was the one they held up during routines. Thankfully, she was never dropped. One fellow cheerleader had wound up with a broken arm and she heard of another who now watched routines from her wheelchair. Karen had always believed herself lucky—until last night.

He was watching her again. At first she hadn't been sure. Often he would be gone for long periods, but then return. She didn't know why he behaved as he did but was sure that he was tall and had very white teeth and striking blue eyes though she had never seen them for he hid himself well.

Sometimes he lay quietly under her bed but most of the time he sat on the balcony just outside of her window. Waiting, with his serrated knife which was bigger than a paring knife. Probably a Bowie. Someday he would use this to kill her family. Mother, father, baby brother. All would die.

This monster had been in her life for a year. Now he started coming more frequently. She thought of telling her mother about him but how could she? He might get so angry that he would kill everyone right then. Just before killing her.

Sometimes Karin did question this fear since she had never actually seen this man. Nor, so far as she knew, had anyone else. As it must be for he existed only in her mind and symbolized what Karen considered to be monstrous within herself: the powerful unrecognized anger which lay deep within the unconscious portion of her mind and struggled to escape its bonds.

While all symptoms are logical, for they merely indicate that something is wrong, some can seem weird. They seem so strange that friends or relatives would react to their description with shock and be unable to provide support or helpful suggestions. Here, professional aid is necessary: to explain how the symptom fits within the person's normal life, and to alleviate or remove it.

Chapter Six

*Not All Childhood Problems Require Psychotherapy
But Some Do*

CHILDREN ARE NOT JUST small adults. While this fact may seem self-evident it was first discovered in the twentieth century by an eminent Swiss psychologist, Jean Piaget. His conclusion was described by Albert Einstein as being "so simple that only a genius could have thought of it." Because children think so differently from adults, they also communicate that they are unhappy in other ways.

1.An unhappy child does not say that they are unhappy

Only very rarely, perhaps once every ten years, has a parent told me that their child said they "need someone to talk to." Instead, unhappy children behave in a puzzling way. They expect that their parents, who are much bigger and more capable, will instinctively know what is wrong and do whatever it takes to fix the problem.

2.Not all childhood experiences require psychotherapy

A symptom, or puzzling behavior, reveals that something is wrong and the child is experiencing more stress than they can tolerate. As a child encounters new experiences, like a new class, they experience stress. Once the demands of this event are overcome, the symptom will naturally disappear.

But if the symptom persists a mental health evaluation should be sought, to determine if therapy is needed. However if no symptom exists, then therapy is not needed. No more than one would bring a well functioning computer to a technician for repair.

3. *Not all child or adolescent problems can benefit from therapy*

Louis' Trashy Girlfriend

Everyone agreed that Veronica came from a no-good family. Her father collected disability payments for an allegedly crippling back condition—though one which didn't stop him from operating a cash payment only, auto repair business. His wife collected disability payments for depression, which she treated with vodka and Coke.

It might have been the alcohol which preserved her youthful looks for in a dim light she resembled Veronica's sister more than her mother, a role which she seldom took seriously. Because of this, fourteen year old Veronica had few rules to follow. The biggest was not to get caught.

Veronica hated school and tried to avoid it, sneaking out early whenever she could. She managed to pass by cheating on exams and getting her friends to do the homework and class projects.

Louis' mother described Veronica as being "trash from a trashy family," and was apoplectic when her son began dating her. Though being two years older, Louis was naive and easily swayed by Veronica's honeyed syllables, gleaming black hair, and the diaphragm which her mother had her fitted for on her thirteenth birthday.

The real reason that Louis was brought to my office was to find him a new girl-friend. Not that I ran a dating service, but his mother was convinced that only an emotional problem would cause her academically gifted son to make such a poor dating choice. I was less convinced after seeing Veronica, who occasionally accompanied Louis and his mother to my office.

Veronica wore the shortest shorts I had ever seen, a tight sweater, and exuded sexuality. On the back of her shorts was written "My boyfriend is cuter." I had no more chance of breaking Veronica and Louis up, even were this my goal, than would a grown chicken surviving thirty days in a slaughter house. Even with the aid of his mother who daily advised her son of the danger of AIDS and other sexually transmitted diseases. "You're sleeping with whoever she already slept with," she exhorted. Happily, they did break up several months later when Veronica latched onto a boy from a more prosperous family.

Psychotherapy can only foster that change in a child's life which they want and are ready for. Some adolescents, even those with severe emotional difficulties, need to have a greater sense of independence and who they are before they can tolerate the dependency which therapy requires.

Chapter Seven

Four Crucial Times When Your Marriage Needs
Psychotherapy to Survive

NOT ALL MARITAL PROBLEMS require therapy. Stress occurs in marriages as well as in individual lives and when the problems diminish the stress will disappear. But some marital problems do not spontaneously resolve themselves and would benefit from professional help.

1. A marriage would benefit from psychotherapy when there are significant communication problems

Ben Does Brussels

It was right after the morning news when Carla *knew* that something serious had happened during Ben's business trip to Brussels. What, she didn't yet know, but she was determined to find out. So the next morning Carla demanded from Ben a moment-to-moment description of how he spent his days in Europe. Which he provided for he wanted their relationship to return to its usual calm.

Carla's initial questioning was bearable: she worked the night shift and their time together was mostly on weekends. But then her work schedule changed and her persistent questioning broke him down. Finally, he told her the truth: that he had an affair while on his business trip in Europe, six years before. This confession caused them to consult me.

I listened and questioned and considered their situation, but remained puzzled. The affair happened long years before. Why were they seeking therapy *now* for this ancient occurrence? Only after the couple left did I understand what was really going on.

Ben had long been angry with Carla because she was very controlling. But he didn't want to raise this issue because he was unsure whether she could change. If he complained, they might divorce. An event which he didn't want because of their three young children. So, while drunk and with reduced self-control, three thousand miles away, he had a one-night affair with a woman he barely remembered. Through this act he expressed the anger towards his wife which he couldn't communicate openly.

2. *A marriage would benefit from psychotherapy when there are differences in how to relate to important issues*

Lilly, Andrew, and Why His Father Shot the TV

Everyone, not only her parents, agreed that Eve was a beautiful child. Even passersby on the street were entranced by her glowing eyes. "Have you thought about her being a child model?" more than one of them had asked Lilly and Andrew, her parents.

Then, just like in Hollywood legends, Eve was seen by an ad agency casting agent who arranged for her audition and first photo shoot. Which was not a simple task for it demanded that Lilly travel from their distant suburb into Manhattan—along with the flow of traffic both ways too. But the money was good and all of it went into Eve's college fund. Plus there were extras: the toys and clothes which she used on the jobs were hers to keep.

The neighbors were jealous. Why wasn't their child chosen? Lilly tactfully explained that looks were only part of the requirement for modeling jobs. And not even the most important for the child must be able to tolerate long boring waiting periods and follow instructions on cue. Though she was just over four years old, Eve thrived at her duties and never objected to getting up before dawn for the long trip into the city.

Andrew was initially hesitant for Eve to model, but her delight at seeing herself in TV commercials reassured him. After the first months he treasured their appearance and bored friends by repeatedly showing their tapes.

But the parents disagreed about discipline. Andrew's ideas derived from his childhood when he never dared to refuse any of his parents' demands. Only once he did: when his father told him to turn off the TV and do his homework. When Andrew ignored him. his father repeated his request. Then he left the room, returned with a pistol, and shot a bullet through the center of the TV screen.

Though Andrew would never behave as crazy with his child, he still held the same idea about parenting: that a child *must* be obedient. Eve was submissive on her modeling jobs but not with her parents. If she wanted to do what they asked, she would. If not, maybe she would do it in an hour or so, though this wasn't likely.

Andrew's remedy was to punish her by refusing to let her play with the dog or forcing her to sit on the Bad Girl Chair for ten minutes until she realized that she had done wrong. But the only effect these measures had on Eve was to make her angry and even more disobedient. Like causing her to "accidentally" spill her milk.

Lilly was more accepting of Eve's misbehavior. Lilly would tell her what she should do and, if it wasn't done, Lilly would do it for her. Thus the family stretched from one disciplinary pole to its opposite, and this tension began to effect the marriage.

I met with Andrew and Lilly for several months, listened to their differing viewpoints about child rearing, and provided my own. Eve's occasionally defiant behavior was normal for a four year old, I informed them, and there are better methods of dealing with it than the parents were using. The child rearing errors they were making were not from malice but because infants do not come with an instruction book, and parenting instincts derive both from biology and childhood experiences.

What Lilly and Andrew needed was counseling to help them become appropriately assertive with Eve, and not to feel inadequate when their efforts didn't work. Even when parents operate at their best, children can sometimes be impossible to deal with.

During some sessions with Lilly and Andrew, I conducted what was essentially their own individual therapy by exploring the childhood roots of their behavior with Eve in order to reduce its present day effect.

3. *A marriage would benefit from psychotherapy when dangerous conditions exist*

Kimberly and Harry Avoid a Shoot-out

The tight t-shirt and ripped jeans emphasized Kimberly's sex appeal. Her phony Rolex and eyebrow piercings were other good touches. She had been on the street for four years and was good at her job. But though her appearance was still convincing, she was getting tired of street life. It was too similar to her adolescence. No wonder I'm so good at it, she thought, it was lucky that I didn't turn out like this.

The previous night, things hadn't gone smoothly. A shooting happened, which nobody wanted no matter which side of the law you were on. She had once shot a guy who was high on meth and coming at her with a knife. Luckily he survived, not that she would have given two thoughts had this worthless shit died. But any shooting, even one which didn't result in death, was best avoided. Unless one enjoyed talking to lawyers for the next few years, in whatever civil suit or departmental action could be thought up.

But it wasn't Kimberly's job which was on her mind that evening as she sat in a Starbucks, nursing her Latte to avoid going home. The fighting with her husband was getting worse and had turned physical. That morning she fantasied a shoot-out between them: both were police officers with weapons readily available. Whether or not her marriage survived, she hoped it wouldn't come to that.

While all intimate relationships have problems, only one demands that the couple separate: when violence exists, for this contains the potential for police and court involvement. Even a simple push can lead to a fall in which serious injury or death occurs.

It is far better to explore the relationship in therapy and find a conclusion which both consider tolerable, than to risk the potential danger from these situations.

4. A marriage might benefit from psychotherapy even after the couple separates

MaryLynne and Jim, A Couple Who Separated Without Knowing Why

The tension between them was worse, Jim thought, as he left the house that morning. Since their marriage six years earlier, they always had the same routine. Up at 6AM, showering together, then breakfast.

Seven months ago, their showering together stopped. Then they began eating breakfast separately when she changed her working hours to start later. Soon they were sleeping apart. Not that it mattered for he had been falling asleep in the living room with the TV on for the past two months. Now, they barely spoke.

So it wasn't altogether a surprise when he arrived home one evening to find that she had moved out. Taking enough of her clothes so he knew that she wasn't coming back.

But MaryLynne hadn't been as bad as some spouses are when they separate. After checking their joint savings account on-line, he discovered that she had drawn only half of the balance. She also left him a check for a half month's rent.

When they married, he had wanted their finances to be handled jointly. But MaryLynne insisted on each paying half the expenses from their separate checking accounts since both were working full-time. Deciding who would manage the family finances would only have led to arguments.

Jim tried not to think about his marriage after MaryLynne left. His job as a civil engineer kept him busy and he no longer objected to working overtime now that he had no reason to go home. A month after she left, Jim got a letter from MaryLynne. She had found a job two states away, rented an apartment there, and asked that he send some things she forgot. Two months later she called again and asked for the remainder of her clothes.

About this time, Jim began therapy and tried to understand what happened in his marriage. We discussed his parents' divorce and his fear of having children, a decision which he and his wife had faced for both were in their early thirties. He could only think of a few characteristics of MaryLynne which irritated him and these seemed minor: that she liked abstract art which he didn't; and that she enjoyed wandering through flea markets while he would have preferred to listen to sports on the car radio..

Two months after Jim began therapy his wife phoned and said that she wanted to accompany him. She came to three sessions, and Jim missed the next appointment. When I called and asked what happened he said that he and MaryLynne had reconciled. None of us understood why they separated, or why they got back together. Yet, somehow, therapy had been a helpful catalyst, producing enough change in both of their personalities for this positive development to occur.

Chapter Eight

Important Mental Health Terms That You Should Know

M**ANY** **MENTAL** **HEALTH** **PROFESSIONAL** terms have become popular and are often misunderstood. *Symptom* is one of them. Yet though sounding complex, the presence of a *symptom* merely indicates that something is wrong. Which is no different from the word's meaning when it is used to indicate an auto's malfunction. And the required next step with both mental health and cars is also the same. To determine precisely what is different from the usual functioning.

Eight Year Old Travis' Bike

Eight year old Travis loved to ride his bike. Though ancient, it was his first two wheeler and had been give to him by his grandfather who rode it when he was a child. The bike was chrome and had a headlight, tail light, and loud trilling bell. Even the name emblazoned on its side—Road Master—promised excitement and the allure of adulthood.

Though Travis was far from neat, a continuing conflict with his mother being his messy room, this attitude did not extend to his new bike. He polished the chrome daily and even cleaned its tires with his father's auto tire cleaner. When Travis fell and the bike got its second scratch (the first had occurred a half century before) he described this event to his mother as if it were a major catastrophe.

The summer drew to a close. Three weeks before school began, Travis stopped riding, polishing, or even being interested in his bike. It now lay at the back of the garage, like other unwanted pieces which had been inherited. But apart from this odd behavior, Travis seemed the same. He ate more than his mother expected and awoke at about the same time. He still talked little about his daily experiences but he never was a talker. Yet this change in his behavior worried her: why did a formerly beloved possession become– so abruptly–just a piece of trash.

Like in medicine, a mental health symptom refers to a puzzling event, which can be just about anything. While anyone would become concerned were a relative or neighbor to speak seriously of murder, the typical unusual behavior is far less dramatic. Perhaps a formerly disciplined person who now behaves impulsively, or a usually lackadaisical person becoming a worrier. Becoming forgetful or overly fearful of germs or insects, or the washing of hands repeatedly. Poorer school grades or a drastic change in eating or sleeping habits. Any noticeable difference which continues.

Everyone has moody days, puzzling behaviors, and says dumb things at times. It is their persistence which indicates that something significant is occurring. Here, what is being viewed is a true symptom, and its purpose is to communicate that help is required.

When evaluating a fever, a physician can usually declare, with a certain degree of confidence, that an infection exists within the body. Or that the presence of the tubercular bacillus indicates the illness tuberculosis. But the correlation between medical symptom and underlying cause is not always certain. A fever can indicate an infection—or heat stroke. A back pain can be caused by muscle strain, stress, or, rarely, a uterine tumor. And the relationship between a mental health symptom and its cause is even less exact than with a physical symptom since the psychological distress it causes is not inside a physical organ but within an unseen, theorized group of processes collectively termed *the mind*.

People often consider *the mind* to be a mystical notion and more in the realm of science fiction than science. But to speak of psychological capacities is no less real than to believe that muscles and bones are involved in movement. Actually, the mind is just as important in movement, for it contains what is termed the *executive function*: the mental ability to control all of a person's physical activities by deciding in advance what should be done.

Even as an infant's bones and muscles are not fully developed at birth, nor are their psychological capacities. These, as does their capacity to use language, develop throughout childhood and adolescence. The extended length of human development, unique among animals, derives from the complexity of the human brain rather than the size of its body.

Such basic abilities as controlling thinking and behavior; experiencing, modulating, and interpreting feelings; developing a sense of who one is, or *sense of self*; distinguishing reality from fantasy ("reality testing"); and others, are gained through a complex continuous interaction between the infant and their caregivers. Who are usually their mother and father but can be others. Through this two-way interchange, errors in the child's perception and behavior are corrected and become part of their ingrained psychological structure.

One of the first lessons which a child learns is the boundary of their body: that their mother is not a part of them. The mother is the most important figure in a child's first two years of life: they are symbiotic in a tight union. Only during the child's third year does the father become equally important. It is his role to break this maternal symbiosis between the infant and their mother and introduce the child to the larger world outside of their family.

A perfect interaction between a child and their parents is impossible, and not essential. The variation in what may be termed "healthy development" is wide, and it is only experiences which are vastly beyond these boundaries that create psychological difficulties.

For example, a mother may be so afraid of intimacy that she becomes anxious when her infant touches her. The baby will sense this and derive the unintended, destructive conclusion that closeness is dangerous. An experience which, if repeated often enough, will cause this judgment to become part of their personality and endure throughout their life.

An even more basic and destructive result occurs when the child develops weakness in their ability to distinguish reality from fantasy, or comes to question their capacity to do so. Conversations such as the following increase the likelihood of this occurring.

Child (to their continually arguing parents): "Why do you and daddy fight so much?"

Mother: "We never argue."

If a young child feels unable to trust the accuracy of what they sense, consider what a profound effect this will have on their later ability to function in the world as a student and a worker.

Mental health symptoms can be classified into three categories: those which derive from *weakness of basic psychological abilities* (for example, being impulsive or having difficulty concentrating); those that relate to conflict between parts of the personality, which is technically called a *neurosis* (as, wanting intimacy but being afraid of it); and *habits* which impede healthy living (such as smoking, overeating, or alcohol or drug abuse).

Psychological symptoms can be further classified into: the *reactive* (those which develop in *reaction to* a stress); and the *internalized* (those which persist even after the precipitating stress is gone). A symptom can have both reactive and internalized elements.

While all stresses produce effects, most do not require professional treatment. People encounter and overcome many difficulties on their own and mature through this experience. They are then better able to cope with future demands.

A reactive symptom develops in reaction to a new stress. When the stress is over, the symptom will disappear. But a stress which has persisted for a long time changes the normal functioning of the mind. Now, therapy is needed to work *inside of the mind:* to behave as a *catalyst* and nudge the mind back onto the path of its usual healthy development.

Thus symptoms, or oddities of behavior, warrant being investigated:
(1)if they persist, last more than a few months; and
(2) if they seriously interfere with normal school, work, or social functioning.

Symptoms can sometimes cause the popular though unlikely fear that one will "go crazy."

Dr. Delores "Went Crazy"

Being an obstetrician, Delores thought that she knew all there was to know about babies until having four of her own. All were under the age of six years. "Two are twins," she would quickly inform high school chums, not wanting them to think she had been t*hat* compulsive in satisfying her long expressed desire for a large family.

But Delores had other worries besides the care of her children. Her husband, an accountant, had been laid off. Her medical group's practice was beset by increased competition and malpractice insurance cost, and reduced income. Now her SUV was dying, along with their elderly German Shepard. Moreover, unlike the auto repairman and her practice, the veterinarian didn't take credit cards.

Dolores found herself eating and sleeping less, and worrying more. Instead of relaxing on weekends, she dutifully shuttled her children to whichever activities parenting experts or her friends insisted was essential to a child's healthy development.

Despite these pressures, Delores kept her appointments with me for she was afraid not to. In recent weeks she been existing on leftovers from the meals she prepared for her children and was barely sleeping. And despite the belief of her internist that she was healthy, she feared that a heart attack was imminent. While shopping she would get anxious, begin sweating, and her pulse would race. Sometimes she would have to flee the store, leaving her intended purchases in the grocery cart.

"I'm afraid that I'm going crazy," she told me at her first appointment. "You're not," I assured her, and then explained anxiety and panic disorder. Conditions which, despite the terror they create, are well understood by mental health professionals and far more amenable to treatment than most people believe.

What people believe to indicate "going crazy" varies. For a person who never cried, the presence of a tear would be enough. Another might require the inability to get out of bed, to work with their usual diligence, or having a persisting crazy thought. Like Leila did.

Leila's "Monstrous Gripping Hand"

Leila felt that her terror began right after she saw the movie with *that* scene. The hand which came from beneath the bed, grabbed the sleeping young woman's leg, and pulled her onto the floor to endure hours of rape and torture. Though the movie had a happy ending as these films go: the rapist was killed and the victim married the detective and began a typical suburban life.

Leila couldn't stop thinking of *the hand*. The first night after seeing the movie she looked under her bed before going to sleep. Thereafter, whenever her boyfriend, Doug, stayed over, she insisted that he look under the bed and into both closets in her tiny apartment before they went to sleep. Which he did though believing that it was crazy. Because he was horny and knew what would happen if he didn't, she thought. This fear of the hidden hand and rapist, which she sensed was irrational, stayed with her for years until she consulted me.

Why do puzzling thoughts frighten more than other problems like having to solve a math problem on a test or decide the best route to drive to a new job? Because thoughts are the end product of what the mind does and mental processes are what enable us to function. So if Leila could become overwhelmed even briefly by such an outlandish fear, what would prevent an even more illogical one from consuming her: perhaps that she was dying, or was not a person but a camel.

Seven Year Old Patty and her Friends

Patty was about the sweetest seven year old you are likely to meet. When I joked with her father that, when she was older, teenage boys would break down his door to date her, he responded, "I have a gun." But the story I most remember wasn't about Patty but of her three young friends.

All hung out at school, being drawn together by their painful rituals. One child feared that she might walk on a line in the sidewalk; a second was unable to view herself in the bathroom mirror when she washed. But it was the third child's unhappiness which most concerned them. This girl had begun to think of killing herself, an act which she would carry out by banging her head against the bathroom faucet in school. To prevent this, her friends would accompany her whenever she went into the bathroom.

Though frightening, such thoughts and behaviors just indicate that our mental lives are more complicated than we feel comfortable admitting. Almost never that we face a dangerous precipice. Thus these symptoms require informed, thoughtful investigation rather than unbridled worry. Discovering the underlying meaning of these odd thoughts and behaviors will liberate emotions and open the path toward a more fulfilling life.

While an uncomfortable experience can be a thought or behavior, it may also be an odd feeling, like being "twisted," as Ron experienced.

The Day When Ron's Grande Latte Didn't Help

Ron always treated himself to a Grande Latte when his day went bad. Though regretting the expense, it usually made him feel better. But that day it didn't. His day got worse.

Twenty minutes after Ron arrived at work he learned that the deadline for a programming project had been moved up two weeks. This was three weeks less than the time needed and if his team made a mistake it wouldn't be only they who would suffer: a military pilot could die. One who did nothing wrong except to trust the skill of Ron's programming department which created the plane's new control system. A flier who didn't know that the bonuses for Ron's department's success went to those upstairs, not the workers. But Ron had dealt with this kind of pressure before and managed to survive.

Two years before, when the survival of the company itself was in question because of a bad acquisition, Ron's department repaired the software they acquired and avoided the threatened lawsuit. Which might have led to indictment and the company's bankruptcy. He and his staff would do this too—pull the rabbit from the hat, get the ship to port, win another for the Gipper—or whatever the CEO chose as his inspirational phrase for that Monday's meeting.

Ron drove his workers as hard as he worked so they didn't complain. Early the following Sunday morning, about the time most people were turning over in bed, the project was completed. The programming wasn't as elegant as Ron liked but he was sure that the program worked and the pilots would survive. Still, Ron felt—twisted.

He couldn't describe this feeling better. Not depression or anger but more like he was being suspended by his waist and buffeted by the wind. He had this feeling before and it went away quickly. Now it stayed, and thereafter he experienced this feeling at odd times.

Not only when he was alone but during business meetings. Even, one morning, right after he and Janet had sex. She said he had a far away look in his face. He didn't respond, not knowing what to say, following his father's advice to not say anything when you weren't sure what to say. What was wrong with him or, using professional terms, what was Ron's *diagnosis*?

A diagnosis is intended to make matters clear, whether it relates to a car needing repair or the human mind. But some diagnoses don't clarify things for patients because, even if they are correct, they are poorly explained.

Mental health diagnoses are classified in two major guides. One is the International Classification of Diseases, or ICD-10, and is published by the World Health Organization. The second, used by most mental health professionals, is the Diagnostic and Statistical Manual of

Mental Disorders (DSM). First published in 1952, it has gone through five revisions, the most recent being DSM-IVR, with a new edition expected to be published in 2012.

Though appearing abstruse, this manual is no different in concept from that which auto repair shops use for it intends to answer the same question of where the problem fits.

Unlike the earlier mental health classifications (DSM-I and DSM-II), which were underlain by the concepts of psychoanalytic and psychodynamic thinking, the present guide is *behaviorally based* and their diagnoses do not associate a problem with an underlying cause. This diagnosis of a problem is called *atheoretical* because it is not tied to any particular theoretical explanation.

For example, to diagnosis someone with Dysthymic Disorder (300.4 in DSM-IVR), the person must have certain symptoms (remember, a symptom is a sign that something is wrong): being depressed for most of the day for a period of two years (one year for children and adolescents); and the presence, while feeling depressed, of at least two of the following: poor appetite or overeating, sleep difficulty; fatigue; low self-esteem; difficulty concentrating or making decisions; or feeling hopeless. If a person's behavior fits within this classification, they are diagnosed with Dysthymic Disorder.

But this diagnosis says nothing about the cause of the discomfort which the person is experiencing. One therapist may attribute it to a "chemical imbalance"; another may relate it to past and present life experiences. Yet both, though of opposing concept, are correct within the framework of this manual. Equally correct, though inaccurate, would be blaming this problem on a magic spell imposed by a relative, or Santa Claus being displeased.

Thus while formulating a diagnosis is essential to gaining insurance payment, learning it tells the psychotherapy patient nothing about how they might change in order to feel better.

These diagnoses, which use numeric codes, are of most value in research and for benefit payment, and constitute both the ICD and the DSM. But, because it is designed to be atheoretical, other information is more helpful when a therapist decides on the treatment which their patient would most benefit from.

Chapter Nine

How A Psychotherapist Decides What Treatment Is Needed

THE FACTORS WHICH A psychotherapist uses to determine what treatment their patient would most benefit from can be described by the acronym LESS: the *Length of time* the problem has existed; the *Ego capacities* (psychological abilities) involved; the *Severity of this problem* on the person's functioning; and the *Support in the environment* which they possess.

1. How long has the distress lasted?

Everyone has low periods in their life. These can be caused by school, family, or work stress. A teacher or boss may be unreasonable, or a child's behavior becomes impossible. Usually these pass quickly and, with this, so does the discomfort. But if the pain persists, then help is needed to overcome it and the longer the pain has lasted, the greater the harm it will have on the mind. Just like a small, untreated infection of a finger or tooth can eventually lead to life threatening consequences. But, just as with a bodily affliction, this is not certain. For while how long the stress has lasted is important, it is just part of the equation and the other three components are equally important.

2. *The ego capacities (psychological abilities) which are involved.*

People generally think that they were always as they are. But, as we really know, everyone was once very different: when they were a child, before they developed into adulthood. Then they were not just smaller but thought entirely differently, and even more so during their infancy. For the basic psychological abilities which each person counts on to enable them to function: their certainty of who they are, or their (*sense of self*, their ability to control their thinking and behavior (*self-control); and* their capacity to control their mood so that their feelings don't fluctuate between the extremes of depression and euphoria, are not inborn. Instead, each of these abilities is constructed during early childhood through the interaction between one's genetically derived, inborn capacities and their parenting environment. Which, for most infants, is provided by their biological parents.

Because no parents are perfect, they cannot provide an ideal experience for their child no matter how much the child are loved. Thus everyone develops *some* weakness in their basic psychological abilities or, as mental health professionals term them, *ego capacities*. Perhaps they will lack self-control and tend to behave impulsively; or have a less than sturdy sense of who they are and be more easily led into unwise behavior by others.

But these are not black and white affairs: that one either has or does not have limitations. Rather, all people have both psychological strengths and weaknesses. If the limitations are minor, they will have little effect on one's life. But bigger ones do matter. For example, a highly emotional person will have difficulty concentrating, be unpleasant to interact with and, despite their best effort, tend to sabotage their opportunities for happiness and job success. This will make it more difficult for them than for others without this deficiency to eliminate their unhappiness.

So when a person's distress reflects *severe* weakness of one or more of the basic ego capacities (the ability to control thinking and behavior, to modulate mood, to construct an accurate, sturdy sense of who they are, or to tolerate feelings), lengthy treatment is required for significant personal change to occur.

3. Severity of Impact on a Person's Life

Michael. the Lawyer Who Couldn't Speak When It Really Counted

Michael always considered *this* incident to define his life though others were more dramatic. Court cases he won against great odds, and his far too narrow avoidance of arrest by the military police the day he went AWOL to keep a date with a girl he had met. Both memories involved women but it was only *her* name which he remembered. Sharon. The woman he should have married. There were three others he would have been satisfied with but she had the two qualities he considered essential in a wife: intelligence and warmth.

Sharon was a second grade teacher. Every day she hugged every child in her class "goodbye" at the end of the school day. Once a fifth grader returned for his hug but was informed that he was now too old. As I have become, Michael told himself. Old and living alone, as a long past lover had predicted that I would. become.

One evening, after he made a helpful statement when Sharon was upset, she embraced him and said, "I want you to stay with me." A marriage proposal of a kind—to which he said...nothing. Not a word. He never proposed to a woman, not then or later. Did Sharon sense his fear when commitment was mentioned? Probably, for she was very perceptive. Maybe that was why *she* proposed. And because she knew that he desperately needed her.

Why did Michael behave in such a self-defeating manner? Because intimacy—that closeness which comes from sharing—terrified him on an unconscious level and wreaked havoc over his life. Not professionally, for he became wealthy, but in the personal aspects of living which were more important.

After that night Michael began feeling emotionally blocked when he was with Sharon. He didn't know what to say to her because he didn't know what was going on inside of him. And he didn't then realize that a crucial opportunity in his life had closed.

Michael's crippling difficulty with feelings and closeness derived from his basic psychological limitation. Other psychological inadequacies, as those which govern the ability to control thinking and behavior, can lead to just as devastating life consequences as effected Michael. Like what happened with Gretchen.

Dr. Gretchen's Medical Mistake

Tom knew that Gretchen was unpredictable but married her anyway. He was both charmed and repelled by what he considered her idiosyncrasies but grew to love her despite them. Even the ones that drove him crazy.

She was different when they first met as medical school students. More controlled and less impulsive. Medical school made students like that for only by being well organized could they follow the innumerable rules and legal requirements governing medical practice. Which included the profession's refusal to tolerate the smallest mistake.

After graduation, both wanted a normal family life so they chose specialties which permitted regular working hours. For Tom this was dermatology; for Gretchen, ophthalmology. They waited until completing their residencies before having children. Within four years, three had arrived: a boy and twin girls.

Whether it was the stress of parenting, her larger practice, or simply the increased fatigue from her new life style, Tom never could decide. But Gretchen changed, though not so greatly that he couldn't recognize her. Her behavior again became unpredictable. So puzzling that, late at night when she was asleep, he found himself questioning whether she was using one of the drugs she prescribed. Tom knew that physicians have the highest addiction rate of all the professions.

One evening he returned home early to find the children wandering about the house while Gretchen, who seemed oblivious of her responsibilities, washed her hair in the shower. This caused their first big argument. Thankfully, this time, the children were OK, but her next misbehavior had greater consequence.

A sixty two year old woman was referred to Gretchen for glaucoma evaluation, the referring optometrist finding her eye pressure reading to be twenty one mm Hg, on the border of what is considered to be normal. This patient was the last of the day and Gretchen was anxious to leave. Thus, after a cursory examination, Gretchen diagnosed the woman as having glaucoma and prescribed eye drops or surgery to bring down the pressure and avoid damage to the optic nerve. An everyday case, Gretchen would have said, had she been asked. But it wasn't routine for this woman.

Bothered by the shoddy examination she received, the woman went for a second opinion to a famed glaucoma expert in a nearby city. Who advised that not only did she not have glaucoma but that she was unlikely to ever develop it.

What she had were unusually thick corneas, each more than three times the thickness of the normal cornea. Which could have been quickly discovered by measuring their thickness, a procedure taking just seconds. This is crucial for the instrument which measures eye pressure, the tonometer, cannot be adjusted beyond the range of the normal corneal thickness. Thus a "fudge factor" must be used when considering its results and for this patient it was three to four.

So her apparently suspicious reading of twenty-one mm Hg was really a normal reading of between seventeen and eighteen. Had this patient used the eye drops or undergone the laser surgery which Gretchen prescribed, her vision would have been irreparably damaged.

Enraged at her close call with disaster, the woman filed a complaint with the state medical board. Which took her action very seriously, particularly since this patient was a State Appeals Court judge. Gretchen's impulsiveness, which Michael once considered charming, now had the potential to end her medical career.

Many limitations, whether psychological or physical, have little effect on a person's ability to do the important things in life: to care for themselves independently, to earn a living, and to gain and maintain enjoyable relationships. Having a limp, requiring glasses or a hearing aid, or having one or another of the usual aches which everyone occasionally suffers, do not interfere with these. But some limitations do.

Since this is a book on mental health I will leave information on physical disabilities to others except to generalize that their effects vary depending on the person. Two people with identical anatomical injuries may behave far differently. One becomes a semi-invalid while the other goes about their usual activities as if unimpeded—though experiencing discomfort to be sure. Which is not to say that having a paralyzed arm or arthritis is equivalent to the common cold.

Similarly, the effects of psychological limitations are not just present or absent. They follow a continuum from barely minimal to crippling. When small, others view them as reflecting a person's idiosyncrasies; if greater, they become their "emotional problem."

As we have seen with Michael and Gretchen, emotional problems can affect two major areas of life— work and love—or just one. Michael's problems didn't affect his ability to work; Gretchen's problems had begun to affect both spheres of her life. Yet many people can separate, *split-off,* their emotional life from their intellectual functioning and do well within that area of their life which is unaffected by their limitations. Thus the grades of a bright yet troubled child might well remain "A."

But when psychological problems are severe, functioning in all areas of living is reduced. Grades go down, work productivity declines, family and social life is diminished. Which people expect with medical problems too. Most people with a mild cold can function satisfactorily as student or employee or parent, but few will attempt these tasks while suffering from the flu.

4. *The Existence of Supportive Structures*

I recently read an interesting study about the countries where those with the most severe psychological difficulties, *psychotic disorders,* receive the most helpful treatment. Not, as one would expect, in modern Western nations. But in countries which are considered "undeveloped," or in "developing" Africa and India. While the Western nations generally provided only hospital or clinic treatment and medication, the poorer countries (and some small European programs too) gave additional services. They arranged housing for patients with their family or relatives, who also tried to find or subsidize jobs for them, and even introduced them to potential mates.

An American study twenty years earlier had found that, when they were provided adequate housing and vocational services, at least half of these severely disturbed, formerly hospitalized patients were living independent lives fifteen years later—and without the need for medication or mental health services!

The Truck Driver, Ten Year Old Linda and Her Gun

Ten year old Linda knew the man was a truck driver though she wasn't sure how. Probably one of her friends mentioned it. Now he wasn't driving a truck but a car. He once offered her candy which she refused though he lived just down the street from her. She learned *that* lesson in the first grade. "Don't ever take candy from a grown-up," the teacher intoned. "What if it's your father?" her seat mate, Patrick, asked mischievously. "Patrick..." the teacher said in a sarcastic tone, rolling her eyes. She and the other children laughed. Patrick was *always* like that: driving grown-ups crazy with his dumb questions though these sometimes caused her to think that he was smarter than everyone.

But that day the neighbor didn't offer her candy but only a ride home, in his beautiful red car. Which still smelled new, like the car her daddy once bought. It would be her mother's, Linda thought. After she killed her father with her grandfather's pistol which she watched him load and remembered how.

The gun was so big that its handle stuck out from her coat pocket. It was heavy too and caused the coat to droop down. This was why, though she knew that she shouldn't, she accepted the man's offer of a ride home. She was tired after walking to and from her grandfather's house.

Linda wondered when to shoot her father. Right after he walked in the door or in the middle of the night while he was sleeping. That would be easier for if her mother was up she might try to interfere. No, she'd shoot him as soon as she saw him, when she arrived home.

Linda had decided to kill her father the night before, after he again came to her room when her mother fell asleep. Now even Linda's pretense of being asleep didn't stop him. Putting *it* in her mouth and moving *it* back and forth until there was that nasty taste. Then he would leave.

Her six year old sister slept in the next room and Linda wondered whether he would do this with her when she was ten too. Maybe he already did and Stephanie just hadn't told her. Then there was Bonnie, who was only three.

Linda was the big sister and it was her job to stop her father. She didn't expect her mother to—not after the screams she heard coming from her parents' room at night. But soon her mother wouldn't scream anymore, and maybe the scary dreams would go away too.

The neighbor had stopped by the side of the road and asked Linda if she wanted a ride home. She nodded, he opened the car door, and she entered with a blank expression on her face. That was the first thing that struck him. Then he saw the gun butt sticking out from her coat pocket. So instead of driving Linda home, he took her to the village's police station where the police chief readily believed her story. Linda's father had been arrested for DWI several times and was well known to the department.

Her father was arrested again that day and Linda and her sisters were placed with an aunt she grew up with.

Along the way she gained teachers who encouraged her. Linda became an accomplished engineer and vowed that she would never become dependent on any man like her mother had been. Had Linda not had this supportive structure—a concerned neighbor, loving aunt, and caring teachers—her life might have taken a far harsher turn.

Every society expects its members to act in certain ways. To be law-abiding, of course; and to behave in line with certain conventions depending on their age. Which means attending school or being employed and able to live independently.

Children and teenagers have parents to help them with these tasks. If they are absent or inadequate, the government tries to provide substitutes in the form of foster parents and structured residences. But adults who have, so to speak, aged out of the system, must depend on friends or relatives for support though these may not be available. And, despite the existence of public services, caring and commitment is still a family matter.

Thus, when contrasting the likely futures of two individuals with similar abilities and difficulties, one can be more hopeful about that person with the more extensive support network, whether this is provided by family members, government agencies, or some combination of these. Though it can be crucial in the lives of some people, psychotherapy alone cannot substitute for this.

Chapter Ten

*Characteristics of Psychotherapists Which
Matter—and Those Which Don't*

THE TERM *THERAPY* HAS BECOME commonplace. Today, there are few service workers who do not add, or try to add, this noun to their job description. They hope to elevate its prestige, ease their tasks, and maybe increase their salary too. Thus we have reading therapists instead of reading teachers and massage therapists instead of masseuses.

But in the mental health field, therapy has a very particular meaning. It refers to the healing of the mind. This includes such matters as resolving emotional conflicts when one is afraid of closeness, or replacing deficient psychological capacities with more mature ones and so becoming better able to control behavior.

While other important changes (stopping smoking, losing weight) can be aided by a mental health professional, those doing this work are not, strictly speaking, engaging in psychotherapy. Which is what people sense for few say that they are going "for therapy" when leaving for their Weight Watchers class.

Studies have found that how psychotherapists view their work has little to do with what their patients find helpful, or even what they actually do. Thus psychotherapists who describe their work differently may actually be engaging in similar behaviors when providing treatment.

Moreover, studies have found that it is the *quality of the relationship* between the patient and their psychotherapist which is crucial in determining its effectiveness.

Thus while a psychotherapist may describe themselves as being "behavioral" or "interpersonal" or "psychoanalytic" in orientation, one can be sure of exactly what they do only after being treated by them. Which is why I rarely refer people to therapists, for knowing them socially tells me nothing about how effective they are in treating particular difficulties.

All professionals have strengths and weaknesses. What makes them a good fit for one patient might bar them from success with another. So while glowing testimonials from former patients guarantee little, negative comments should be taken seriously. For it may, but not necessarily does, indicate that something very wrong occurred during therapy. And that a therapist is likable, which most are, merely indicates that they exhibit the courtesy and good marketing technique which one would expect of any successful business owner. Not that they have the skills necessary to heal, which is *the* goal of psychotherapy.

Keeping these cautionary words in mind, therapists can be placed into two major classifications: those who work with individuals and provide individual therapy; and those who work with groups and treat several people (usually six to eight) simultaneously. Some therapists may do both individual and group therapy, and a person can have individual therapy with one clinician and group therapy with another. They might also be engaging in marital therapy with a third therapist, with the couple being seen together to improve their functioning, but this situation is uncommon.

So one way of describing a therapist is by considering how many patients they treat simultaneously, whether one or more.

Therapists can also be categorized by whether their patients are children, adolescent, or adult, with some treating all ages. But special training is needed to treat children and adolescents for a therapist must behave far differently with them than they do with adults—as every parent would expect.

Though we were all once children, interacting with a child is a skill which must be re-learned. Because society frowns on what it considers immature behavior, most adults have lost their childlike capacities though some would be helpful even to grownups. Enthusiasm, the capacity for wonder, and the spontaneity to explore are productive abilities for those of any age.

Non-professional Ways in Which Therapists Differ

1. The Sex of the Therapist

I was in a supermarket trying to decide whether to buy olives when the mother of a twelve year old telephoned me. Her daughter had been evaluated by a female psychiatrist who the mother didn't like. Could I see her? I agreed, and the girl and her parents came to my office. While their daughter sat in the waiting room, I spoke first with her parents alone.

"I think my daughter would be more comfortable with a female therapist," the mother said quickly.

"If you told me that on the phone I would have worn a dress,." I replied.

The parents smiled, and I evaluated their child. Despite my recommendation for treatment they never returned, just as they had earlier rejected what the female psychiatrist advised. What the mother disliked about that doctor was her refusal to reveal everything which the child told her, which was the proper professional way to behave.

This situation was clear: whether the therapist was male or female, the mother *did not want* her child to receive therapy.

This is often the case when a parent seeks a therapist of a particular sex for their child. By their behavior this parent is also revealing *their* unconscious emotional conflict with men or women and not their child's level of comfort with professionals of one or another sex..

All psychotherapists (and people) have both male and female characteristics, and a patient will relate to whichever of these are needed at a particular moment in treatment.

I once treated a delightful, very smart, five year old girl who, after I explained the nature of scary dreams, responded, "I know *that*." Her mother had deserted the family when she was two years old and she lived with her father. He tended to date single mothers who were less maternal than him and wound up being a mothering figure for their children too.

Yet for a few patients the sex of the therapist *is* relevant. If a patient had particularly destructive childhood experiences with their mother or father they may feel most comfortable with a therapist of the opposite sex. Which is not to say they can only progress with that therapist but that the initial interview might be more comfortable and thus more likely lead to their continuing in treatment.

Nor, and this may surprise some, is the sexual orientation of the patient an important issue, for both heterosexual and gay patients usually have identical worries: about fidelity and communication in their relationship, and parenting issues.

2. The Age or Physical Attractiveness of the Therapist

Another demographic of little importance is the therapist's age or physical attractiveness. Whether in their seventies or twenties, the age of the therapist has little to do with their capacity to heal. Though the younger clinician is often less effective because of their limited experience. More than one older physician has remarked to me that "young doctors tend to be too aggressive." But lengthy experience can also just mean that decades long errors are being repeated.

Experience in conducting psychotherapy, like that with any skilled activity, is important. But it is the right kind of experience and how one has related to it that is crucial.

Some psychotherapists relate to their work as if it were a religion and they were a high priest who conducts healing rituals. Thus they consider experience to be irrelevant since they regard treatment as consisting of a patient interacting with *them*, regardless of that person's uniqueness. And if the patient fails to improve the fault also lies with *them*, for one who has been ordained and is carrying out a historic ritualized procedure is, by nature of this, infallible.

But a therapist who has treated difficulties similar to yours and benefited from their earlier mistakes *is* more valuable. Not that they were unhelpful in their earlier years but, with increased experience, their capacity to heal has become broader, more consistent, and effective as their ability and perceptiveness have developed.

Research in a variety of fields has supported the finding that taller or more physically attractive people tend to be perceived as more competent and are more financially successful. I do not doubt this is true with psychotherapists too, and also that it is irrelevant to their capacity to heal.

3. The Therapist's Appearance and Office Decor

That business appearance does matter is a well accepted notion. It is exemplified by real estate agents, most of whom drive impressive cars.

I once joked with a patient that I hoped, even after his therapy was completed, he would continue to park his Lexus in front of my office in order to improve my professional image. On another occasion the surgeon/father of a child I was treating apologized for his obviously expensive suit, an uncommon sight in my suburban area, saying that he hadn't had time to change out of his working clothes.

Yet unlike physical attractiveness, a therapist's appearance is significant for it, like their office, indicates personal choice and may convey important information which should not be ignored.

Years ago, a retired police officer was greatly upset by his fourteen year old son's desire to wear an earring, a common sight on today's teenagers. As are slashed or baggy pants, skimpy shorts, the wearing of male pajama bottoms by girls, or facial piercings. But while acceptable for a patient, most people would feel uncomfortable consulting a professional who dressed similarly. Because their appearance would not be what was expected, it would interfere with establishing the minimal level of comfort required to share confidential material.

A psychotherapist cannot change whether they are tall or short, beautiful or homely, and everyone knows this. But to deliberately *choose* an atypical characteristic raises question in the mind of the prospective patient as to exactly who the therapist is, and this question should properly relate only to the patient.

The same applies to the decor of a professional office. Though inevitably reflecting the psychotherapist's individuality, it should not hinder the development of the therapeutic relationship. What is acceptable at home may not be wise in a place of business, or on an office website.

I once read an outstanding short story by Jeffery Deaver which described a blind date. The woman was hesitant for she had not dated in many years and unbeknown to her, her date had just strangled another woman. The twist in this story was that while it appeared he was about to murder her too, he was really a hired killer who the woman was contracting with to eliminate her tiresome, controlling husband so she could begin a new life. This tale so impressed me that I determined to see if I could write something similar. I think that I did, though today there is little market for brief fiction.

Within fifteen hundred words my story told of a woman who, after being traumatized as a child, was advised by her therapist to "confront your fears openly."

Which she did, leading to horrifying consequences. Though the story is basically feminist, describing how this woman became assertive, and the last line invites laughter, its most positive figure is a serial killer. One who, alas, does not belong on a psychologist's website. Even if friends who read my story said that, once begun, it is impossible to put down. But all had advised against my publishing it online, saying that it was too different from the mental health advice on my website and would puzzle or even frighten potential patients.

Yet no therapist can totally conceal their personality; nor would they want to. Some years ago there was a notorious photo on the cover of Vanity Fair magazine: that of a naked, very pregnant actress. While it did not shock me, and despite the magazine's excellent written content, I would not keep that issue in my waiting room though I also did not believe that this picture would upset any child. But their viewing it would bother me, for I believe that children, to the degree possible, should be shielded from adult matters.

Other information about a therapist is also useful. Is the temperature in their office comfortable and are there enough chairs. Do they offer beverages, and are they receptive to changing appointments because of illness or hazardous driving conditions. In short, do they relate as would any caring person to another, whether client or not.

With some of these matters there is no definite answer. Therapists, like all people, behave individually, and no one choice is best so long as it is informed and considered.

Some therapists do not offer beverages in their office feeling that, if the patient wants one, they can bring it from one of the many coffee shops in most urban areas. While these are available in my suburban area too, they are not as convenient as in a city. So I offer beverages: water, juice, and regular or diet soda but not hot coffee, fearing that it might spill onto a children.

Years ago I was treating some adolescent girls in a therapy group. Though I made sure that water and soft drinks were available, they pleaded for snacks, saying that they were hungry after school. So I provided these, and it became a project unto itself.

Some girls preferred vanilla cakes, others would eat only chocolate. Even whether the chocolate covered peanut butter bars were wafer or hard coated became an issue. As did the flavor of the potato chips (sour cream and onion was OK but never taco). Though I sometimes felt as if I was running a grocery store and not a therapy group, the girls did change for the better and this is what was most important.

While I felt comfortable providing snacks in this group's therapy, I only occasionally do so with my individual patients. Like the gangling athletic teenager who also said that he was hungry after school and requested potato chips—but not the snack cakes which I provide for the girls. Thereafter, I kept chips on hand but only for him and another teenager. And rather than gorge on them as I feared, they ate only a handful each session. What was important was not the snack but its meaning: that I cared. These teenage boys were in foster care and didn't have real parents. My other adolescent patients did.

There are other considerations in offering snacks: having food in the office might attract insects; and a child could have a food allergy or gorge on it. Also, mothers have very definite ideas about what their children should eat and my asking their permission could place them in a bind and hinder their commitment to their child's treatment. But patients are welcome to bring food with them, just as some children carry a beloved small figure or stuffed animal.

I once did an informal, non-scientific Internet survey among psychologists seeking their policy on providing snacks to patients. Almost all did not, though some put out candy at holiday time. So my offering drinks is atypical, and reflects my intuition more than professional consensus. That doing so might aid the interaction between therapist and patient but it is not something which is essential to therapeutic progress.

Chapter Eleven

Choosing A Psychotherapist From Among the Eleven Major Brands

BECAUSE PREJUDICES AFFECT CONCLUSIONS, before describing these psychotherapies I should state my own clinical orientation. It consists of several general beliefs deriving from different though closely related treatment philosophies.

First, is the idea that *why* a psychological symptom developed is crucially important, as are early life experiences. Then, that the mind consists of psychological capacities, and conscious and unconscious elements.

Finally, that because of the innate inertia of all biological structures, every personality change creates resistance. So the larger the change which is attempted, the greater will be the difficulty. Much like it is easier to repave a road than to build an entirely new one.

I also believe that physical contact between patient and therapist, apart from a handshake if the patient desires, is not helpful and can be risky. This guideline alone places me at odds with a small number of therapies who are termed "body oriented," which will not be covered in this chapter..

There is one further guideline which I believe is important: that if a new treatment method is proposed, there must be a logical connection between it and well accepted effective treatments. For example, Freud's notion of the unconscious had a long history in philosophy and literature, and his original procedure involved the then conventional intervention of hypnosis.

As previously stated, therapists may describe themselves as individual or group therapists; or by another name: psychoanalytic or Sullivanian or behaviorist or psychodynamic. Those who find it difficult to classify their work using one of these terms may call themselves "eclectic," meaning that their work reflects elements from several theories of treatment and they choose what they believe is the most helpful part from each for a particular patient.

Psychotherapy Treatment Methods ("Brands" of Psychotherapy)

1. *Psychoanalysis and Psychoanalytic Psychotherapy*

Psychoanalysis has been publicly revered, criticized, and part of American culture since the nineteen twenties.

Though it was long the treatment of choice by the wealthy, and considered the gold standard against which all mental health treatment methods are measured, it is not. Rather, it is both a theory of psychological development and a treatment method. A therapist can accept some of its dogmas and reject others, particularly since it considered suitable for relatively few patients.

The basic concepts underlying this method of treatment are well known and have been popularized in movies. These include: the *unconscious; repression,* or the making unconscious of a forbidden thought; the *resistance* to these thoughts through such psychological defenses as fears (*phobias*); the tendency to transfer early life emotions onto later experiences, or *transference;* the tendency to repeat a troubling behavior until the emotional need which underlies it is met (the *repetition compulsion*); and the belief that people behave to maximize their pleasure in line with the *pleasure principle*, this however being constrained by reality, or the *reality principle.*

Though many of these ideas date to ancient times, it was Sigmund Freud who devised the term "psychoanalysis." He replaced the earlier use of hypnosis to treat emotional problems with that of *free association* in which the patient is required to speak freely whatever comes into their mind.

Whether one accepts or rejects them, these theories demand understanding for psychoanalysis has sought the most complete understanding of human behavior and influences fields ranging from art to warfare. As a noted child development researcher, Charles Wenar, once remarked, "To really understand human behavior, you must go to psychoanalytic theory."*

*personal communication

Central to psychoanalysis is the concept of the *unconscious*: that there is a part of the mind which effects behavior without awareness. The unconscious is considered the underpinning of psychological life. A small part of it is *the conscious*, thoughts of which we are aware, often just briefly when we consider something.

During early childhood when our mind is rapidly developing, experiences are imprinted within us, much as happens with many animals. The most important of these experiences are those with our parents and other adults who, because of their far greater abilities and our dependency upon them, seem like Gods to us.

But some of the things which we learn are incorrect and interfere with our ability to have a satisfying life. For example, parents who fear new experiences will, without conscious intent, teach their child this fear. So when this child reaches adulthood they too will hesitate when confronting change. They may explain their puzzling tendency with the illogical conclusion that such behavior is safer or provide another apparently plausible reason. Any explanation rather than admitting that their behavior is motivated by unconscious forces.

And if they do momentarily relate their behavior to their parents' fear, they will likely repress this knowledge: force it from their conscious awareness back into their unconscious. Why do they behave in this way? Because, having experienced their parents as Gods throughout their formative years, this view has become exalted and protected from criticism.

When conflict between an unreal image of parents and real world events occurs, it is kept from awareness by *ego* or *psychological defenses,* which attempt to maintain calm when beliefs and feelings conflict. This is the major function of all the psychological defenses: to reduce the person's feeling of distress so they can function normally. Because childhood beliefs and behaviors are woven within the fabric of one's adult personality, they must be defended and maintained regardless of the psychological cost.

A gifted psychiatrist/psychoanalyst wrote of his treatment of a surgeon who, because of his destructive early family experiences, felt compelled to sexually expose himself in public when he was an adult. He was, symbolically, showing-off to his mother as might a young child, despite the self-reproach, disgust, and huge professional risk which this behavior caused.*

Long-term ingrained fears and erroneous beliefs can be healed through psychoanalytic therapy because the therapist becomes a trusted figure, much like parents are throughout everyone's childhood. Then, when self-defeating attitudes or incorrect perceptions are exhibited, these are corrected by the therapist, and change.

Though identical concepts underlie psychoanalysis and psychoanalytic psychotherapy, these treatment methods differ with regard to the frequency of treatment, the techniques used, and the patients they would benefit.

*Lindon, John A., Does technique require theory? *Bulletin of the Menninger Clinic,* 1991, 55,1, pp.9-11.

Freud is now considered to be a far less rigid and austere psychoanalyst than his disciples pictured him and later tried to emulate. One modern analyst made no comment when a mother spoke of her fear that her ill child might die, after which the patient ended treatment, considering her doctor to be inhumane.*

Freud even spoke with his patients of subjects far from their personal problems. He was particularly gifted in interpreting dreams and, from them, sometimes predicted the existence of long buried family secrets which investigation later confirmed.

During psychoanalysis the patient is treated three to four sessions per week. Psychoanalytic psychotherapy sessions are less frequent, usually once or twice a week. Also, the stress of psychoanalysis, during which long periods of silence occur, requires that a patient, though suffering, have enough satisfaction in their life and good enough control over their behavior to tolerate this frustration. During psychoanalytic psychotherapy there are fewer periods of silence, these are briefer, and far more emotional support is given by the therapist.

But these treatment methods are not black and white affairs. One is not better than the other for: they are intended for different types of problems.

*Lohser, Beate, and Newton, Peter M., *Unorthodox Freud: the View From The Couch,* New York City: Guilford Press, 1996, p.193.

Moreover, therapists differ and the boundary of what has been considered "psychoanalysis" has increasingly expanded, with greater acceptance of the analyst expressing empathy. The esteemed, traditionally trained psychiatrist and "gifted psychoanalyst" I referred to earlier, John Lindon, M.D., Ph. D., who achieved remarkable results with unusually disturbed patients, described himself, early in his career, as being a "wild therapist" because of his willingness to alter his treatment methods depending of the needs of his patient.

2. *Jungian Psychotherapy*

Jungian psychotherapy derives from the ideas of a Swiss psychiatrist, Carl Jung. Originally a disciple of Freud before breaking with him, Jung developed his own theories of behavior and treatment but kept the basic concept of the unconscious as being the primary motivating force in human activity.

Jung believed that the best way to investigate the mind was through a study of dreams and folklore. He sought to reconcile the patient's life with what he termed universal *archetypes* which all people possess. These are tendencies to behave in particular ways and make up the *collective unconscious*, which is revealed in religion, art, dreams, and myths.

These archetypes are considered to be as real psychologically as the human arm is biologically, with both having developed through evolution. Jung believed there is an innate need for self-realization, much as psychoanalytic psychotherapists believe that there is an innate tendency towards psychological health.

For Jung, mental illness arises when a person has difficulty achieving their individuality. This is termed a *shadow,* an unconscious complex which includes a person's rejected aspects. This shadow may have both desirable qualities (as warmth) and destructive qualities (as brutality). One task of Jungian therapy is to make these tendencies conscious to avoid their being projected onto others, a task similar to that which psychoanalytic psychotherapists perform.

Though Jung's concepts have gained interest in many fields, he was primarily a treating psychiatrist and followed his theories with only some of his patients. With others he used his own brand of psychoanalysis with the goal not being "treatment" for the patient, for he considered this to lie within the realm of psychotherapy, but rather for them to discover who they are and to achieve their final cohesive maturation as an individual.

3. *Interpersonal Psychotherapy*

Harry Stack Sullivan, the founder of the Interpersonal Psychotherapy movement, was one of the most influential psychiatrists of the twentieth century despite his graduation from a diploma mill medical school.*

*Perry, Helen Swick, *Psychiatrist of America: The Life of Harry Stack Sullivan*, Belkap Press of Harvard University, Cambridge, 1982.

Sullivan was a lonely child who was born into a desperately poor farming family in upstate New York. He gained little affection from either parent. Though an excellent high school student, he dropped out of college and disappeared for two years during which it was long speculated that he was hospitalized for schizophrenia. At nineteen, he began study at the Chicago College of Medicine, a school which closed in 1917, the same year he graduated.

Sullivan's early clinical work revealed his talent for treating patients who were previously considered incurable and unreachable by psychotherapy. Through his Interpersonal Therapy, during which these patients were provided a corrective emotional experience, the rate of healing significantly increased. He believed that mental illness derived from the distorted ideas about relating which people carried over from their childhood. Thus the role of the therapist was not to behave as a blank screen, as did the typical psychoanalyst, but to actively participate and to point out, in a warm accepting atmosphere, the errors in interacting with other people which the patient had been making.

Though considering himself a psychoanalyst, Sullivan emphasized social factors and joined with other dissidents from Freudian theory to found the Washington School of Psychiatry. After World War Two he helped to establish the World Federation for Mental Health.

Sullivan greatly influenced psychiatry throughout the nineteen-thirties and nineteen-forties, being a leading force in opposing the use of Electric Convulsive Treatment (ECT) and psychosurgery which were gaining in popularity. Despite this he is little spoken of today perhaps because, in a sense, most present therapists are inherently Sullivanian and pay great attention to their patients' relationships.

4. *Existential Psychotherapy*

Existential psychotherapy derives from the concept that because all people are alone, their life will lack meaning unless they make choices and take responsibility for their decisions. The existential therapist believes that each person must create the standard by which they live. Yet doing so involves a basic conflict for while making decisions arouses anxiety, being courageous and doing so adds meaning to a person's life. Thus the role of the therapist is to enable the patient to make healthier decisions, a process that will gradually reduce their anxiety.

This treatment derives from the nineteenth century philosophical beliefs of Kierkegaard and Nietzsche, who reached identical conclusions from opposite poles. Kierkegaard was a minister who believed that if people live passionately, they will find meaning in life through their struggle. This goal could be enabled through faith and trust in God.

But for Nietzsche, God was "dead" and an old-fashioned concept. He believed that people should discard conventional standards and, by using their free will, live as they would, creating their own rules.

Both Kierkegaard and Nietzsche emphasized the importance of courage, personal choice, and freedom in day-to-day life.

Existential psychotherapists are far less concerned with the patient's past than therapists who follow psychoanalytic or interpersonal treatment methods. While early life events may be considered, the emphasis in existential treatment is the patient's present and future. That they gain awareness and behave with greater freedom, responsibility, and courage to surmount their anxieties, which derive from their sense that their existence is threatened. Yet, even during intense suffering, existentialists believe that life can always have meaning.

5. *Gestalt Psychotherapy*

Like existential psychotherapy, Gestalt psychotherapy focuses on the patient's present life and emphasizes personal responsibility. But it also addresses the interaction between therapist and patient, and the patient's social relationships and how these have developed.

During Gestalt psychotherapy the patient becomes aware of what they are doing, changes it and, through this process, comes to live more in the present, discarding the incorrect beliefs and self-defeating feelings of their past. Like all psychotherapies it strives to enable the patient to realize their creative abilities and thus gain greater fulfillment.

Gestalt psychotherapy is an action oriented therapy. For example, while a psychoanalytic therapist might encourage a passive patient to talk about her husband, the Gestalt therapist would ask the patient to imagine that the therapist *is* the husband and to speak assertively to him. They might also focus on the breathing or mannerisms of the patient when speaking about different matters. The Gestalt therapist tries to resolve difficulties by paying attention to how they are expressed in words *and* behavior, not just verbally.

Problems are seen as representing a fixed way of relating to experiences which derive from one's past. The goal of therapy is to make the patient more responsive to the present, an outcome which can only be achieved if the therapist rejects any conception of how the patient should ultimately be. Healthy personality change occurs through identification with present experience and not rigid beliefs about life. It is considered that the more a person ignores present experience, the more their life will remain the same.

Gestalt therapy also differs from psychoanalytic therapy is emphasizing that the patient must create their own interpretation of experience rather than adopt those of the therapist. Discovery and experience, not accepting the interpretation of the therapist, is a major difference between the two treatment methods.

Gestalt means *whole* and indicates that the patient must be viewed as part of their entire experience, and that fulfillment can only be gained within this greater framework. While to become a Gestalt therapist requires particular training, each therapist will behave differently depending on how they have integrated their experiences. Some therapists emphasize body work, others less so.

6. Primal Psychotherapy

Primal psychotherapy is based on a simple concept: that unhappiness originates from childhood trauma and, to overcome this, the pain must be re-experienced. Which cannot be through traditional talking methods since this uses the mature reasoning areas of the brain while the source of the early imprinted pain derives from more primitive brain functioning.

This *primal pain,* which causes the adult distress, begins in the first three years of life and results from inadequate parenting. By re-experiencing these pains back to the first trauma which occurred at birth, healing is considered to occur. During primal therapy, the patient experiences a connected feeling between past and present, and meanings become attached to feelings. Since emotional difficulties reflect a repression of feelings, it is the experiencing of them which heals. Intense emotions will be felt after which the patient gains insight into their life.

Primal therapy has been criticized on a number of grounds: that it is simplistic; that people cannot remember infantile experiences; and that too much faith is placed in emotional catharsis, a relief which may be temporary since the mere expressing of powerful feelings is not considered sufficient to resolve them.

7. Neuro-linguistic Programming (NLP) Psychotherapy

Neuro-linguistic programming was one of the New Age treatments which arose in the nineteen seventies. It was devised by Richard Bandler and John Grinder whose focus was the effect of language, thinking, and behavior on the success of personal relationships. They theorized that neurological processes, language, and ways of relating, have been learned and programmed in the course of one's life and that these can be altered to meet with greater success in achieving personal goals.

Their major concept was that learning effective personal interactions can produce "magical" results by granting a person (so to speak) better software for their brain. Thus their first book, published in 1975, was called *The Structure of Magic*. It was based on their studies of the work of the eminent Gestalt therapist, Fritz Perls, the influential family therapist, Virginia Satir, and the noted hypnotist/psychiatrist, Milton Erickson.

Soon Bandler and Grinder began claiming that their method was not only effective as therapy but could be used to increase the likelihood of success in business by: knowing what you want; flexibly trying different behaviors; and noting and adopting those which are successful in furthering you towards your goal.

In later years there were legal battles over the ownership of the NLP trademark with little consensus over the best practice or length of training required for proficiency in its methods.

Critics state that NLP is more a lucrative industry than an effective, researched, and structured treatment method. That it uses vague scientific sounding terms and analogies to gain legitimacy; and that there is no evidence to support its claims of effectiveness as a therapeutic tool or in advancing business or social success.

8. Transactional Analysis (TA) Psychotherapy

Transactional analysis, or TA as it is called, was devised by a psychoanalytically trained psychiatrist, Eric Berne, in the nineteen fifties. It has strong roots in psychoanalytic and interpersonal theory with its emphasis on the importance of early life experience on later behavior, and the need to pay attention to the give-and-take of relationships in order to change one's life.

But while psychoanalysis emphasizes the making conscious of unconscious motives, TA's major focus is how people interact, whether the *scripts* which people follow are helpful or maladaptive. If unhelpful, they were termed *games*, and TA asserts that the lives of most people could be changed simply by becoming more aware of their behavior patterns and altering them.

An adult is considered to have three *ego states:* Parent, Adult, and Child, all deriving from early life experiences. Too stressful childhood experiences create these symptomatic games in later life.

TA games have unconscious scripts. These are ways of relating which were originally rewarded by parents or other powerful childhood figures. Thus a script which contains the commandment, "Don't be close!," will cause its possessor to reject intimacy as an adult.

Problems may also occur when adults interact with two different ego states. For example, a supervisor who instructs a worker to complete a project will use an Adult Ego State, or grown-up way of relating. If the worker responds, "Stop telling me what to do," they are using the Child Ego State. This clash of ego states will cause garbled communication and conflict. Similar difficulties can occur in marriages.

TA insists that people with virtually any problem, once they figured out their scripts and changed them, could "be OK."

TA is basically a therapy which seeks to use "what works" within the framework of its basic model: the *Parent, Adult, Child Ego States;* the *Transactions*, or communication between people which contain positive (enjoyable) or negative (painful) consequences; and the *Injunctions*, or messages which are built into scripts (as, "Don't grow up"). These and *Redefining*, the distorting of reality to conform to ingrained scripts; and *Games,* lead to social interactions which proceed towards a predictable result.

Berne died in 1970, before the TA movement expanded. Some later techniques, as the attempted "reparenting" of schizophrenics using techniques which alleged profound physical and emotional abuse, would likely have shocked him.

Berne wrote two popular books on TA, *Games People Play,* and *What Do You Do After You Say Hello.* Another widely read TA book, *I'm OK, You're OK*, was written by his friend, Thomas Harris.

9. *Hypnotherapy*

The inaccurate ideas which are held by many people about hypnosis have been framed by the old movies they saw on Turner Classic Movies. A Sherlock Holmes or Hitchcock film in which the hypnotist twirled a watch and forced the subject to do or to reveal what they otherwise would not; or a similar scene from a modern X-Files episode. But rather than being unsavory, the capacity to be hypnotized reflects an ingrained part of the human condition and thus is as old as humanity itself.

Hypnosis is simply an altered state of consciousness in which attention is paid to only a select experience. For example, an infant taken to the ball park may naturally tune out the noise. This selective attention is hypnosis.

Hypnosis is used in medicine for many conditions: to help cancer and burn patients cope with pain; to ease the pain of childbirth or dental procedures; as an anesthetic during surgery, if none is available as in wartime; to help lower blood pressure, lose weight, and stop smoking. Even to eliminate warts, for these are caused by a virus which the body's immune system has the power to kill.

When used medically, hypnosis is safe and has no side effects. Despite this benefit, it is not widely used because it takes time to prepare the patient—far longer than a simple injection of anesthesia. Ninety percent of people can be hypnotized for medical purposes. But only ten percent of this group are such good hypnotic subjects that major surgery can be performed using only hypnosis as the anesthetic. Ten percent of people can't be hypnotized.

A rapid test of hypnotic susceptibility is asking whether a person became so greatly involved in reading as a child that they would tend to lose themselves in a book. These people are usually good hypnotic subjects.

The British Medical Association, the American Medical Association, and the National Institute of Mental Health have endorsed the use of hypnosis for both medical and psychological difficulties.

Techniques which are used in hypnotherapy include: enabling the patient to *recall and re-experience traumatic memories* (following an accident or battlefield event); *guided imagery*, when a patient is provided a relaxing experience; *post-hypnotic suggestion*, when a patient is encouraged to behave in a certain way; and *visualization*, when a patient is told to imagine an outcome, following the concept that this is then more likely to occur.

Although hypnosis is an accepted and safe treatment method, it is not widely used in psychotherapy. I can explain this reason best by telling a story.

During my training as a psychologist I had a medical school course in hypnosis which, many years later, I still consider valuable both personally and professionally. It was taught by an English psychiatrist who, in his practice, would hypnotize disturbed adolescents and implant in them the suggestions that they felt better, more secure, and confident. These teenagers did improve—but only briefly.

Many psychological difficulties arise over a period years and have become part of a person's ingrained personality. It is not reasonable to believe that these difficulties could be ameliorated without underlying change. While symptoms like anxiety can be reduced by hypnosis, it should only be used while the problems which cause it are being resolved.

Moreover, hypnosis cannot provide that insight to a person which will enable them to construct a calming, more logical sense of who they are; or grant them the personal relationship with the therapist which is crucial in healing. So while hypnosis can be a helpful adjunct during psychotherapy, it should not be considered the whole of treatment for emotional difficulties.

I consider the greatest value of hypnosis to be with medical conditions, and to enable relaxation and stress reduction. For these, it should definitely be more widely used.

I offer to virtually all of my adult patients a self-hypnotic relaxation CD which I have personally used for more than twenty-five years. The induction procedure is derived from a research study which related the effectiveness of the body's immune system to the development of cancer, hypothesizing that stress reduces the body's innate ability to kill cancer cells, a theory which is widely believed today.

I first used this self-hypnotic procedure myself, while working as a hospital administrator and managing a problematic staff. During this time I began getting pain in my neck at the end of each day. My interpretation of this symptom, that the employees were giving me "a pain in the neck," provided no relief. After reading this research study in an issue of the American Journal of Clinical Hypnosis, I made a tape of the induction procedure which was used. I listened to it twice, the pain disappeared and, like they say, the rest is history.

Several cautions should be followed when considering hypnotic treatment. Because hypnotists are not licensed, anyone can title themselves a "hypnotist." Also, one should not volunteer to be a subject for hypnosis in a club. While these hypnotists are often skillful, several research papers have described subjects who, after their experience, wound up in a hospital's Emergency Room with frightening, apparently life threatening symptoms. It was later discovered that they had, months before, been hypnotized during a stage performance and not all of the hypnotic suggestions given to them were extinguished.

If hypnosis for medical or mental health difficulties is sought, a referral can be gained at the website of The American Society of Clinical Hypnosis (*www.asch.net*), an organization which trains physicians, psychologists, social workers, and other professionals in hypnotic techniques.

10. *Rational Emotive Behavior Therapy (REBT)*

Rational Emotive Behavior Therapy (REBT) was one of the first cognitive behavioral therapies. It was devised by a psychologist, Albert Ellis, in the 1950's. Ellis' lifelong interest in changing behavior might have been predicted from an event in his adolescence. Realizing that he was shy around women, Ellis forced himself to speak to one hundred women in one month. Though not getting a date, he felt that through this experience his fear of being rejected by women decreased.

Although trained as a psychoanalyst, Ellis developed his own theory which he termed Rational Therapy (RT), its name later changing to Rational-Emotive Therapy and then to Rational Emotive Behavior Therapy (REBT). Its basic premise is that what most influences people is not an unhappy event but what they think about it, this conclusion being influenced by earlier life experiences. Thus, effective therapy lies in confronting irrational beliefs and replacing them with healthy, optimistic thoughts.

Which is not to say that some events, like learning of a serious illness, are not traumatic, but rather that their painful effect can be reduced by REBT. While agreeing that early life experience plays a major role in later behavior, REBT does not encourage the patient to explore the past as does psychoanalytic psychotherapy but focuses on changing current thinking. In this way, behavior, feelings, and self-defeating ways of relating will be modified.

Ellis postulated three core irrational beliefs: that a person must always be successful and win approval or love; that a person must always be treated fairly or nicely; and that a person's life must always by enjoyable and without stress. He believed that holding any of these beliefs will inevitably lead to anxiety, depression, and feeling worthless.

During Rational Emotive Behavior Therapy the therapist and patient develop a working relationship to explore problems and set goals. This includes eliminating behaviors which unnecessarily upset people and learning how to lead a happier life. By gaining insight into initial problems, the patient can generalize this knowledge to other areas of dissatisfaction.

There may be homework exercises during which the patient practices what they fear and behaves assertively against beliefs which cause their unhappiness.

A basic concept underlying REBT is that of *behavior modification* which refers to the popular human notion that a painful consequence will reduce the likelihood of a behavior occurring while a pleasurable result will increase its probability. In psychological terms these are called *reinforcement* and *punishment*.

Behavior modification emphasizes: defining a problem as a specific behavior which can be measured; altering the environment to effect change; and then measuring the result so, thereafter, only effective punishments are used. Thus there first must be a *functional behavioral assessment* which answers the essential questions of what the undesired behavior is, what came immediately before it, and what followed..

Because these concepts are easily understandable, and apparently implemented, programs embracing this theory have been instituted in residential treatment settings, substance abuse programs, schools, prisons, and places of employment. While procedures based on this theory do work, it is only when the environment is tightly controlled (as in prisons), and then for a limited period of time.

Critics of behavior modification insist that it is reductionist: that human behavior is far more complex than can be explained or modified by a simple pain/pleasure principle except under extreme, atypical conditions. Interestingly, behavior modification works with dogs but not with cats; and with intellectually limited children but not those having close to or above average intellectual ability. This is probably because behavior modification so simplifies the environment of cognitively limited children that they can more easily negotiate it.

Though not defined specifically, all theories of psychotherapy have behavior modification elements for every patient is well aware of what their therapist most approves and tends to behave accordingly.

11. *Sex Therapy*

Sex Therapy is a specialized talk therapy with both counseling and educational parts. While other therapies deal with broader life issues, sex therapy tries to resolve only sexual problems and usually, though not always, between couples. It is brief, lasting no more than several months, and highly directed. Participants are provided information, emotional support, and physical exercises to practice at home.

Sex therapy is conducted by those who are licensed as a psychiatrist, psychologist, social worker, or nurse, and received additional specialized training in sexual problems. Being an unregulated field, anyone can call themselves a "sex therapist." Because this "counselor" may be untrained and unlicensed, one who simply advertises their services, caution should be exercised in choosing a sex therapist.

Couples seeking sex therapy may not be going for the reason they initially believe. Valid reasons are because of sexual inhibitions or dissatisfaction with their sexual intimacy; or wanting to become freer to speak about sexual matters. But a couple's real problem, like with some who seek marriage counseling, may be very different.

I once treated a couple in their thirties who consulted me because of their self-diagnosed "marital problems." But I quickly concluded that there was nothing wrong with their marriage, or even with any of their children, which sometimes underlies what troubles couples. Instead, they had both experienced bizarre childhoods: events so strange that they would be termed unbelievable in a novel. At that point in their lives, these early developmental experiences were effecting them. So though they came to my office together, the treatment which I provided them was, essentially, individual therapy.

Similarly, when people seek "sex therapy" their underlying dissatisfaction may not be sexual. When problems occur in a marriage the first thing to go is the sexual relationship or, as has been said, the largest human sexual organ is within the head. This is also the last to recover. One can quickly judge how healthy a marriage is by comparing the present frequency of sex with its frequency when the couple was most intimate. A great difference, in the absence of such major factors as the birth of a child, illness, or unemployment, indicates that communication problems must be addressed—and these are usually not sexual. Thus, like with every mental health symptom, a sexual problem may indicate other difficulties.

Chapter Twelve

How Psychotherapy Heals

ALL PSYCHOTHERAPIES, WITH the exception of such body oriented treatments as Reiki*, reflect one or a combination of *therapeutic postures,* or healing interactions. These are specific ways in which therapists relate to their patients to foster emotional and personality change.

The Relationship Psychotherapeutic Posture

When using the *relationship psychotherapeutic posture* the therapist interacts with the patient as would an ideal friend: listening without comment; informing without prejudice; and being always available.

Calvin's Messy Life

Calvin knew that his life was a mess. Just thinking about it hurt, for he felt that at sixty-two his life should go smoother.

---

*Reiki is a holistic therapy which is believed able to foster physical and emotional well-being by using a (hypothesized) universal *life force* to effect healing. Access to this force, which stimulates the person's natural healing capacities, can be gained through an *attunement process* performed by a Reiki practitioner, who holds their hands on or near the patient.

Both of his parents were seriously ill in Los Angeles and he flew there regularly to see them. Being in their late eighties, Calvin knew that their health would improve only temporarily. His relationship with his girlfriend of three years was falling apart and he wasn't sure he wanted to try to save it again. Moreover, he had developed Lyme Disease; and the income from his long prosperous brokerage business was way down because of the stock market collapse. No one was investing these days and judging by how poorly his clients' accounts had done, he half-seriously considered hiring a bodyguard.

In the past, Calvin, on his own, could manage his parents' health problems and resolve the issues which periodically arose after his divorce. He was sure that he could handle his business problems too but didn't feel that he could now manage everything without an ally. A person to talk to who wasn't involved in his life and didn't have a stake in it.

He had spoken freely with his father, a retired Protestant minister, in the past, but considering his present health issues this wasn't an option. Nor was his brother, an alcoholic who was in and out of rehab. And since one decision concerned his girl-friend, she was out too.

Calvin was a strong person. Without the aid of therapy he had managed, over the years, to make significant changes in his life. He had learned to restrain his impulsive tendency which caused him to act violently when provoked, as when he knocked down a worker snorting cocaine on the job. And he now behaved more maturely when confronting his ex-wife's illogical demands.

But when too many problems cropped up simultaneously—the business downturn, his health issue, having to decide whether to continue his relationship with his girlfriend, helping his ill parents and adult children—Calvin recognized that he too needed help. An objective person with whom to assess his life. One who could be an ideal friend, which is how a therapist behaves when he adopts the *relationship psychotherapeutic posture.* As I did with Carl too.

Carl, The Teenager Who Could Not Speak

Fifteen year old Carl got "A's" in school, performed whatever chores were requested by his parents, and worked weekends as an usher at the the local movie theater. He presented the image of a perfect teenager—except that he had barely spoken with his parents for nearly two years.

"He is an ideal boy," was the way the school principal described him, to the detective who was investigating the telephoned bomb threats which Carl had made to the school. That was when other disturbing aspects of his life became known. His fascination with guns, explosives, and Nazi paraphernalia; and his social isolation. Carl had no friends; nor had he begun dating though several girls expressed interest in him.

During his mental health treatment (which was mandated by the Court), I reduced Carl's loneliness by discussing teenage movies; and told him stories about other adolescents, including their initial difficult dating experiences. Like the fourteen year old who, after being overheard describing a European exchange student as "pretty," was told by his girl-friend that she was dumping him. But they had planned to see a movie on Friday night, he objected. "Can't you wait till after then?" The girl agreed and they saw the movie together. Then she dumped him.

By adopting the relationship psychotherapeutic posture, behaving as a friend to Carl, I reduced the isolation of this friendless boy and lowered his stress level, this intervention enabling him to function better so he could begin to make the psychological changes he needed.

The Psychoanalytic Psychotherapeutic Posture

Nowadays everyone has heard of psychoanalysis: the treatment in which a patient lies on a couch, faces away from the therapist and speaks freely. This type of therapy is comparatively rare, and helpful to only a small number of people.

But the p*sychoanalytic psychotherapeutic posture,* which is widely used, differs from psychoanalysis and refers to a particular way in which a therapist can relate to their patient during psychotherapy.

Here, the therapist explains the patient's troubling symptoms by relating them to their early life experiences— thus making sense of what seems inexplicable and terrifying. For example, being scratched by a cat when one is three years old can lead to a lifelong fear of pets even if the early experience is forgotten. Through this *psychoanalytic psychotherapeutic posture* the therapist helps the patient make links between their feared thoughts and feelings such that these become understood, and their life again makes sense.

A Fireman's Heart Attack—Or Was It?

Todd was six foot four and built so broadly that he seemed to fill a room. Though his face was unlined, his prematurely gray hair made him look older than forty-three. Todd was a fireman and loved his job, even after many of his friends died on that terrible day in 2001 when the World Trade Centers were attacked and collapsed. "I might have been in the rubble, not picking through it," he remarked philosophically at our first appointment.

It took Todd a long time to begin therapy. After canceling the first two appointments he vowed to keep his third appointment and did. I asked him my usual questions. He was married, had three children, and all were doing well. Though some colleagues reported health problems related to their work, he had none. But things which never frightened him in the past now did: like being in a room from which he couldn't immediately exit. Then he would start feeling warm, his heart rate would shoot up, and the fear that he was having a heart attack would arise. At first this happened only when he was in a crowded room; recently it began occurring elsewhere.

It has been said that soldiers, police officers, and firefighters find it hardest to begin therapy and Todd was no exception. Despite widespread public education about mental health problems, there remains a stigma about receiving treatment for them. To have lung cancer after self-destructively smoking for forty years is acceptable. But not a panic disorder even if, as with Todd, it derived from his heroism on September 11th.

Now he was even more frightened than *that day* when, he later told others, he was just following routine.

Which is what good training does: enable one to cope with dangerous, frightening situations automatically. Only when it was over, with the Towers having fallen, bodies being removed and smoke clearing, did he think of what might have been. That he could have been crippled or become ashes...nothing.

Todd also had a problem staying asleep. He would become awakened by dreams in the middle of the night, not with a vision but the sensations of heat and pressure.

He had begun worrying about his health too. Apart from his yearly physical exam, the results of which shamed his overweight physician, he rarely saw a doctor. Colds, flu, and backaches, he recovered from quickly without medical aid. But when the red rash on his chest appeared, he hurried for an evaluation. Shingles, the doctor quickly diagnosed, and it was probably related to stress. "I can give you medicine but because of the potential side effects it's best to see if it goes away on its own." And, like Todd's usual medical issues, this soon disappeared too.

Two months later, when Todd felt completely normal again, he started to notice things which he had never paid attention to before. Feelings of warmth or cold; rumblings in his stomach and mild muscle aches. Things which everyone experiences daily and ignores but he began worrying about. He sometimes feared that he was developing something fatal: a rapidly spreading cancer, or imminent stroke or heart attack.

At first, these thoughts were fleeting and he would quickly push them from his mind by involving himself more strongly in duties on his job or engaging in unnecessary worry about his children. But one day, soon after he arrived at work, he couldn't escape "it," as he had begun to think of these concerns about his health.

He was seated at a desk and completing his daily log when *it* hit him. The fear that he was having a heart attack. And not just *might* be having one but that it was actually occurring. Suddenly he felt warm and sweaty. He became afraid to stand up, fearing that he must surely faint, being unsure of whether he was more concerned with dying from a heart attack or appearing weak before the other fire fighters.

Todd managed to control his feelings and none of his colleagues noticed anything unusual. But when this fear returned while he was at home, his wife insisted that he go to the local hospital. There, upon hearing the words, "heart attack," the medical personnel sprang into their emergency routine, relaxing only when their tests revealed the real facts about his condition.

His symptoms—increased heart rate, feeling of warmth, odd bodily sensations—reflected a panic attack, the severe anxiety attack which could mimic the symptoms of many medical conditions. They gave him a tranquilizer and strongly advised that he seek therapy. Which was, finally, when he kept his appointment with me.

Self-control was important to Todd. He had always tried to ignore painful feelings and to do what needed to be done. This attitude worked for many years but the level of stress created during and after the World Trade Centers attack was something new. It was too great for him to ignore no matter how hard he tried. So, within the unconscious portion of his mind, symptoms were created: anxiety, panic attacks, and the fear of imminent death. But though apparently illogical and mysterious, their intent was helpful: to *force* Todd to make the changes in his life which were needed in order to relieve his stress and avoid harm. For, were the stress to continue, both his mental and physical health would deteriorate.

The possibility of "going crazy" is a widespread and understandable fear since severe mental illness greatly reduces the ability to function normally. So, demanding attention, this unconsciously created worry *forced* Todd to seek the psychological treatment which he long feared but had become necessary. Through the *psychoanalytic psychotherapeutic posture*, Todd came to understand his fear. This, in conjunction with my providing other therapeutic postures and his use of the self-hypnotic relaxation CD I provided him, caused his worry to permanently disappear after two months of therapy.

The Supportive Psychotherapeutic Posture

Mary Studies Her Husband—and Leaves Him

Mary's suspicions began long before she called me. Her husband, Jake, was on a business trip and failed to call early in the morning as he usually did. She found out where he was staying by telling his secretary that it was a family emergency. When she phoned him at his hotel she heard a woman's voice in the background. Two hours later she again called the hotel. After lies to the desk clerk, Mary learned that Jake was registered with "his wife."

It was only then that Mary allowed herself to accept what she long suspected: her husband had been unfaithful throughout their eight year marriage. Now she understood why the frequency of their sex had diminished from daily to barely once monthly, and that they rarely spoke. Even her pregnancies hadn't improved the relationship though he was affectionate with their children..

She remembered hints of the truth. The condom wrapper she found in the car, along with the blazing red lipstick, a shade which was far different from hers. He was having an affair, was her initial thought. But he explained away the condom and lipstick by saying that he let his secretary borrow the company car when he was away. A girl barely out of her teens—you know how those kids act. He would talk to her.

But Mary knew when Jake lied and she needed to decide what to do. Should they try marriage counseling? But Jake had refused this suggestion in the past. There was nothing wrong with their marriage, he insisted, but if she wanted to waste money for *her* therapy it was fine with him.

Mary got a pad and began writing, numbering each element in the decision she had to make. If they separated, she would have to get a job. Two families living apart could not live as cheaply as one, all of her divorced friends insisted. They also informed her how strongly a husband could resist supporting their family—particularly when they were starting a new one.

Mary last worked six years before, until she began "showing" during her first pregnancy. Most of her job, completing research applications for the Federal Drug Administration, could have been done at home and e-mailed in. But, though a start-up, the pharmaceutical company where she worked was conservative and her boss refused her request. So when her maternity leave was over she decided to remain a stay-at-home mom. With her graduate degree in organic chemistry and joint undergraduate degree in English and chemistry, other companies might rush to offer her a job. Not only drug companies but businesses which produced technical newsletters, and professional societies. And if she could work from home, there wouldn't be the expense of child care.

Mary's conclusion about her marriage was just as logical. She liked but no longer loved or trusted her husband. She also needed to be tested, to see if she contracted a sexually transmitted disease from him. It was this realization which decided the matter. "I'm out of here," she wrote across the bottom of the page.

So when Mary consulted me, she had already determined to end her marriage. What really bothered her was how easily Jake accepted her decision. "I would have liked for him to try to talk me out of it." We discussed her family situation, the plans she made, and I provided information about the normal stress she was experiencing, thus supporting her emotional strengths rather than trying to change her personality.

Just as people have particular artistic or mechanical abilities, they have unique psychological strengths and limitations. One person may be more sensitive to feelings and another be better able to bear pain without complaint. When using the *supportive psychotherapeutic posture,* the therapist strengthens the patient's present capacities, enabling them to better cope with their stress without changing their underlying personality. As I did with Ivan too.

Ivan, before Jail

No one would envy Ivan's life after the few minutes it took to change.. The time for a judge to accept his guilty plea for fraud and sentence him to six months of weekends in jail, and a stiff fine. Though were it not for the effective testimony which he gave against his bosses, the real thieves, his sentence would have been far harsher. Years in prison and not weekends in the local jail but this was bad enough.

Ivan would have to leave his young children, and his wife who had recently been diagnosed with multiple sclerosis. Moreover, the only thing that he was really guilty of was trying to support his family by holding onto his job.

Ivan had long felt uneasy about the company's financial records but whenever he raised this issue, his boss said that everything was fine. Their outside accountant had always approved them and who was he to question that professional judgment? Ivan was six years out of college but still lacked the CPA certification and MBA degree which would enable him to get a real corporate job. One where he wouldn't have to work for this family enmeshed company where everyone important was a relative. So Ivan continued to sign every form that was placed before him, even those which, deep down, he knew that he should not.

One day a sophisticated shareholder anonymously mailed his well-documented questions to the state Attorney General's office. Maybe in another administration nothing would have happened. The letter would rest on an overloaded desk before being filed away forever. But the political winds were changing, particularly for those who dreamed of becoming governor or United States senator.

So when Ivan was invited for an informal chat with this state attorney, he finally did the smart thing. He borrowed money to hire the best lawyer he could find, told everything to the government investigators, and agreed to wear a wire. This was why his sentence was so light, despite the size of the fraud which ran into the hundreds of millions.

Twenty-four weekends in jail. Forty eight days away from his wife and children. Forty five days more than he had ever been. And Ivan had read what happened in jails: assaults and rapes. He didn't think that he would survive one weekend in jail let alone twenty four.

In treating Ivan, my major task was not to explore those unconscious and practical factors which kept him from doing what he had known was unwise. Rather, it was to support his current ability to cope with the stressful (jail) situation he was shortly to enter. As we spoke, he became calmer. Particularly after reading a book written by a formerly incarcerated lawyer which told how a prisoner could survive their imprisonment. I also told Ivan stories about other patients I treated who had survived, without incident, their prison experience. All for far longer periods than his would be. One person viewed his incarceration as having changed his life for the better though, certainly, there are better ways to accomplish this. And occasionally over the years, I had evaluated prisoners in county jails, and I shared my perceptions with Ivan.

I spoke with Ivan for a half-dozen sessions before he began serving his sentence and periodically on weekdays thereafter. His perception of jail life was similar to that of the other prisoners I had spoken with: the worst aspect was the boredom. During these months he was hired as an accountant with a non-profit organization. Where he still worked several years later, as he informed me in a Christmas card.

A therapist using the *supportive psychotherapeutic posture* helps the patient to cope with the demands on their life just as the person is. The therapist avoids raising other emotionally charged   issues and conflicts—which would present more stress—until the current crisis is over.

The Replacement Psychotherapeutic Posture

Andrew, The Perfect First Dater

Only when Andrew reached thirty-four did he decide that something was seriously wrong with his life. Not his career, for he owned a thriving insurance agency, just his personal life. He considered himself an interesting person and at least reasonably attractive—several women had described him as being "good looking." Still, none of his relationships lasted longer than two months. That was when he always seemed to find some reason to end it.

He didn't think that his problem was sexual for there had been no issues there. Nor could it be social inadequacy: he had no difficulty in meeting women, a task which he pursued as avidly as he did the sale of a high commission annuity to a retiring millionaire. Yet as soon as he felt close to a woman, when she spoke of they being "a couple," things started going wrong.

He would find things that he didn't like about her: her perfume or the newspaper she read. Even his realization that these objections were nonsense didn't reduce their effectiveness.

Then would come his comments. The worst of them still caused him to cringe. While lying in bed with a woman after having sex, she said, "This is the best relationship I ever had." To which he instantly responded, "It's the worst I ever had. It's going nowhere." As bad as a punch in the stomach. Seven months later, still wishing that he could take back these words, Andrew phoned this woman and learned that she had recently married.

It didn't require a psychologist to diagnose Andrew's problem. Most people after hearing his dating history would accurately describe him as being terrified of intimacy. The experiences which caused him to panic were the feelings of closeness and sharing and dependency which develop within a committed relationship. While the roots of these difficulties lie in the earliest years of a child's life, their later healing cannot be with the same parenting figures for childhood is then passed. Instead, during psychotherapy, the patient comes to internalize an image of the therapist and carry it with them on a twenty four hour/ seven day per week basis.

It is this image which heals a person's psychological deficiencies by *replacing* their inadequate ego capacities with more mature ones. Through this process, Andrew's minimal capacity to tolerate feelings was increased and he became able to tolerate the feelings of affection which he was earlier unable to. This removed the emotional limitations which had been devastating his personal life..

Scientists no longer doubt that early developmental experiences are crucially important in forming a person's personality. Nor is there any question that major changes can be made later during adulthood. But this is not a simple task. The mind functions conservatively and is loathe to change—except when it is effected by a powerful catalyst. This is what psychotherapy is.

There are reasons why early life experiences have such great effect. The brain is then developing rapidly and particularly susceptible to being influenced. Also, parents have great power over their children: controlling all rewards and punishments, and interceding between them and the world. For these reasons many children, even when they become adults, still hold the same opinions as their parents and often behave similarly, as the ancient phrase attests ("chip off the old block").

But just as highways can be reconstructed rather than just repaved, the human personality can be transformed—if a powerful enough agent is used. Love is one, and its power has long been recognized. The gaining of an authentic religious conviction is another. So is the experiencing, for a long period, a powerful external structure. One which, like parents, tightly controls rewards and punishments and behavior, as within a military or police career.

Similarly, incarceration, in a few instances, can have a positive effect though for most inmates this possibility is small and why the recidivism rate is so high. Incarceration and criminal attributes are discussed in Chapter Twenty Five.

For authentic personality reconstruction to occur, an experience similar to early childhood is required. During this intervention, the psychotherapist is available whenever needed and provides an accepting attitude within a relationship characterized by dependency, continuity, and warmth. Or, as therapists say, a *replacement psychotherapeutic posture* is provided.

All of the elements of the replacement psychotherapeutic posture are present in the other three therapeutic postures. Only one is unique: the fostering of *psychological regression,* or creating the feeling of being a very young child. Some regression occurs naturally during all therapy for it involves interacting with a parent like, authority figure (the clinician) within the family resembling structure of the therapy office.

Because, unlike with adults, it is not comfortable for children to discuss their concerns at length, play therapy is used with young patients. Here, involvement with board and card games, coloring books, and imaginative play with stuffed figures occupies the time. But, though resembling ordinary play, this is *therapy.* During this activity, personal conflicts and worries are discussed and relieved for play is the natural mode of communication of children.

Children can easily regress, to the degree they need do so, during this therapeutic play. Then, like adults, they behave normally upon leaving the therapist's office.

By experiencing the *replacement psychotherapeutic posture,* weakened psychological abilities such as the capacity to control feelings, mood, behavior and others, are replaced with more mature ones, this enabling the patient to permanently function better.

These four psychotherapeutic postures (supportive, analytic, relationship, replacement) are not used alone. They are interwoven throughout each moment of every therapy session in order to foster the most extensive psychological healing.

Upon learning of these psychotherapeutic postures you might consider a therapist to be a cold, calculating person. One who, only after long observation and with great deliberation, reacts with the correct therapeutic posture, then becoming silent until the time arrives to present another response.. But a therapist's behavior is more that of a well-trained public speaker than deliberating machine.

Like most people I was always terrified of giving speeches. I still remember the fear I experienced in high school when, with shaking hands and halting voice, I stood before a class to give a required speech. Even having to read aloud before others frightened me.

Years later I gave my first speech as a psychologist. While I had prepared my talk and the audience was receptive, things didn't go well. Two members of the audience argued and, I feared, might even come to blows. I realized that if I were to continue public speaking I would have to learn how.

Operating by instinct, I practiced my talk numerous times. I even indicated on the notes which I would bring to the lectern when I would tell amusing stories. You might expect that with all this preparation my speeches would seem wooden but the opposite was true. The more I practiced, the more spontaneous they appeared and the better able I was to control interruptions and respond to questions from the audience—even those which were far afield and unexpected. I successfully coped with these challenges because I was so well prepared that I was in complete control of the information I was presenting.

Similarly, an experienced therapist does not tell themselves, "Now is the moment to relate to this patient as a friend (or as an analytic or a mothering figure). Their appropriate reaction occurs spontaneously and is based on their sense, deriving from their experience and intuition, of what would, at that moment, be the most helpful interaction. Which may be to say something and what it should be, or to remain silent.

Therapists use various terms to describe their clinical technique: *psychoanalytic* or *cognitive-behavioral* or *interpersonal,* or some other. But regardless of what phrase they use, these four therapeutic postures (analytic, relationship, supportive, replacement) are the basis of all psychological healing.

If the correct psychotherapeutic posture is used, the patient will feel relief and comfort. When there is an disjunction between the psychological needs of the patient and how the therapist relates to them, the patient feels uncomfortable and concludes that their therapy is not going well. Crucial to being an effective therapist is having the ability to sense which therapeutic posture best "fits" a particular patient during each moment of their treatment, and how to present it. With greater experience this skill becomes second nature. As is implied in my occasional joke to patients: that I have been doing therapy for so long I can do it with my eyes closed—and sometimes do.

Chapter Thirteen

The Lowdown on Psychotherapy Fees: Two Important Questions and Twelve Warning Signs

Since the cost of my therapy will be determined by its duration, how long should I expect that it will last?

Asking how long therapy should last is analogous to asking how long the treatment for a medical condition will. Most would say, particularly with children, until the illness is healed. But medical and psychological problems do differ. Aside from suicide, and this a relatively rare event, people do not die from psychological problems though their functioning may be crippled. And with both medical and psychological disorders, the earlier the condition is diagnosed and treated, the better will be the result and less expensive the treatment. For with early treatment, less damage is done to the developed or developing mind and personality, and less pain will be experienced by both the patient and their family.

Just as the techniques for treating children differ from those for adults, so are the factors which enter into how long their treatment will last. Because children are dependent on their parents, the treatment of children may end earlier than they or their therapist feel is necessary.

Some parents can only tolerate mental health treatment for a certain length of time. One mother ended her child's treatment after three months, giving the explanation that her progress was not rapid enough. When

I thought about this I realized that she had earlier ended her older son's treatment after only three months too—just as she previously did her own. This mother could tolerate a little—but not too much—change.

Another mother, as I described in an earlier chapter, brought all four of her problematic sons for therapy, with none of their treatment lasting longer than six weeks. When the immediate family crisis was over, so was their treatment.

Some parents justify their behavior with popular philosophy. One father ended his seven year old daughter's therapy with the words: "don't fix it if it ain't broke." When I began treating his daughter she was terrified of asserting herself and so frightened by social activity that she would vomit before leaving the house to visit a friend. During her first session in my office she spoke so softly that I could barely hear her.

Five months later, when the school principal accidentally omitted reading her name in the auditorium, she yelled from her seat to remind him. Yet despite the positive changes, I felt that she had further progress to make in order to avoid problems which I feared would arise during her adolescence. But the father disagreed and his position was a reasonable one.

Sometimes, with both children and adults, more progress cannot be made at a particular point in their life. An adolescent may need to develop a clearer sense of who they are before they can tolerate further personality exploration; or an adult must end a painful relationship.

Thus therapy should be regarded as being an experience with which one can periodically engage: to aid with basic developmental tasks as gaining better self-control; or when making important decisions, like whether to divorce.

Therapy is a limited and not a lifetime endeavor. It will rarely last just four sessions or extend to ten years. Most frequently it lasts from several months to several years. Yet no matter how greatly involved in therapy the patient is (and often it is the most important experience in their life), therapy must always be regarded as a catalyst towards more meaningful living, not a substitute for life itself.

While this statement is generally true, some early developmental experiences can be so destructive and the resulting social development may be so limited that, for some people, therapy may not only be their essential element towards personal change but represent the only human contact, apart from parents and siblings, which exists in the individual's life. They may have great fear of intimacy, or have never gained the sense that comfort is possible in human relationships.

Is expensive therapy better than therapy which costs less?

Depending on whether one has health insurance and its nature, therapy can be expensive. Lacking coverage, the cost of each session may range from ninety to three hundred dollars. But if covered by insurance, the patient is only responsible for the co-payment, which may be ten dollars—or fifty. With one insurance plan, the patient's portion of the fee was higher than that of the insurance company, causing me to wonder whether their plan should even be termed insurance.

Because insurance plans vary greatly, therapists usually investigate the coverage before the first session. This is why they ask those annoying but necessary questions which patients resent.

The insurance identification number, plan telephone number, name of the insured and their address, and the patient's date of birth. This is done because these are the questions which are asked of the therapist when they telephone to request benefit information or authorization for treatment.

Be assured: every therapist would far prefer that there be no co-payment required, and that prior authorization is unneeded. But those who rely on insurance must comply with the demands of their plan—if they expect to be reimbursed. Yet the provisions of some plans are so difficult to understand that, if I phone the company twice, I may receive two completely different answers.

Some therapists don't participate in insurance plans. They resent the lower fees, the unpaid time to complete paperwork which is required, and the sometimes strange requirements for reimbursement, as that the patient complete unvalidated questionnaires. Having said this, as insurance companies have become more familiar with mental health difficulties, they became easier to deal with.

Many plans no longer require prior authorization for treatment and, for those that still do, this often consists of a brief, one or two page form which can be faxed every three or six months. This policy is logical since the total cost of psychotherapy is a very small percentage of insurance payments. Even with the unlimited outpatient psychotherapy available in many insurance plans, according to future American government regulations, I doubt this cost would rise by much considering how great the fear of psychotherapy is. A study in France asked whether a person would undergo psychoanalysis if it was free. More than ninety percent of the respondents replied that they would not.

The popular aphorism, "you get what you pay for," is not true with regard to psychotherapy for this treatment involves both science and talent. Thus the fee charged tends more to reflect public belief in the qualifications of the therapist. While it is generally true that increased experience leads to greater competence, this is not certain. Some clinicians have, without awareness, been making the same mistakes for much of their career. Thus size of fee is far too simplistic a measure to use in determining choice of therapist.

Fees can sometimes be reduced by negotiation with the therapist. Many will be flexible if the patient lacks insurance or has financial problems. Also, many states now have free or very low cost, excellent health insurance plans for those lacking coverage. These are sometimes better than are provided by many employers.

Fees are also determined by the therapist's profession though there is no primary profession for psychotherapist. A therapist may have a degree in medicine, psychology, social work, nursing, or the clergy. Since all charge for their services, there is competition among the groups.

Psychiatrists tend to be the most costly, followed by psychologists, social workers, nurses, and the clergy in that order. But there are exceptions to this general rule: a cleverly marketed practitioner of one discipline may charge more than a less business knowledgeable member of another.

The following information is also generally true, though there is broad variability among members of these groups.

Psychiatrists view emotional problems as a type of illness, with symptoms to be medicated away with drugs or such physical methods as Electro-Convulsive Treatment ("shock treatment"). Though he was a physician, Freud believed that the training for medicine and psychotherapy were incompatible: physicians must lose their attitude of focusing on the disease and relate personally in order to be effective as therapists. Some psychiatrists, particularly those with psychoanalytic training, have been outstanding as therapists.

Psychology is most closely related to psychotherapy since it has always concerned itself with psychological processes. It developed the humanistic and existential approaches; and emphasizes the achievement of potential while discouraging the stigma of emotional difficulties. It developed the concept of behavior modification.

Social work has historically been most involved with family therapy and effecting changes in society to benefit the individual.

The basic degree of a therapist can be an M.D., Ph. D. or Psy. D., M.S.W., R.N., or D.Div., but none of these, in and of themselves, indicate proficiency in psychotherapy.

Nor does membership in a national society such as the American Psychiatric Association or the American Psychological Association. Many psychiatrists today have minimal training in psychotherapy* and most psychologists are not clinicians.

The fields of social work, nursing, and clergy are just as murky and the titles by which therapists call themselves (Psychotherapist, Psychoanalyst, Pastoral Counselor, Marriage Therapist, Family Therapist, Child Therapist, Counselor, Sex Therapist) are not legally protected so there is a need for caution when choosing a practitioner.

The frequency of treatment also determines the cost and effective therapy does not always follow the notion that more is better. Some patients who benefit from once weekly therapy sessions do more poorly with more frequent treatment for it creates too great stress for them. The reverse can also be true, with more frequent therapy being beneficial. One teenager I treated, who was coping with an alcoholic father, his own intermittent use of cocaine, and grave school difficulties, made far greater progress when he agreed to increase his therapy sessions to twice a week. Thankfully, his insurance coverage permitted this.

*Wallerstein, Robert S. The future of psychotherapy. *Bulletin of the Menninger Clinic,* Fall 1991, 55:4.

Therapy can sometimes be reduced to every other week if finances are limited, though this is not optimal and often too greatly stresses the psychological resources of the patient. Less frequent, monthly treatment, is not usually helpful, except just before treatment is ended. The gulf between sessions is then too great to foster and maintain therapeutic progress

Therapists who insist that progress can only occur with more than two sessions per week may be more interested in filling their schedule or acceding to their personal philosophy of treatment than responding to their patient's needs.

I once heard a talk by a psychoanalyst who proudly described the progress of a patient from early in his career. This girl had four therapy sessions each week for five years, her mother was seen once weekly and her father once monthly. Yet I treated a child with apparently equivalent difficulties once a week, also speaking with her parents alone for a few minutes each session. Eight months later her parents terminated treatment, being well satisfied with the outcome since their child's symptoms had disappeared.

Why did this doctor involve the child in lengthy psychoanalytic treatment? Being tactful, I didn't ask. Maybe because he then needed an analytic patient for his training, or from the mistaken belief that psychoanalysis is the gold standard against which all psychotherapy must be measured.

Research has shown that even young children are conscious of price though more so with toys than grocery items. Perhaps because toys are more expensive or parents more often refer to cost when purchasing toys. Most adults, even those who are wealthy, do consider price and sometimes follow popular philosophies when deciding on a purchase. "You pay for a bargain later." "A price can be too good to be true." "You get what you pay for."

While these proverbs can be accurate when purchasing tangible items such as a car or laptop or house, psychotherapy is different. Even if it shares some of their marketing techniques, like having an impressive office and the practitioner being expensively dressed. Neither of which has anything to do with the business of therapy, though a shabby office or clothing would cause thoughtful customers to pause. But beyond conventional appearance, other factors apply.

A fifty thousand dollar auto may be five times as reliable as a ten thousand dollar one, but no professional would dare to assert that therapy costing ninety dollars a session is one third as effective as that costing three times as much. It is far more likely that the clinician with the higher fee practices in a less competitive market or has a more publicized reputation, though the latter also has little to do with effectiveness since it is usually determined by the amount of research published or how exalted their job title is.

Because therapy is both an art and a science, professional degrees and years of experience are important but should not be the sole factors when considering its worth. Like medical treatments, healing is cheap at any price, and failure can be costly. What price should be placed on becoming a more capable parent, better at one's work, or be more likely to achieve intimacy? Many would consider these goals to be priceless.

Yet getting one's money's worth is an important consideration. But if price does not indicate the quality of therapy, what does? How can you be sure that the therapy you are receiving, or considering the purchase of, is or will be effective? Not a waste of time and money—or far worse.

While playing catch as a five year old, I had a frightening experience. The ball rolled into a dimly lit alley in which several grownups stood. Whether it was the dark or their presence I'm not sure, but I suddenly became too frightened to enter the alley and retrieve my ball.

Years later, as an adult, I read Gavin deBecker's book, *The Gift of Fear,* which explained this. He referred to the natural protective instincts which all people have, and emphasized the importance of following them—if one wants to remain safe. Similarly, each person has natural protective instincts which can safeguard them from inadequate *toxic therapists* and the destructive mental health treatment they provide. Sensations which, erroneously, we too often dismiss as being "discourteous" or "illogical." But these are instincts which deBecker strongly advises that we should trust.

Eight years ago I was advised to have expensive dental work. Before doing this, the dentist asked that I consult a periodontist to evaluate my gums. The appointment with this specialist was at 8:30AM and I arrived early. While sitting in the waiting room, I heard him returning phone calls from other patients. His voice strongly resembled that of an employee who I once had to fire because of his lying, self-centered ways.

The periodontist evaluated my teeth and pronounced his verdict: my gums required treatment costing three thousand dollars. This would require three sessions, he later amending this to two. As the doctor spoke I grew increasingly wary because of his resemblance to my past employee and because his recommendation had changed so quickly. I said that I'd consider his advice and get back to him.

I then sought a second opinion from an elderly periodontist who taught at a major university. He advised that I did *not* require periodontal surgery but merely a better cleaning that I had been receiving. "Young periodontists can be very aggressive," he concluded, adding that he considered the recommended dental work to be unwise too.

Since then, this dentist has been cleaning my teeth—which remain fine. When I need other dental work, I've consulted a colleague he recommended and have referred people to both.

Four Reasons Why People Don't Trust Their Instincts When Choosing a Psychotherapist

1. *They believe that they are entering an experience about which they know little.*

Knowing little about a field does not mean that a person cannot distinguish desirable from poor businesses. Everyone does this daily, as when they choose one supermarket or gas station over another.

I recently chose to buy gas at a newly constructed station for it had a far larger newspaper selection and, more importantly, a free air hose to refill tires. One that always worked unlike those in competing stations which charged for this convenience. The free coffee which the new station gave during their first months was an incentive but not the deciding factor.

As I earlier stated, I know virtually nothing about how an auto operates and for me to attempt to fix it would place both myself and other drivers in danger. But I can recognize a quality operation in the automotive field, just as you can when choosing a therapist. And just as free coffee alone would not keep me going to a gas station, an attractive office or face should not be important factors when choosing a therapist or deciding to remain with them.

2. *They feel desperately unhappy and helpless.*

A person who feels desperate should be exceedingly cautious about their choice of therapist for when feeling this way a destructive therapist can cause greater harm. Yet even when they are most unhappy, a person does make adequate decisions. Before entering the therapist's office they decided when to go, how to travel, how to pay the fee, and had likely already checked whether the treatment was covered by their health insurance.

3. *They feel so relieved after making the initial appointment that they feel they will never find another therapist to treat them.*

A person thinks this way because their unhappiness is causing them to feel dependent. Like a child who believes that they can have only one set of parents. Or one therapist for this role contains parenting elements. But while a child cannot choose their biological parents, an adult is free to choose one—or another—therapist. And there are many more therapists than supermarkets, which is a frequent choice for all.

4. They are afraid of becoming depressed were they to leave their first choice of therapist.

Feeling depressed indicates, among other things, that one is conflicted between choice "A" and choice "B." Thus, being stuck in the middle, these people give up, do nothing, and *depress* their feelings. But making a new choice will lift this depression and cause the person to feel better.

Stop, Before Going: The Twelve Warning Signs of Ineffective Therapists

Not all odd happenings are important. To paraphrase Freud, sometimes a cigar *is* just a cigar. But some observations should cause a person to hesitate and to use this information to influence their decision. A traveler feels uneasy about walking through a darkened alley, chooses not to, and thereby avoids the mugger awaiting their next victim. While this example is dramatic, choosing an inadequate therapist can be equally as dangerous for it can result in lengthy unhappiness or worse.

The most publicized but comparatively rare therapist fault of seeking intimacy with their patient is easily detected (this issue is discussed in Chapter Fifteen), but other indicators of ineffectiveness are more subtle. Which is to be expected for the quality of this complex treatment reflects three elements: talent, scientific knowledge, and training.

1. A Therapist Is Ineffective When They State Too Quickly That They Can Help

Everyone wants to hear that they can be helped with their problem. What is wrong with this? Nothing—except when it is asserted by a therapist who knows little about their new patient. A therapist who makes this statement while lacking important basic information is akin to a Mac computer expert expressing an opinion about a Windows software problem or a bicycle mechanic who advises about car repairs. They don't know enough about the situation they confront.

The promise of help should be given only after the full extent of the patient's problem is revealed which includes knowing all of their strengths and limitations. This is not something which can be accomplished during the first therapy session and maybe not even the second. Until this information is gained, the only honest answer given by a therapist can be that they have helped others with similar difficulties—but can guarantee nothing. Nor can any psychotherapist assure progress by their patient for psychotherapy is a *catalyst*, or activator, and the psychotherapist controls only a few of the many elements entering into personal change.

2. A Therapist Is Ineffective When They Don't Explain A Painful Symptom

Just as human difficulties are no longer believed to be influenced by magic, neither should the aid which therapy provides. Rather than being magical, it is a technique with a scientific basis and possesses as much validity as does the prescription of an antibiotic for a bacterial infection. Because it is scientific, every symptom which the therapist confronts has an explanation—one which can and should be provided using simple language.

If, by the end of the first session, you are not provided an explanation of you or your child's symptoms, what is wrong and should be done, and your questioning does not produce this, then you should seek treatment elsewhere. Which is not to say that all difficulties can be fully explored in one therapy session. Where evidence of mental retardation or neurological impairment exists, the needed evaluation may be lengthy. But this too should be so well explained that the patient is comforted and relaxed about the further procedures—not more anxious than when they arrived.

3. A Therapist Is Ineffective When The Patient Feels Continually Uncomfortable

Therapy is usually but not always an enjoyable experience for learning painful truths and confronting personal anxieties can be difficult. But the anxiety or depression which then arises should be brief and followed by a feeling of comfort, greater self-awareness, and increased self-control. If the pain persists for more than several days then the therapist's interpretation was inappropriate, it having been inaccurate or not optimally tailored to the patient's present needs.

4. A Therapist is Ineffective When Their Patient Is Not Making Progress

A therapist is a skilled worker who is consulted with the expectation that progress will be achieved. Which may be the reduction or elimination of a symptom, like being afraid of flying, or a more general change in life: feeling less anxious or depressed, being more confident, having clearer goals, or reduced marital conflict.

Most people will feel more comfortable after their first therapy session because, even though their life is still the same, they have described their problem to a professional and expect to to be helped with it. But if change doesn't occur after a reasonable period of time, then seeking a new therapist should be considered.

Here the operative term is "reasonable." While one would not expect for a lifetime's collection of frustrations, bad habits, resentments, emotional conflicts and bad decisions to disappear within several months and perhaps not even several years of treatment, the explanation for the lack of progress should be available. And, other things being equal, the more recently a symptom developed, the more quickly it can be expected to disappear.

Stress arises from various causes: a difficult work, home, or school situation; or trying to achieve an important developmental goal, like dating successfully as a teenager. If the stress is too great then a symptom, or the sign that something is wrong, will develop.

Which can be anything: increased anxiety or panic attacks, depression, illogical worries or behaviors. When the stress disappears, so will the symptom and for a recently developed one, treatment may not even be needed.

But if the stress has persisted for a long period of time, the symptom will remain even after the stress has been removed. This symptom has now effected the ongoing development of the mind and therapy is required to work inside of the patient's mind to produce change.

For example, because of too great stress a person may develop panic attacks. If they had no prior mental health treatment, this symptom usually requires only two to four months of once weekly therapy; some people find that psychotropic medication is helpful in alleviating the discomfort. But if the panic attacks have occurred for years, then the treatment required may be far longer. And success with some goals, as achieving a happy marriage, can never be certain since they depend on factors other than emotional well-being.

While personal change through therapy will never be as rapid as is desired, a general time frame for the length of treatment can usually be given, though it may never be requested. People who are receiving effective therapy will sense that they are improving, and be able to note their progress in their improved daily interactions and greater feeling of well-being.

5. A Therapist is Ineffective When Their Patient Feels That They Can't Live Without Them

Jonathan, After Eleven Years of Psychotherapy

Jonathan's therapy had lasted too long, his one friend told him. This man knew him since their high school days and they now lived in the same apartment complex. "Eleven years. That's longer than you've known me," he repeated, though not unsympathetically. *His* therapy had helped him through a bad time after his too youthful first marriage broke up. But that was years ago. Since then he re-married, had three children, and was promoted *twice* at his job. Even while Jonathan's life remained the same. Like the furniture in his apartment: white painted crates holding his books and a coffee table constructed of a plank across sawhorses.

Jonathan wasn't satisfied with his life. He continually complained about this to his friend and his older sisters. He didn't want to be so lonely. Why otherwise would he be in his therapy which cost twenty percent of his salary? To which Jonathan received their persisting reply:

"If your life hasn't changed in eleven years despite this therapist's help, maybe it's time for a new one." But Jonathan wouldn't listen. The therapist was wonderful! Only when he was with him, did he feel alive. Jonathan even refused a promotion because it would have forced him to move to another city. He couldn't imagine life without this therapist.

Therapy is an intense experience for it contains the elements of authority and dependency made more powerful by psychological regression which causes the patient to feel that they are once again a child. This is why a competent therapist will not allow the patient to become excessively dependent for they might then consider themselves to be incapable, alone, of making *any* decision.

Thus a therapist should occasionally emphasize the limits of their collaboration with their patient. Stating that while the patient has problems in certain areas of their life, they are fully capable of coping with day-to-day issues. And with these, no discussion during therapy is needed.

Some psychological regression is needed during therapy because only through this experience can healthy development occur. After these changes are made this experience or, as it is termed professionally, the *transference*, will gradually disappear.

Therapy is an important life experience. One so significant that, at times, major decisions should be avoided while personality changes are being made. But this must be the patient's choice and not the therapist's decision. Therapy continues along with life, not in place of it. The purpose of therapy is to change one's life, not attempt to live it through the clinical experience. Which, after all, is only a prototype of human interaction and why it is called *therapy.*

When a patient feels they cannot live without a particular therapist and that another cannot help them equally well, it indicates that something wrong is going on in therapy. The therapist's narcissism, their exalted unrealistic image, is paralyzing the patient's development and not letting them grow. However, under certain circumstances, a particularly gifted therapist *may be* the only therapist who can help that person.

6. *A Therapist is Ineffective When Their Patient Does Not Feel Understood*

One of the most important capacities which all therapists should possess is the ability to make their patient feel understood: that the therapist knows who they are and why they came for treatment. When the patient begins to doubt this, progress in treatment is just as unlikely as would be the healing of a medical condition after the doctor makes an incorrect diagnosis.

Misunderstood Leila

Leila was a forty-nine year old single woman whose life had long revolved about her job as nursing supervisor in a large hospital. After several administrators were charged with embezzlement, Leila's therapist, noting her downcast look, suggested that she was worried she might be charged too. The therapist insisted on this interpretation even after Leila heatedly denied it.

Living an honest, ethical life was more than a mere phrase for Leila, this fact being well-known to her friends. She never exceeded the speed limit, and completed her tax forms so conservatively that she received a refund most years. Money which she found on the street would be donated to charity.

So the therapist's wrong interpretation, one which he pressed in the face of Leila's denial, indicated to Leila that he didn't really understand her after all.

7. A Therapist is Ineffective When Their Patient Feels Putdown

Emily Ends Therapy and Writes a Book

Emily wasn't sure why she didn't like her therapist. He dressed professionally and was always on-time and courteous. Still, he always seemed to make her feel that she wasn't on his level. A feeling which became stronger when she told him that she planned to write a book. He didn't ask her to expand on this topic: the type of book, or whether she had written before. Instead he smiled indulgently, as one might with a grandiose child, and said softly, with more than a little disbelief, "You're going to write a book?" That was their last session. Emily did write her book, which won rave reviews and good sales even before her TV interviews.

A therapist does not often have knowledge of other fields. And even if they do, one can never be so certain of a person's abilities that it is helpful to discourage their goals.

8. A Therapist Who Violates Boundaries Is Ineffective

When people hear that a therapist has "violated boundaries" they usually think they had sex with their patient. An act which is forbidden by ethics and law for a very good reason. Because of the great influence which a therapist has over their patient, the patient's agreement to be intimate cannot be freely given. But there are other, equally damaging ways in which a therapist can behave, and all are considered to violate boundaries.

These include when a patient is used by the therapist to satisfy *their* needs: sharing intimate details of their life, or doing business with them. But the proper behavior, particularly in small communities or under unusual circumstances, is not always clear. In rural areas where few mental health resources are available, a therapist may not only treat a person but wind up buying a car from their dealership or having them repair their tractor.

A psychologist, embedded with a military unit in Iraq, would occasionally sleep beside the men he was treating, an occurrence unknown in civilian practice. Here, this psychologist's behavior was ethical because of the exceptional circumstance and that his goal was always the welfare of his patients. Which can become compromised when proper patient/therapist boundaries are violated, the therapist's interests become primary, and their patient is living through their therapy rather than gaining a more fulfilling life apart from it. Which was what happened with Paulette.

Paulette, Who Some Said Loved Her Psychotherapist

Not being gay, Paulette would have found laughable the notion that she loved her therapist though there were similarities in her feelings. She thought about her often and began to dress as she felt the therapist would approve. She also shared really intimate details of her sex life, things she never even told her friends. But her therapist did the same, and sometimes Paulette felt that they were buddies rather than patient and therapist. So Paulette wasn't surprised when, after she despaired that she had nothing to do on a holiday weekend, her therapist suggested that they see a movie together and then go shopping. Which they did.

Paulette considered her therapist wonderful and could not conceive of living her life without her. Which can happen when proper therapist/patient boundaries are violated: the patient will fail to mature from their treatment and remain stuck in it, without ever knowing why.

9. *A Therapist Will Be Ineffective When Their Behavior is Markedly Unconventional*

Therapists, like dentists and medical doctors, usually behave traditionally. So much that it can cause them to make errors of judgment. A man in his fifties once called me for treatment. He previously called a psychiatrist who became frightened after listening to his story and had refused to treat him. He advised him to go to the local hospital's Emergency Room. What scared this doctor? That the man mentioned he had been in jail thirty years before.

When consulting a therapist a patient should feel no differently than when they are meeting with a dentist or medical doctor. A great gulf between these experiences should be questioned though there may well be a sound explanation. One psychologist had a foot condition and needed to wear slippers. But this is the exception. A psychiatrist/psychoanalyst suffered from a rare cancer which ultimately proved fatal. But despite his intermittent personal discomfort, none of his patients suspected this until his medical condition so worsened that he was forced to close his practice. He concealed his pain from his patients, not wanting to burden them with his private concerns.

Therapists behave conventionally to increase the comfort of their patients so they will be better able to reveal their true thoughts and feelings, which is never easy.

10. *A Therapist Will Be Ineffective When Their Office Decor Doesn't Reflect Their Patient's Needs Too*

Therapists' offices usually reflect themselves. Some hang pictures of animals and nature while others have photos of family members. Some offices are cluttered, others not. And they may be filled with expensive antiques or cheap, long-lasting furniture. Mine falls into the latter category. I once placed expensive inherited furniture in my office waiting room. But then quickly moved it out after one child carved his name into the piano lid with a nail and another made pencil holes in a leather chair.

These office peculiarities are irrelevant to the course of treatment and should be ignored—or tolerated. But other, smaller ones, reflect personality characteristics which may affect treatment. Like if the temperature of the room is set according to the therapist's comfort alone, or there are persistent burned-out light bulbs in the waiting room. If a therapist doesn't care about their patients' physical comfort, do they really care about them?

11. *A Psychotherapist Will Be Ineffective If They are Unreliable*

Amy, Who Decided That For A Psychotherapist To Resemble Freud Just Isn't Enough

Amy believed that her therapist looked exactly like a therapist should. Tall and elegantly dressed, his slim fingers and beard made him resemble the Freud of vintage photos. Were it twenty years earlier he would be smoking cigars too, she thought. Despite which, she wasn't sure that she liked him for he continually changed her appointments.

The appointment they originally decided on was Tuesdays at 5:30PM. Which was perfect since she left work at five and it was a brief walk to his office. But over the seven months since they first met, she had seen him only twice at that time. He would always call in the morning and want to change her appointment to a later one or another day. Sometimes he had no other openings that week so she didn't see him for two weeks. When she suggested that they change her appointment time permanently, he said this wasn't necessary.

Amy wondered if he treated other patients the same. Was he changing her appointments to accommodate new or higher paying patients?

It wasn't only about this that he was unreliable. When she needed a report for the court he had faxed it to her lawyer late. So despite his impressive appearance, Amy didn't think that she could work with him any longer.

Predictability in therapy is required to allow patients to risk the major emotional turmoil which occurs.

12. *A Therapist Is Ineffective When Confidentiality Is Not Maintained*

A hallmark of medical treatment is that what is told to the doctor remains confidential. But this creed has become frayed in recent years, mostly because insurers have the expectation that they should know what they are paying for. Even though the topics discussed during therapy are more intimate than the symptoms of most medical problems and, were they to become public, might cause great personal damage.

Grave insecurities, marital and work dissatisfaction, sexual diseases, substance abuse, frightening fantasies, are all discussed in the therapist's office. Which is why most therapists take confidentiality very seriously. But some therapists, perhaps wanting to impress their colleagues, discuss their cases with them. While this can be helpful in gaining professional support or advice, identifying characteristics must always be well disguised. One group therapy patient was justifiably concerned when her therapist offered to tell her why another member had left the group. "If he was so willing to tell me about this other patient, what might he be telling them about me," she perceptively remarked.

Chapter Fourteen

Is Medication and Not Psychotherapy the Solution For Your Unhappiness?

MANY YEARS AGO A MOTHER brought her problematic eight year old to a medical school child psychiatry clinic. The mother was given several pills, a small dose of a mild tranquilizer, and told to bring her child back for the therapy he needed. When she failed to appear, she was phoned and asked why they had not returned. She said that her son's behavior changed so greatly after taking just one pill that he no longer required treatment, a result which the prescribing psychiatrist stated was impossible. But it would not have surprised those doing drug research for some important findings have been long known but little publicized.

A study by Maurice Rappaport in a 1978 issue of International Pharmacopsychiatry, reported that patients in psychiatric hospitals who were treated with a placebo in the hospital and no medication after their discharge showed far greater improvement than those treated with psychiatric drugs. The difference in improvement was staggering, with those receiving medication being re-hospitalized nine times as often.

The October, 1989 issue of the American Journal of Psychiatry reported on a comprehensive study of psychotropic medications by staff at the Harvard Medical School and McLean Hospital. They were able to find only five research studies which were scientifically valid and concluded that, with regard to treating people in the acute phase of schizophrenia, the improvement was the same no matter what drug was used, whether anti-psychotic, anti-anxiety, or narcotic. Thus the importance for all patients was the drugs' sedating effect.

They also found that in some studies placebos performed as well as medication, and suggested that the patients' improvement resulted from removing them from their difficult home situations.

In the late 1980's a large scale study of Ritalin was described in the American Journal of Orthopsychiatry. This medication and similarly reacting drugs are commonly prescribed for Attention Deficit Disorder, a condition which is discussed in Chapter Twenty. This research, conducted at a major medical center, was unusually thorough and involved the psychological testing of hundreds of children and interviews with their parents and teachers. Despite the teachers' belief that those children receiving medication were doing better, they were not. They did, however, tend to be quieter, to be smaller, and to weigh less. Following this finding, Ritalin was no longer prescribed at the medical center, a situation which, because of the large amount of advertising done by the pharmaceutical industry, has almost certainly changed.

These research observations emphasize that the use of medication for emotional distress is not a simple black or white affair. As with all invasive medical procedures, caution and knowledge are strongly advised in their use.

During my first year in private practice a patient in her early forties described the stress from her pressured insurance company job and from having to single parent her disturbed teenage daughter. During her first session she spoke so continually that I began feeling jittery myself.

While psychologists in several states can now prescribe mental health or, as they are professionally termed, *psychotropic* medications, then none could, and I thought that, were I legally permitted, I would whip out my pad and write a prescription to alleviate her pain. In those days drugs were considered even more magical than they are today. Being unable to, I offered to refer her to a psychiatrist for medication. But she refused my offer and said that when she was anxious in the evening she far preferred a glass of wine. Which did seem much the better solution for, while we spoke, her anxiety gradually disappeared.

This is what usually happens when people talk about their problems and the incident caused me to realize how powerful psychotherapy can be. Which is not to say that psychotropic medications are never helpful. Like all drugs, they may be helpful; unhelpful and have no significant effect; or be harmful and cause reduced functioning. And, as with psychotherapy, the skill and knowledge of the prescribing doctor or nurse (in some states nurse practitioners can also prescribe) is an important factor.

It is only humane to want to reduce pain and medication sometimes meets this need, helping those who have limited control over their behavior and present a danger. But just as hospitalization is sometimes an excessive and ultimately unhelpful reaction, so too can prescribing medication. For despite the occasional rapid comfort which it can provide, there are drawbacks.

Psychotropic medication can produce side effects ranging across the physical spectrum from mild lethargy to sexual problems to persistent, debilitating neurological effects. Some of these may not be predictable for long-term studies of psychotropic medications are rare. Even valid, short-term studies are few: those using a double-blind technique where both the patient and the researcher do not know which patients receive the real drug and which the placebo.

Another risk of using psychotropic medication is that the patient gains the incorrect notion that the source of their problem is external rather than inside their mind: that change must come from without and not within. While children are particularly susceptible to this belief, so are some parents. They fear to realize the role which parenting and unconscious factors play in human behavior and prefer to place their child on powerful medications, even those which were never tested on children, rather than to have them involved in psychotherapy.

One mother told me that she would rather for her child to have a brain tumor, since "it could be cut out," rather than to suffer from an emotional problem. Her knowledge of both medical and psychological disorders was equally naive.

While medication may alleviate some symptoms of distress, it cannot resolve the personality problems or emotional conflicts which cause them. For these only psychotherapy—the personal engagement with a trained professional—will work.

The Complex Role of Psychotropic Drugs in Psychotherapy

The use of psychotropic medications has greatly increased in recent decades. Problems which were once considered part of normal development—shyness, school difficulty, worrying—are being medicated, with little authoritative information about the physical or psychological effects of these drugs on development.

A friend, as a personal experiment during his psychiatric residency, took a small dose of a then popular psychotropic drug. The profoundly disturbing sensations which followed caused him to be exceedingly cautious about prescribing them throughout his career.

The gold standard for drug research is considered to be the double blind test. A medication is prescribed or not to patients with the same illness, and the difference is noted between those receiving the drug or the placebo. But few such studies have been performed with psychotropic drugs. Apart from being expensive, patients and doctors are well aware of who is receiving the drug for these produce different sensations and side effects. Thus the research staff might relate to the patient who is receiving the actual drug differently from those taking the placebo, and this would effect the results, making all these findings must be suspect. Moreover, most drug company research is completed in several months and significant side effects may not develop until years into the future.

Several years ago I developed a mild case of conjunctivitis ("pink eye") and had it evaluated, though knowing that a physician's general response to this condition is "with treatment it goes away in a week, without treatment it takes seven days." Most cases of conjunctivitis are viral not bacterial, and an antibiotic will not help with these. Still, without testing to note which condition I had, an antibiotic was prescribed. But before taking it, I investigated this drug.

The difference between the effectiveness of this medication and a placebo was not great. Ninety three percent of patients improved with the drug; sixty two percent improved with the placebo. And the drug's potential side effects, though infrequent, were significant. Needless to say, I didn't fill the prescription and the condition spontaneously cleared up in a few days. Yet ten years earlier, when I developed a more severe case of conjunctivitis, I did use medication and it greatly relieved my discomfort.

Despite the need for caution, medication can be valuable in mental health treatment under certain circumstances.

1. *Psychotropic medication should be considered when potentially dangerous behavior exists*

Everyone does impulsive things occasionally. An angry child may run from a classroom or even from the school, while an angry adult may rage at a slow driver and tailgate them for miles. If, despite psychotherapy, this potentially dangerous behavior persists, medication should be considered as an adjunct to therapy.

2. *Psychotropic medication should be considered when a person is experiencing significant pain*

Some people tolerate discomfort better than others. But when despite psychotherapy, the pain interferes with a person's functioning, medication should be considered.

The Potential Side Effects of Medication

While all drugs have side effects, not all people experience them. Yet for some, they may be so uncomfortable that the drug will be discontinued.. Studies have shown that the usage of between one third and one-half of all prescribed drugs are stopped because of their side effects; and the longer the medication is taken, the greater is the likelihood that this will occur.

A good general rule is that if the benefits of taking the drug are vastly greater than the side effects experienced, the drug should be used. If the side effects are equal to the benefit, one should be cautious in taking the drug. And if the drug's side effects greatly exceed their benefit, the drug should not be taken.

Medication has not always been accompanied with a helpful attitude by the prescribing physician. Even the phrase "compliance with treatment" implies an authoritarian rather than collaborative relationship—and it is one in which the patient assumes all of the risk! It has been suggested that the term "adherence" be used, to emphasize that the patient is free to control their treatment. Moreover, for a patient to cooperate with long-term treatment may not accord with human nature for this role, even when the patient is viewed as being a consumer of the medical service, contrasts with the powerful desire for individual autonomy.

For a psychotropic medication to be helpful, even if it is the perfect drug in the most effective dosage, there must be regular contact between the patient and a trusted prescribing physician who can detect troublesome side effects. For this, the physician must possess a sensitive, open-minded attitude, in order to create a cooperative working relationship and avoid a power struggle.

Some patients develop fantasies about the medication they are taking. Those who fear taking any drug may become anxious as soon as it is swallowed, believing that the typical symptoms of nervousness which result (sweating or feeling cold; dryness of the mouth or stomach distress) are caused by the drug, They then stop taking it though the medication was blameless.

Others may view their medication as being a magical potion and feel instantly better after taking it. Or they may carry a tranquilizer with them, the mere knowledge that they have it available if needed enabling them to remain calm.

Certain factors decrease the likelihood that medication will be successful: when many medications are prescribed; if the dose is inadequate or the patient is particularly sensitive to an ingredient; if the side effects change or are severe; or if treatment must stop because of a medical condition or pregnancy. The cost of the medication may also be a factor.

Moreover, the beneficial effects of psychotropic medication are often slower to develop than are their distressing side-effects. And "distressing" is no understatement for these can include: neurological problems; feeling tired or sleepy; being unable to concentrate; sexual problems; weight gain; blurred vision; heart problems; stroke; urinary and bowel difficulties; restlessness; anxiety; and others. Obviously, the decision to use psychotropic medication is no small matter.

One unhelpful psychological side-effect is the belief that the prescribed medication will change the patient's life. No drug, no matter how potent, will increase a person's psychological abilities. It may make them less tense and more comfortable, and so better able to deal with their duties. But other—internal--changes must occur for them to become more capable of intimacy and to obtain a life filled with joy. Unfortunately, no medication to produce these changes has yet been produced or is likely to become available.

There are two opposing camps concerning psychotherapy and medication. One asserts that mental health symptoms derive from an unknown or hypothesized brain malformation or insufficiency, much like diabetes is caused by the body's inability to produce enough insulin or to use it effectively. Thus insulin and/or other medications are provided a patient who can then, usually with some restrictions, go on to lead an essentially normal life.

Similarly, one who suffers from anxiety, depression, or mood swings, requires medication to reduce or eliminate these symptoms. Psychotherapy is considered helpful in maintaining compliance with the prescribed medication and reducing the normal stress which accompanies change. Some extremists believe that every undesirable thought and feeling derives from bad brain chemistry. This is one pole of the debate.

At the other extreme, all mental health symptoms are considered to reflect basic psychological weaknesses which govern the ability to control thinking and behavior, modulate mood, develop a sense of self, and others; and/or emotional conflicts revolving about intimacy, self-assertion, or another matter. It is considered that these difficulties can only be healed through psychotherapy, with medication being helpful, if at all, as a minor adjunct to the psychotherapy by enabling patients to get through a rough period.

To summarize these opposing positions: one views medication as being essential to behavioral change while the other views psychotherapy as essential with medication having minimal importance.

While the modern family of mental health drug were first produced in the nineteen fifties, the use of substances to improve mood and feelings is as old as human history. Ancient societies used herbs and foods with psychedelic properties, these sometimes being incorporated into religious rites. Hallucinogenic mushrooms such as Amanita muscaria ("Fly Agaric") is such an example. St. John's Wort, which is widely used in Europe to treat depression, is another example.

Psychotropic drugs fall into several classes.

1. Antidepressants such as Lexapro, Prozac and Zoloft, which are prescribed for depression, anxiety, and other disorders.

2. Antipsychotics such as Thorazine, Abilify, and Risperdal, which are prescribed for psychotic disorders such as schizophrenia.

3. Anti-anxiety drugs such as Valium and Xanax.

4. Stimulants such as Adderall, Ritalin, and Concerta, which are used to treat attention deficit disorder (ADD).

5.Mood stabilizers such as Carbolith and Depakote, which are used to treat manic disorders.

While it is logical to treat a mental health condition with a psychotropic medication designed specifically for it, this is not easily done. First, psychotropic medicines tend to have widespread bodily effects and can cause harmful changes in areas unrelated to the disorder. Thus antipsychotic drugs may cause deteriorated teeth because they reduce the natural flow of saliva, or significant weight gain. Other potential side effects of these drugs are more severe: diabetes; agranulocytosis, a dangerous reduction in the white blood cells; tardive dyskinesia, the repetitive, involuntary movements of the lips, face, or legs; or seizure.

While antipsychotic and antidepressant drugs can have particularly worrisome side effects, all psychotropic drugs produce systemic change. Unfortunately, even children are not immune to their inappropriate prescription.

In 2007 nearly four hundred thousand children were treated with Risperdal, a powerful antipsychotic drug intended for the most disturbed adults. Why were these children provided such a dangerous drug? To help them concentrate in school, a condition for which it was never approved by the government. This use was strongly criticized by a federal panel in view of the drug's serious risks (great weight gain, metabolic disorders, permanent muscular tics).

Much of the theory underlying these drugs is myth and not science, a marketing tool. For example, the "chemical imbalance" theory which is used to market antidepressant drugs derives from the belief that depression is caused by low neurotransmitter (catecholamine) levels, serotonin being one of them. Which sounds reasonable except that the serotonin level of depressed, suicidal patients and that of normal people is the same. Moreover, a recent major study found that anti-depressant medications were only marginally better than a placebo, and that even this minimal effect was likely too high.*

What these drugs do is to make people less likely to behave impulsively which, admittedly, is important. Though they do not cure depression, or encourage a person to think seriously about the events in their life which are causing it. This, depending on the philosophy of the prescribing physician, may be their greatest detriment: encouraging people to believe that they can make complex life changes by taking a pill, without having to struggle with the difficulties of emotional change and personality growth.

Psychotherapy Psychosomatics, 2010, 79 (267-279)

Though lacking a curative effect and producing potential side-effects so great as to be legally actionable, psychotropic medications, "by affecting biological substrates to reduce disorganized and disruptive behavior," can enable some severely disturbed patients to "continue their lives with minimal disruption."* Which can be a major benefit.

*Robert O. Obourn, M.D., Director, C. F. Menninger Memorial Hospital, *Bulletin of the Menninger Clinic*, 47(3), 1983, p. 274

Chapter Fifteen

Answers to the Three Important Questions Which Patients Never Ask

If nothing is permanent, then why bother trying to change?

In thinking about the relationship between patient and psychotherapist we must consider time. That each of their contacts is time-limited, with some being too brief for the patient's comfort and others too lengthy for the therapist's. This reality reflects the limitations in the therapeutic relationship and the pain these sometimes occasion. Which raises the ultimate question: if nothing is permanent, then why bother trying to change even if not doing so produces boredom and refutes a basic law of development. For, as living creatures, we are geared towards growth and dislike goals which cannot be reached or are final.

The task of the psychotherapist is to place their skills at the use of the patient. In a room, for a time, and within a relationship in which demands, manipulation, and greed are absent.

An interaction guided by openness and honesty and hope within which the patient is free to choose to change or not. This novel experience creates a place of inner peace. One which can be maintained after the therapy ends, making it a priceless experience even if the goals are not fully achieved.

Why do some psychotherapists sexually abuse their patients?

The popular explanation for this uncommon event is sexual attraction. Though, like with much such information, this impression is mostly wrong. Not that the attractiveness of the patient is unimportant though this reflects a very individual choice. But this unethical and, in many states, illegal behavior derives from complex psychological factors, most of which have nothing to do with sex.

Often these therapists are acting out the cultural myth that an impulsive, substance abusing man needs only a good woman in order to settle down, like is depicted in so many movies. Most such intimate relationships are between a male therapist and his female patient though these also occur between female therapists and male patients and those of the same sex. I know of two female therapists who married their male patients: one was alcoholic; the other, a lawyer, was severely disturbed and long unemployed.

Despite the great risk, these relationships occur because of the same factors which underlie all self-defeating behaviors: an interplay of unconscious motives and needs and reasons which may have little to do with sex.

1. A therapist who never gained a feeling of importance from his mother may seek this from their patient in the emotionally charged, isolated atmosphere of the therapy office. Thus, through the mechanism of *counter-transference* in which a therapist projects childhood feelings onto their patient, the therapist relates to the patient as he did to his mother decades before,

seeking to satisfy emotional needs which remain unfulfilled.

2, The therapist may be lonely—love-starved—and convince himself that *this* relationship with a patient is different, unconstrained by ethics or law for both are "star-crossed" and meant for each other.

3. The therapist may be angry at the facility he works or institute he is training and, indirectly, be acting out his angry feelings in this forbidden way.

4. Because every successful treatment involves an end to the relationship between therapist and patient, the therapist may try to avoid their natural feeling of grief by maintaining the relationship in a continuing affair.

5. The therapist may be responding to the patient's unconscious need for warmth and longing to be loved which, though being expressed in a sexually provocative way, is misinterpreted by the therapist.

6. The patient may unconsciously wish to merge with the therapist they idealize and become stronger, not recognizing that real strength can only be gained from emotional growth. This possibility may increase if the therapist believes in the curative power of love, a childhood fantasy of many who concluded that their lives would be improved had they been better loved by their parents.

7. The therapist may be angry at the patient who fails to improve despite the therapist's best efforts. Thus, despairing, the therapist may then act out their frustration in a sexual manner.

So, like many puzzling behaviors, what seemed simple at first glance may be amazingly complex.

Why do people become psychotherapists?

Certainly not to make money, which is what many people think. Psychiatrists have near the bottom income of all the medical specialties though their training is just as long. While in the years following World War Two, fifty percent of a psychiatrist's residency training was spent learning psychotherapy, this has become reduced by nine tenths.* So psychiatrists who practice psychotherapy must gain additional education in training institutes, which can be expensive.

To become a clinical psychologist requires at least five years of graduate school training; and though a social work degree can be gained in two years beyond the college degree, these practitioners often seek further training too. Thus when considering the cost of education and the future prospect of making less money than workers having far less training, other motives must be in play.

For some therapists, like many who go into medicine and nursing, it is the desire to heal based on childhood experience with an ill relative. Others may have experienced painful childhoods and want to help others avoid them. And some may simply find no other field of study to be as interesting as human behavior.

*Wallerstein, Robert S. The future of psychotherapy. *Bulletin of the Menninger Clinic,* Fall 1991, 55:4.

Chapter Sixteen

How to Choose a Great Psychotherapist (Hint: Ignore the Usual Advice)

FINDING A GREAT PSYCHOTHERAPIST demands as much personal research as does the search for any highly skilled worker. But not in a magazine, where being named "best" may indicate little more than being personable and having good marketing skill or public relations contacts. Recently, one perennial favorite of a noted "Best Doctors" list, "a highly respected Manhattan shrink" and founding chairman of a hospital psychiatry department, was successfully sued by his patient who was awarded $650,000. She described her five years of treatment as being "a living horror."*

Nor can one rely on a clinic or university counseling center since their therapists are usually inexperienced and the match of patient to clinician is most often made for administrative reasons: who has an open slot in their schedule or needs a person with a particular problem for their training. Moreover if a mismatch is made, changing one's therapist at these settings is no simple matter. And they usually have elaborate intake procedures so it may be weeks or even months before treatment can begin.

---

*Dareh Gregorian, "Voyeur shrink set up patient's trysts to hear salacious details," *New York Post*, 10 October 2010.

With an individual practitioner, treatment starts far more quickly and a change of therapist can be accomplished with just a phone call. Yet the same difficulty exists: how to choose a good therapist from all those available. And make no mistake: it is a matter of choice, not desperation.

The popular but unhelpful advice is to seek a referral from a trusted physician. Yet while physicians are knowledgeable about the body and write fifty-nine percent of mental health drug prescriptions*, a practice which has been criticized, they often have little insight into emotional difficulties or understand how complex psychotherapy is.

Recommendations by other community leaders are no more helpful. These referrals (by a religious figure, school official, etc.) are actually less accurate since they are too often based on knowledge of the therapist socially, or derive from the therapist's professional reputation which is largely based on research or their professional position rather than how well they conduct therapy. And while one can be a good researcher *and* effective therapist, both skills are not often found in the same person.

*Based on a study of 472 million American prescriptions for psychotropic drugs, conducted by researchers from Thomson Reuters and the United States Substance Abuse and Mental Health Services Administration, reported on September 30, 2009.

Similarly, choosing a therapist because they are on the panel of an insurance company or member of a professional organization is no guarantee that you will be satisfied with their treatment. What it comes down to is that there can be no substitute for your personal investigation of the therapist, one with whom you will be sharing the most intimate details of your life. Today, this initial study can be done quickly using the Internet. Like with traffic lights, the information you gain can be placed in Red, Yellow, and Green categories.

The Red Warning Signal in Choosing a Psychotherapist or Danger Lies Ahead:

Be wary if the therapist is unlicensed or has lost or given up their license in any state. The latter is an uncommon event and their clinical error or misbehavior must have been great for it to happen. But even here, these mistakes may have had nothing to do with the quality of the therapy which was provided but arose from other behavior. Ethical issues, like giving an opinion regarding child visitation or custody without evaluating *both* parents; providing information without the proper signed consent; or fraud in insurance billing. Not whether the therapist was capable of fostering healthy psychological change.

Despite this, I suggest being exceedingly cautious about consulting a therapist who lost their license in another state or previously in the state where you live though, admittedly, licensing authorities can made unfair judgments.

The Yellow Warning Signal in Choosing a Psychotherapist or Maybe You Should Keep Looking

Although every therapist was once inexperienced, experience does matter. A seasoned clinician will make a quicker, more accurate diagnosis, and the therapeutic relationship will be more comfortable. Having said this, psychotherapy is both an art and a science, and receiving treatment from a gifted beginner is a far better bet than gaining it from a sixty year old with only average ability.

The Green Signals in Choosing a Psychotherapist or Clinicians to Try

1. Recommendation from a trusted friend

That a friend is enthusiastic about a therapist is always a good sign. Yet even if a therapist helped your friend, there can be no certainty that they will be able to help you. Problems differ, as do personalities. And the therapist may have changed and become affected by their own life stresses.

While it is true that, with experience, therapists become more effective in treating a wider range of problems and personalities, each has their quirks and limitations. For example, those who are most effective with children and prefer working with them might not feel comfortable treating adults with major substance abuse issues for the emotional demands are too different. And while one can work productively with patients one dislikes, just like a surgeon can operate successfully on people with any personality, this is not the best situation.

I once treated a man in his forties who I didn't like. Not because of his arrogance or that he betrayed his wife, but because of the nasty remarks he made. Still, he made good progress in the several months I treated him but I was glad when his therapy was over.

People are perceptive and a therapist's true feelings will soon be sensed. So they don't usually treat patients who irritate them for long.

2. A Positive Change You Noticed in your Friend or Relative Following Their Therapy

Probably the best recommendation is when a friend, relative, or their child, has changed for the better after therapy. Even if their problem was different from yours, their positive experience indicates that the therapist knows what they are doing and can quickly judge whether they can help you. And, even if they decide against treating you, your next choice will be better informed because of this contact.

Because psychotherapy is an individual exploration, there can be no "start and remain in treatment" cues: you must continually evaluate the adequacy of your treatment. The best that can be said, following your first several sessions, is that the therapist appears knowledgeable and effective. Your judgment whether to remain in treatment should be reserved until you have greater experience with them.

A Common Source of Misunderstanding In Therapy

Probably no issue arouses so much discomfort for both therapists and their patients as whether to charge for missed appointments. Each sees it from a different viewpoint.

Therapists view the issue as follows. In medical practice, a physician might schedule a half-dozen patients for the same time slot so the absence of one has little financial effect. But a therapist reserves a specific block of time for each patient. If they don't come and insufficient notice is given, the therapist loses income.

Patients interpret the situation more simply: why should I pay for something which I didn't receive? Particularly if my reason for missing the appointment is a good one: my child got sick or the weather made driving hazardous.

Because both sides are right, whatever is done tends to lead to ruffled feelings.

There is another important but unspoken factor: the ability of the patient to pay. With wealthier patients who populate psychoanalytic practices in large cities, paying for missed appointments has traditionally been the norm. Elsewhere, less affluent patients resist paying for missed appointments despite the logic of the therapist's explanation.

There are no hard and fast rules and mine are probably more lenient than those of other therapists. So long as the patient gives reasonable notice, I do not charge no matter what reason they use. Some excuses I never question: poor weather, because people have different tolerances for driving and it is better not to risk an accident; their illness or that of their child; or the death of a friend or relative.

I do charge when I feel that I am being taken advantage of, as when appointments are repeatedly missed. However since skipping appointments indicates a lack of seriousness about treatment, rather than charge I generally end the patient's therapy when it occurs. But I also tend to be easy about taking patients back.

This is my policy and follows from my general feeling that charging for missed appointments creates so much resentment that it affects the success of treatment. It is also unfair since it more greatly affects people with tight finances for missed appointments cannot be billed to insurance.

Other therapists approach the matter differently. Some permit one or two missed sessions and charge for the rest; or offer a make-up session for later that same week and, if it is kept, charge only for this appointment and not for that which was missed. As with most complex human affairs, there is no right or wrong approach or a solution which satisfies everyone.

Chapter Seventeen

Cheer Up! You've Arrived For Your First Therapy Session

People begin psychotherapy when their life is in crisis. An important relationship or their job is endangered. They cannot decide whether to attend school, move to another town, or some less precise worry which is more important: what they want to accomplish in life, or who they really are.

Contrary to popular belief, few people who enter therapy do so from the fear that they are going crazy; and many leave their motive for treatment for their therapist to figure out. Which is always one of their primary tasks regardless of what the patient initially says.

Apart from the sometimes incorrect information which they gained from movies, or analogies with their past medical treatments, people who are new to therapy don't know what to expect in their first or later sessions.

During the first session there will be the required business forms to read and sign, a task taking no more than two minutes. These consist of information about the therapist's privacy practices, a statement which is required by federal law; and a form documenting your receipt of this; a form permitting the therapist to release personal information about you to to needed parties (usually an insurance carrier and possibly your physician). There will also be a form which permits the therapist to receive insurance payments for your treatment ("Signature on File"), in addition to the co-payment which is your responsibility.

What then follows depends on the particular therapist. Some therapists and all clinic settings have questionnaires which new patients are asked to complete explaining why they are seeking treatment and describing their symptoms. I don't, preferring to obtain this information through the many questions which I ask during the first session.

These questions concern the patient's general health; whether they are taking any medication, their marital status and if the marriage has problems; whether they have children and, if so, their names and ages; their education, job and if there are work difficulties; their opinion of their parents and siblings and if they are now close; whether they ever had mental health or substance abuse treatment; the degree to which they use alcohol or drugs and whether they smoke; and if they ever had suicidal or homicidal thoughts. Finally, what brought them to my office. To reassure them, I explain that my questions are basic and asked of all new patients.

It is not only their answers but their behavior which is important. Do they speak fluidly and exhibit good self control? If they seem anxious or depressed, can they control their behavior or are they jumpy. Are their answers brief, as if they never consider such matters; or lengthy, indicating that they tend to think deeply about their life.

Do they seem to have a clear sense of who they are, or do their opinions change depending on what another person said? Do they answer questions directly, or ramble and raise irrelevant matters? Before they leave, I provide information how therapy sessions usually go and, to the degree I then understand them, explain what is causing their distress and any symptoms which puzzle them.

After only one therapy session a person should feel a little better for they have determined to solve their problems and acted on this decision by describing them to an expert on human behavior. So, with their aid, they now expect for their life to improve.

Should You Schedule A Second Session?

Patients do not always feel better after their first therapy session. Perhaps their expectations were too great, or they weren't yet ready to engage in therapy. Some people see three or four or even more therapists, for one session each, before they feel comfortable about treatment. Which they will then pursue with their next clinician, who may be no more competent than was the first they consulted.

Or perhaps the original therapist was not a good choice: they spoke too much or not at all; provided too little or apparently erroneous information; were emotionally cold or too solicitous; had upsetting personal habits such as biting their nails, had a nervous tic, or put on hand cream while speaking.

For whatever reason, there may be poor "fit" between the person and this therapist. At this point, two choices exist. For the patient to return for a second session, describe their discomfort and see how the therapist responds and if their feelings then change. Or, if their discomfort was very great and they feel *more* anxious after the first session, to seek a new therapist with whom they will be compatible.

A therapist who senses a patient's ambivalence about treatment usually suggests that a second session not be scheduled without their further consideration. Therapists do not want to treat someone who is ambivalent about therapy for progress will be lacking, appointments will be missed, and both parties will feel dissatisfied.

However if it is only the patient who feels uncomfortable, they should not hesitate to seek another therapist. The mind operates very quickly and can come to decisions without awareness. Though not all of these will be good ones, an instant dislike or sense of disconnect is too important an instinct to ignore. But the patient should analyze this feeling to be sure that it is the therapist's behavior which caused this and not their own fear of treatment.

Those beginning therapy have a war going on inside of their mind. Part of it wants to change while another element fears change and will use any means to stop this. Which sometimes includes misinterpreting the behavior of the therapist in order to create a feeling of distrust and encourage the termination of treatment.

"Wait!" their unconscious mind tells them, as the anxiety which they experienced before their first session drains away and with it their reason for making this appointment. Such people may not schedule another therapy. appointment until their distress returns. Clearly, deciding on a therapist and beginning therapy is a complicated matter.

Your Second Psychotherapy Session and Thereafter

Like with many medical problems, there is no predictable path with how healing will progress. While with a well-trained and talented therapist most emotional problems can be healed—to the extent that personality, intellect, and time permit—this is not certain.

Psychotherapy is a catalyst. It encourages healthy change to occur but cannot guarantee that it will. Life intervenes for good and ill. An isolated man may become more open to intimacy but his life would remain unchanged had he not met the warm, interested, and available co-worker. A woman changes greatly—only to be diagnosed with terminal pancreatic cancer.

Several beliefs underlie all brands of psychotherapy: that warmth and good intentions alone do not heal; that psychological symptoms are related to treatable causes; and that the relationship between therapist and patient is crucial to the success of treatment. Most psychotherapies would add another factor: the need for an increased understanding of the the patient's unconscious motives.

As therapy progresses there will be ups and downs. A patient may erupt with anger because of something the therapist said. They may even vow to end therapy only to change their mind a few minutes later. This apparently illogical behavior reflects the war going on inside of their mind: the struggle over whether to allow themselves to risk change or to remain as they are.

Because therapists understand that personal change is a momentous undertaking, they accept behavior during sessions which would be condemned by adults. Like speaking of and to stuffed animals as if they were alive;

expressing emotions with a vehemence unrelated to the situation; lying in a fetal position on the floor; or refusing to leave at the end of the session.

"The unconscious is very powerful and you have to respect its power," a psychiatrist colleague once said. But while respecting the power of the unconscious a patient must also try to control their emotions with logic and reason when it threatens to overpower.

It may seem that with all of this seething emotion psychotherapy must be a painful experience but this is not true. If conducted properly, psychotherapy should, on the whole, be enjoyable, for where else can a person speak freely, without consequence, of whatever concerns them. A place to reveal the humiliations and disappointments and fears which all have experienced. A setting where these can finally be laid to rest and for healing to occur. There are few greater gifts in life than this.

Your Child's First Psychotherapy Session

As was earlier stated, symptoms (the sign that something is wrong) can be placed into two categories: *reactive symptoms* which are caused by a recent stress, and *internalized symptoms* which derive from long-term stress.

While therapy will reduce or eliminate both types of symptoms, those which are caused by longer term stress will require more treatment. With recently developed childhood symptoms, therapy may not be needed. Positive change will occur by eliminating the stress, as through the parent's intervention with a bully or unresponsive teacher or another situation. Then the symptom (lowered school grades, sleeping or eating problems, a nervous tic) will naturally disappear.

While the theory underlying psychotherapy with both children and adults is identical, the techniques differ greatly. Because extended conversation with an adult is not natural for a child, another means is used. This technique, *play therapy,* is well understood by children because it is similar to their usual activities: board games such as Chutes and Ladders and Connect Four; checkers and chess; card games including War and Go-Fish; coloring in coloring books; completing picture puzzles; and imaginative interaction with stuffed animals.

Yet despite these activities, the topics of conversation during this play sometimes differs little from that with adults during their therapy: why they coming for therapy, nightmares; and painful experiences with peers.

Because children are young, some progress should be noticeable after just several sessions though it will not be great. The child may be a little calmer and more cooperative, and seem happier. The reason for these positive changes is that the child's life has again begun to make sense. They were unhappy, their parents recognized this and involved them in an enjoyable activity after which they feel better. Which also increases their ability to meet the reasonable demands of their parents.

Evaluating how long therapy will last is also different for children than with adults. A year of treatment for a five year old is twenty percent of their life. Thus, because of their youth, it will produce greater change than will a similar period for an adult.

Because children are dependent on their parents, so is their treatment. It frequently ends as soon as the presenting symptoms are eliminated, which may be well before the needed psychological changes can be made. This termination may occur even with very disturbed children. Psychotherapy can arouse irrational fears in even the best intentioned parents.

How Long Will Your Psychotherapy Last?

The exact time when therapy should end can be no better defined than when it should begin. My first literary agent, an elderly lawyer, advised me that a book gets written when a writer feels they must do so. The same is true for therapy: patients remain in therapy for as long as they feel they must.

Ideally, therapy ends when both the therapist and the patient conclude that it should. Which is to say that as much progress as possible has been made at that point in the patient's life with the most important goals having been achieved. But therapy may also end because of relocation or financial reasons. And, with children, because the parent (but usually not the child!) cannot tolerate further treatment. Thus with psychotherapy as in life, the ideal is not often attained.

A woman in her thirties, who I treated during the intermittent periods when she was living in the United States, told me that her last therapist said she should keep in touch with him. What did I think of this advice? I replied that therapy was a treatment for certain difficulties and, when these were resolved, there was no need for further contact though therapist usually welcome hearing from former patients. This viewpoint made sense to her as it always did to me.

Though there are friendship and parenting elements in therapy, a therapist is neither a parent or a friend. They are a trained professional who enters a person's life to do a job and leaves when it is completed. Though, just as with valued relatives, teachers and others, their memory may persist for a lifetime.

As people age, new difficulties and challenges arise. Divorce, child-rearing, work stress, even chronic illness or disability. The distress aroused by these situations may benefit from additional therapy even if it formally ended years before. There is no certain answer whether to consult the same or another therapist. The patient may conclude that mistakes were made in their former treatment and a new therapist is preferable. Or they may prefer one who did not know them then, when they were more vulnerable and troubled. Or the earlier therapist may be unavailable. Then the guidelines in this book for choosing a therapist should be followed.

Psychotherapy is a special relationship between two people. An interaction overlain by the therapist's expression of hope, warmth, and caring during their joint inquiry into the patient's life. It is a noble, even sacred journey on which they embark.

Chapter Eighteen

Eleven Annoying Psychotherapist Behaviors and Why They Happen

THROUGH AN INTERNET SURVEY, complaints were gathered about the behavior of therapists which most annoy patients. While several are innocent and tend to be misinterpreted by patients, the rest are inexcusable.

1. A therapist who is late for or misses appointments.

Since therapists work on a one patient per time slot schedule, I would think that relatively few therapists are routinely late for or miss scheduled appointments. When this happens with me it is usually just a five or ten minutes lateness and virtually always because of an earlier patient's behavior: they being late because of traffic or another reason. And other things can happen too for people aren't machines and illness occurs.

I once left the office early with flu like symptoms, feeling worse because I was unable to see a teenager who had driven from another county to see me and waited in the parking lot. A psychiatrist I know had to end a session early when he sensed that he was having a heart attack.

Most therapists are conscientious but those who regularly miss or are more than a few minutes late for appointments may be indicating a lackadaisical professional attitude which it is best to avoid. Or they may be considering closing their practice and their behavior reflects this.

2. A therapist who eats during sessions

Apart from drinking water, juice, or diet or regular soda, drinks which I offer to all patients though some bring their own, I have never eaten during a session. But I don't object to patients doing so, whether they are children or adults.

People lead rushed lives and if eating during the first few minutes of their therapy session makes attendance easier or more comfortable then it is fine with me. Having said this, it is rare for patients, whether children or adults, to eat during therapy sessions.

Years ago I conducted a therapy group for teenage girls and provided them snacks but never ate them myself, feeling that to do so would interfere with my ability to concentrate on what they were saying.

3. A therapist who yawns during sessions

Probably there is no more common but incorrect conclusion about therapist behavior than that yawning indicates being bored with a patient. It can reflect many things. Feeling tired from inadequate sleep. A poorly ventilated room. Or having sat for too many hours and needing a break, the yawn being a brief seventh inning stretch.

Which is not to say that some patients are not tiresome, particularly those who repeat complaints which have been addressed many times. But here the therapist should try to engage the patient differently so that they gain control over their distress and reduce it.

4. A therapist who speaks of their personal life

People come to therapy because of their personal concerns, not those of the therapist. Which is so obvious a statement that many would question why it need be stated. But being a therapist is a difficult task. For though it requires that they interact with the patient honestly, the relationship also contains an element of deception of which both are aware.

One person speaks of intimate, even sexual matters, yet there can be no intimacy between the two of them. They meet regularly just like friends do and the therapist is concerned with their patient's physical comfort: Do they want a drink? Is the room too warm or cold? Are they over their recent illness? Questions which even some spouses ignore. Yet despite these friendly aspects, the two participants are not really friends.

The therapist's questions reflect more than professional courtesy since comfort and trust are required to enable the essence of therapy: the internalization of the therapist's image by the patient in order for healing to occur.

Though a noble task, working as a therapist has a built-in danger, as when a lonely therapist wastes time in speaking of their life rather than that of their patient. Yet some personal revelation by the therapist is inevitable for people cannot always be speaking of "problems." Relaxation, by speaking of other matters, is needed.

Moreover some patients, particularly children and teenagers, may be unable to speak of their personal matters, and their therapist's questions will elicit only very brief or single word responses. With these patients, silence is not an option since it creates too great stress. Nor are some children and teenagers receptive to bridging the gap by playing games. Here, the skilled therapist will tell stories: disguised experiences from the lives of others to educate them about human behavior; or humorous, minimally revealing stories from their own lives. Like the seventy nine dollar Mercedes I unwisely purchased as a graduate student, or what I heard at a psychology conference.

The difference between these personal references and those deriving from therapist loneliness or narcissism is their goal: whether it is the patient's needs—or their therapist's—which motivates the telling of them.

5. *A therapist who is difficult to contact*

I once knew a highly regarded psychoanalyst who successfully treated people with the most severe emotional difficulties. His commitment to their care was so great that, when on vacation, he would spend several hours a day speaking with them on the phone. His wife considered these his "telephone vacations."

All patients would prefer their therapist to be like him: willing to speak with them whenever they feel the need. I agree, though whether it derives from my training with this doctor or what I learned thereafter to be the most healing I'm not sure.

I believe that therapists should be continuously available to their patients. They should *not* leave a telephone message referring them elsewhere to cope with their crisis, as to a hospital's Emergency Room. This behavior infuriated me when I worked as a hospital administrator. "A doctor should care for their own patients.

Not refer them to the ER when they go on vacation," I would insist, though to no avail.

Therapists behave differently. Some, when they are not in the office, are immediately paged with all telephone calls which are quickly returned. Others do not return phone messages for many hours or even days. And many still refer people to that old stand-by: the Emergency Room of the local hospital. Before beginning treatment, one should check which of these options is followed by the therapist.

Closely related is whether the therapist makes themselves available to speak with patients outside of their session. My position is that I would rather defuse a potential emergency early than have to deal with its ramifications later. So I tell all patients to call me whenever they feel the need. Despite this suggestion I am phoned infrequently except to re-schedule appointments. When patients feel that they can gain immediate help, they rarely need to do so.

Most of the phone calls which I do get are not true emergencies. A child refusing to go to school or having a severe temper tantrum; or a husband distraught over his wife's accusations. But some are. Like that from the parent of a teenager who stood on the balcony and spoke of suicide; or the woman whose husband threatened to kill her and was wandering about the house with a pistol. A therapist who is unwilling to receive phone calls will not learn—until it may be too late—which of these situations their patient confronts.

6. A therapist who is distracted by their phone or laptop

What every patient wants is the continuous, undivided attention of their therapist during each session. But this creates two conflicting goals. How can a therapist be continuously available by phone to a patient they are not with and also attentive to the patient they face? Here, like with other human situations, compromise is necessary even if the notion of continuous attention is a fiction, an ideal which can be only intermittently achieved.

During a session, a therapist may be distracted by thoughts of their family or a backache. Perhaps a noise from the waiting room causes them to momentarily wonder if the next patient is exceptionally early or they made a scheduling error. These brief lapses of attention do not hinder the progress of treatment anymore than does the temporary inattention of a mother make them a bad parent or causes their child to feel unloved. Therapy is an ongoing, vibrant, developing interaction, not a series of discrete, disjointed events.

Whether to answer the phone during sessions is an issue about which therapists disagree. Some, including me, feel that a therapist should always be available. That brief advice given during a (rare) true emergency can avoid extensive distressing developments. Moreover, a greatly upset patient can become calm after hearing the therapist's voice and their few words. Consider how upset you were while awaiting a physician's call about your frightening symptoms or test results or those of your child.

If requiring more than a minute, most therapists will offer to call back at the end of their ongoing session. Patients willingly accept these rare interruptions for they understand that someday they might need this service. But tolerating these calls does not mean having to listen to a therapist speak with their broker or of another personal matter. Those interruptions are an entirely different matter and unacceptable.

The other point of view is that no interruption is acceptable during a therapy session. These therapists refuse to answer the phone and rely on an answering machine to do so. While understanding their position, I feel that it causes the therapy they provide to be considered more a ritual than treatment method. But this is just my opinion. There is no research to say that one procedure is better than the other. Some therapist behavior simply reflects what they feel most comfortable with.

Using a laptop to take notes is another taxing issue. I have sometimes thought of using my keyboard, the AlphaSmart Neo, to take notes. This is a small two pound, silent machine with a six line screen and is the size of a small netbook. Anything typed on this can be quickly exported via a USB cable into a computer's word processing program. I use this to write during my free time in the office and elsewhere. But I decided not to use it during therapy sessions, sensing that it would not feel comfortable for the patient and would reduce my ability to concentrate on what they were saying. Thus I still rely on pen and pad to keep notes for this technique seems less obstructive.

While an increasing number of physicians do use laptops, particularly those in the larger medical groups, this behavior tends to be resented by patients who, too often, go nearly unseen while the doctor pecks away.

7. A therapist who expresses racial, religious, lifestyle, or other personal preferences

Everyone holds prejudices, ranging from their conclusions about people with extensive tattoos or who love horror movies to members of one or another political party. Being prejudiced is part of the human condition and enables the mind to more rapidly fit people and circumstances into categories and for the person to remain safe. While these can be false, some prejudices are sensible.

If a person approaches you on an urban street holding an unsheathed knife it would be prudent to follow your conclusion that they are dangerous and to flee. This is one of any number of judgments which are automatically made. Is that girl really interested in me? Can I trust that man in my apartment on our first date? Many familiar judgments are based on prejudice or pre-judgment: the experience one had with people with similar characteristics even when scientific evidence was absent.

So while it is normal to hold personal prejudices, for the therapist to bring theirs into the therapy session—since they are non-scientific—*is* wrong. Even telling amusing stories can be problematic: since their appeal is individual, they may arouse unintended discomfort.

I once gave a talk on public speaking to my local Chamber of Commerce. There, I advised against telling religious and political jokes or stories because the speaker could never be sure of the reaction of the audience. As an example, I told the only religious anecdote which I feel comfortable telling anywhere.

One evening, as a new resident of St. Louis, I drove along a poorly lit road. While trying to make a left turn, I beached the car on the divider. An auto holding four huge men pulled up beside me. The driver left the car. As he approached me, my fear of robbery increased. "What's wrong?" he asked, and I explained my situation. With that, he waved his friends over and gestured to them. Then, without another word, they lifted my car from the divider and placed it on the ground. I felt relief and gratitude. "Let me pay you," I gushed, but my offer was refused: "There's a revival meeting at the St. Louis auditorium tomorrow night. Come!"

Being human, it is inevitable that therapists exhibit idiosyncrasies, as through their dress or office furnishings. But these should not be so startling that they interfere with the process of therapy.

A person enters therapy to resolve their emotional conflicts and gain a healthier personality. Not to become a clone of the therapist. For this reason, and contrary to some popular belief, the sex, age, religion, or ethnicity of the therapist is almost always irrelevant to the progress of treatment. It is the competence of the therapist which is important.

A person who is ambivalent about therapy may use one of these characteristics to reject treatment, but this is a different matter.

8. *A therapist who keeps a pet in the office*

I have never had a pet in my office. Some might regard the stuffed animals there as being substitutes but for me and my young patients they are our friends. And, if inadvertently hurt, they repair quickly and don't hold grudges. But dogs and cats demand attention; can be hurt accidentally or otherwise; or might trigger an allergic reaction. And few therapists could maintain positive feelings towards a patient who, repeatedly, "accidentally" hurt their pet. For these reasons I do not think that pets belong in any therapist's office. Some therapist's disagree, particularly those with an office in their home which may be a small city apartment. Or a therapist might feel that their pet gives their office the informal quality they prefer. A pediatric dermatologist I know brings her dog to her office, insisting that he isn't a problem for her patients or staff, but I wonder. For safety, health, and the personal comfort of many including myself, I still maintain that pets are best kept out of the professional office.

9. *A therapist who permits physical contact*

While there is no question that sexual contact between therapists and patients is inappropriate, some therapists consider hugs to be acceptable. I don't, though recognizing that this social practice between even mere acquaintances has become common. Though there are social elements in therapy, it is always a healing and not a social relationship. Moreover, physical contact between the therapist and their patient detracts from an important treatment goal: to learn to communicate better by using words to describe thoughts and feelings.

Which is not to say that all physical contact should be forbidden. A grateful patient may want to shake hands at the end of the session and this is fine with me. But when a child wanted to hug me "goodbye" I quickly stopped her saying, "Nope, can't touch. But you can hug Marvin or Dorothy," they being two of our stuffed animal friends. Being persistent, the girl said, "I hug my aunt goodbye," and I replied, "I'm not a relative." This child tended to hug all adults, even strangers, but ended this inappropriate behavior after several months of therapy.

10. *A therapist who takes notes during therapy*

Therapists must keep notes: this is a legal requirement and for very good reasons. Without a written record there is no evidence of what occurred and no therapist has a good enough memory to accurately remember events from more than a day before. Sometimes, issues can arise about treatment which occurred years before. Once a patient phoned and requested a receipt covering payments she had made to me for her child's therapy seven years earlier. She wanted to submit this to the Family Court. I have occasionally had to write reports which required my notes from several years past.

Patients understand that these circumstances occur and object only when the taking of notes seems more important than the therapy. During the initial evaluation session, when many questions are asked, I write several pages. Thereafter, two-thirds of a page or a bit more usually suffices.

One therapist has stated publicly that, in the interest of confidentiality, he maintains no notes of therapy sessions. I would not feel comfortable consulting such a professional. Nor, I think, would many people, though keeping mental health notes confidential is crucially important since they contain information about intimate thoughts and feelings. Happily, these don't become public except during rare court proceedings.

Though records can be subpoenaed by any attorney and routinely are during child custody disputes, these attempts virtually always fail. On the few occasions when I received a subpoena for records, I responded by faxing a letter to the attorney stating that the records which they requested were privileged by state regulation and could not be released without a judicial order or the patient's written consent. I never heard from these attorneys again.

However, there is one type of court case in which the patient must agree that all medical records, including mental health records, be surrendered. This is when claim is made for damages due to alleged injury. There are other exceptions but these are rarely encountered by therapy patients: when child abuse exists; or when a serious threat is made against the president or another person.

The confidentiality maintained in therapy is, in most states and with a licensed practitioner, as good as that which lawyers enjoy. Which is as good as it gets. But, like most things in life, it is not absolute.

11. *A therapist who watches the clock excessively*

In 2009 there was a hugely disruptive upheaval in New York State when the entire legislative process came to a halt. This widely criticized event originated, reportedly, in the annoyance of a billionaire who became angry when the legislator with whom he was speaking seemed more interested in writing on his Blackberry.

Therapy patients can feel just as upset when, as they pour out their anguish, their therapist glances too frequently at the clock. Though their therapist may not be uninterested but merely suffering from a cold or another temporary malady which can claim people. So understandably, they just want to be home.

Many people feel that listening to personal troubles is exhausting but that is not the major task of a therapist. Their job is to allow their mind to freely associate, make connections between the patient's past and present experiences, and then to speak to relieve their pain and aid their psychological development. When a good association is made, both the patient and their therapist feel energized, much like the winner of a competition.

While an occasional glance at the clock merely indicates that therapy is a business contract for a finite period of time, the therapist's continuous concern with time does reveal cause for concern. Then, for whatever reason, their mind is not involved in the therapeutic process and they have broken the treatment contract. With this as with all puzzling therapist behavior, the most obvious remedy is also least followed. Asking the therapist "why" may well gain information which settles the matter ("I'm expecting an important phone call." "I have to leave on time because of a babysitting problem.").

Excessive clock watching by the therapist *can* indicate that they find the patient uninteresting. And, since boredom indicates not being in touch with feelings, its presence may also reflect *the therapist's* depression, which it is important for them to realize.

Therapists are particularly vulnerable to depression because, unlike others, they cannot simply walk away from those who upset them unless they end the therapeutic relationship. Hearing about a particular patient's feelings and fantasies may arouse the therapist's anxiety, their fears and fantasies about aging, mortality, and other life issues. Here the clock watching symbolizes their wish to end these painful associations by retreating psychologically. And, as with patient behavior, recognizing this is the first step towards change.

Two Suggestions to Make Your Psychotherapy More Comfortable

1. *Can I invite my therapist to my wedding or other joyous event?*

Such a request puts a therapist in a bind for while there are friendly elements in the therapeutic relationship, the participants are not really friends. They have a business relationship and the therapist is paid for providing clinical services, not socializing.

Also, any social contact between a therapist and their patient may, no matter now innocent, be looked upon unfavorably by state regulators. And even if the occasion is a joyous one and not a suspect activity like seeing a movie or going shopping, how should the therapist relate to others at the event? Certainly not by identifying themselves accurately for to do so would violate patient-client confidentiality which is a serious matter indeed.

So for the best interests of all concerned, it is wisest for patients not to make this most understandable request and to keep separate their social and therapy activities. Helping a patient to improve their social life is a therapist's job; becoming part of that social life is very definitely not.

Having said this, there are other, equally valid viewpoints, particularly in small towns where therapist and patient may pass each other regularly; and with an isolated person whose long clinical work with their therapist may have provided their most meaningful human experience. Which is just to say that the ethical and professional guidelines which therapists must follow, though attempting to be logical and protective, may seem overly rigid to laymen.

2. Is it alright to ask my husband/wife/child what they talk to their therapist about?

No. The spouse and parents of patients often feel threatened when treatment begins. They are afraid that it will cause them to lose the closeness they share. But their understandable question, "What happened in therapy today?" or "What did the therapist say?" should never be asked for, if they are answered, the patient will no longer feel free to speak in therapy of how they really feel. And it is this behavior which will, eventually, improve all of their relationships.

Chapter Nineteen

Psychotherapy for Habit and Eating Disorders

Psychotherapy for Habit Disorders

SOME PEOPLE BEGIN THERAPY not because they are dissatisfied with their life but to eliminate a particular habit, usually smoking or over-eating. Which is no small business. Virtually all physicians have treated patients who behave self-destructively: smoking while recovering from a heart attack or otherwise sabotaging their treatment following another medical catastrophe. Perhaps following a diet which exacerbated their diabetes, or heightens the risk of developing cancer.

I once treated an eight year old girl with severely crooked teeth, Despite this, her parents had difficulty finding an orthodontist who would accept her as a patient because of her nearly continuous thumb sucking at home, in school, and on the playground. When another student asked why she did it, the girl explained, unashamedly, "It's a habit." Though her thumb sucking was not the reason she was brought for therapy, it remained after her other problems disappeared.

Getting rid of a habit, which can be defined as a recurring persistent behavior, is not easy because they serve a valuable function. They provide rapid enjoyment and relaxation in a simple manner which is entirely self-controlled. When a person is tense or unhappy they need only light a cigarette or drink beer or eat the entire Sara Lee chocolate layer cake which awaits them in the refrigerator. They will quickly feel better until later, when remorse over this behavior sinks in, perhaps accompanied by a hoarse throat or indigestion or their DWI arrest.

Habits are difficult to eliminate no matter how greatly motivated the person is. They have existed for a long time; are effective in their major task of reducing tension; and are tightly ingrained in the pattern of the person's life, perhaps being strengthened through association with their friends or spouse. Moreover, habits are self-reinforcing: the more they are engaged in, the better they are at reducing stress.

The most effective therapist for habit difficulties understands and can provide coping strategies to aid in eliminating it; can help to discover the reason for it; and can reduce the stress which it satisfies. How long this therapy will take depends on the motivation of the person, their satisfaction with other areas of their life (family and job or school), the usual level of stress in their life, and the habit itself.

Whatever treatment is used will take time. Some advertised hypnosis programs promise to eliminate smoking or over-eating after just one session. I knew one person for whom such a program worked: an office secretary who wanted to lose weight. But she was so well-motivated that anything she tried might have worked.

I have also known smokers who suddenly stop smoking, as well as a heroin user who also quit cold. These are the exceptions. For most people, ending an undesired habit is a drawn-out, psychologically and sometimes physically painful process. It is important to be honest with oneself about how difficult this change is for there will be inevitable setbacks: sneaked smokes, snacks, alcohol, or drugs. One should regard progress as being akin to learning how to type. Initially there will be increasing speed, this then remaining the same or even slowing for awhile. But further progress will follow.

I have found that the most effective means of losing weight, both for myself and my patients, has been to count calories religiously: not to eat anything for which the calorie count is unknown.

The calories needed to support a particular weight depends on whether one is a man or a woman and their activity level. For a pound of weight to be maintained requires between twelve and fifteen calories. Thus if one wants to weigh one hundred fifty pounds, the calories of food necessary to maintain this weight, for a man of average activity, would be approximately twenty-two hundred and fifty (one hundred fifty times fifteen), and for a woman who is primarily sedentary, about eighteen hundred calories (one hundred fifty times twelve).

If one eats healthfully and avoids processed foods, both calorie counts allow for a large amount of whole grain foods, fruit, vegetables, and fish, Processed foods tend to contain large amounts of sugars, fats, and salt. Moreover, eating them are addictive. The frequent advertising jingle, that it is difficult to eat just one, is true—but not for the reason which is suggested.

Psychotherapy for Eating Disorders: Anorexia Nervosa and Bulimia

Until it is understood, every mental health symptom is frightening. But while the vast majority, like anxiety, are painful but not deadly, anorexia nervosa, if inadequately treated, can result in death. The term derives from the Greek and means "loss of appetite." This condition has the highest death rate of all the mental health disorders, it being estimated at between eight and eighteen percent.*

Few behaviors seem as illogical for anorexia nervosa *forces* a person to ignore the basic biological imperative of eating, which is essential to life. Though considered a modern illness, anorexia nervosa has a long history. During the nineteenth century, frail, gaunt women were typically diagnosed as being "neurasthenic" or "consumptive." They were thought to suffer from another of those mysterious maladies which afflicted women, who were then sent to health spas for treatment.

*Hsu, L.K.G., *Eating Disorders*, New York: Guilford, 1990.

The person suffering from anorexia nervosa becomes obsessed with their weight, which they continually reduce through extreme dieting, excessive exercise, or by taking laxatives or diet pills. Most, by far, are adolescent females though men and adults may also develop it.

Anorexia nervosa is most prevalent in Western societies, and among members of particular occupations like dance and modeling which demand thinness. While influenced by public perceptions of beauty, it primarily reflects an underlying psychological disturbance revolving about self-esteem and family issues, with sufferers carrying the current societal ideal of beauty to an extreme.

Those suffering from this disorder have an intense fear of gaining weight. They hold a disturbed image of their body and refuse to acknowledge the importance of good nutrition in maintaining health. The absence of menstruation is common, along with physical effects which may include headaches, fatigue, dry skin, stunted growth, and metabolic abnormalities leading to heart disorders.

The person becomes obsessed with food, their sense of who they are being determined by their weight. Increasing thinness is viewed as better, and their concept of the optimal body shape becomes associated with all that is feminine and good. Yet though more than three quarters of American women were found to be dissatisfied with their weight,* relatively few develop anorexia nervosa.

*Harris, Louis, 1987, *Inside America*, New York: Random House.

These people are also governed by the erroneous belief that control over their eating is synonymous with controlling their thoughts and feelings. Sensing the hostility of others to their irrational, dangerous behaviors, they are secretive about their weight and eating and exercise, and withdraw from social activity.

Bulimia nervosa is the other major eating disorder. This is characterized by binge eating followed by purging oneself through self-induced vomiting, the use of laxatives, or the attempt to compensate for eating through prolonged exercise.

While those suffering from anorexia nervosa may also exhibit bulimic behavior, most bulimics tend to be of about average weight in contrast to the emaciation of anorexics. They also have slightly greater insight into their behavior. But bulimia can cause serious physical problems, most notably severe tooth decay due to excessive vomiting. Several public figures, including Princess Diana, have reported their sufferings from bulimia, which is sometimes induced by stress.

The major distinction between anorexia nervosa and bulimia nervosa is the presence of binge eating, for in both conditions there is excessive concern with body weight and shape. Anorexia nervosa is diagnosed when the body weight decreases below fifteen percent of the ideal.

Eating disorders are treated both in hospitals and in the outpatient therapist's office. Hospital treatment, which may be prolonged, is reserved for medical emergencies when the life of the person is at risk. In the hospital the patient is educated about their diet, body, and sexuality, knowledge which they often lack despite their pretense of sophistication. The staff thus attempts to move the patient's focus from eating to broader issues.

In some hospitals these patients help to prepare meals and are encouraged to taste healthy foods which they may be phobic about. Some patients may embrace their personalized version of vegetarianism and eat only a few foods. Hospital meals are structured and observed; bathrooms may be locked to discourage purging; and socialization after eating is fostered.

The patient is encouraged to note the warning thoughts and behaviors which lead to relapse. They learn to identify their feelings and how to nurture themselves, and are encouraged to explore their lives more deeply. They learn to view recovery as a long process, and to be easier on themselves. Tolerating each failure as being inevitable, then learning from it and growing.

Depending on the severity of the patient's eating disorder and the other emotional problems which may exist, hospitalization may last from one to three months. Yet even after the eating difficulty comes under control, significant conflicts remain.

The patient must become comfortable with feeling pleasure, as that which is associated with eating. They must develop a clearer sense of who they are, and separate emotionally from their parents.

Often, symbolically, the conflict over food reflects the unconscious longing to merge with and gain emotional support from their mother, which they feel they lacked. Thus their repeated eating/food refusal/purging behaviors reflect their unconscious, healthy longing for independence. Though being reflected in an immature fashion which can never gain them the autonomy and love they seek.

Because these conflicts and the associated psychological deficiencies develop in the earliest years, the healing of eating disorders is difficult. Because of the possibility of death when conflicts are acted-out, treating these patients creates great stress for their therapists, who tend to burn out.

The successful therapist must recognize the powerful unconscious conflict which the eating symptom reflects. And, though it is dangerous, that the patient's resistance to change reflects their fear of losing their sense of who they are. Which, though fragile and incomplete, is better than having to confront the world with *no* personality–being no one.

The successful therapist recognizes that therapy is not only interpretation but also waiting and providing "active attention": the time and empathy necessary for the patient to develop their unique autonomy. Thus this therapist provides a safe, continuous, non-threatening "holding environment" within which the patient can grow.*

*Winnicott, D.W., 1965, *Maturational Processes and the Facilitating Environment: Studies in the Theory of Emotional Development*. New York: International Universities Press.

An experience which can be readily understood for it is similar to the childhood experience granted by effective parents who are reliable; emphasize the child's needs and not their own; create warm, helpful interactions so the child feels understood; and are better attuned to the real world than is their child so that their puzzling experiences can be interpreted and their fears relieved.

But the parent-like elements of therapy can only be analogous to those experienced during infancy for the adolescent or adult eating disordered patient is no longer a child, and what they needed early in their life is far different from what they later require for their psychological healing. Just as the infant's beneficial, life-enhancing breast feeding would, if performed on an adult by a therapist, be bizarre and destructive.

Parents naturally recognize this distinction when tolerating babyish behavior in a two year old but condemning the identical behavior with the child's older sibling. It is this need to provide the minimal, essential, continuous limits over the dangerous behaviors of the eating-disordered patient—without infringing on their struggle to create a healthy independent identity—that makes their treatment so difficult.

The potentially dangerous behavior of other mental health conditions is relatively rare and brief; that of the eating-disordered patient may exist for years, causing continuing stress on the patient's family and their need for emotional support too.

Chapter Twenty

Psychotherapy for Childhood Difficulties

PARENTS OFTEN RELATE DIFFERENTLY when seeking medical than mental health treatment for their child. Few parents would ask a five year old their opinion about getting a vaccination yet this same child's opinion of therapy would be influential. Which tells you how ambivalent parents can be about involving their children in psychotherapy.

Unlike adults, when a youth is unhappy they don't speak of it. Instead, they behave in a puzzling manner to indicate their unhappiness. This symptom is also intended to communicate to their parents that they need help though they do not yet know what this involves. So when parents suggest that they consult a therapist, the child feels torn. Though needing *something*, they fear that this new person will treat them like others have done: criticize them or boss them around, tell them what they should do. Which, the child knows, is not what they need or want.

And *what is* a therapist anyway? Someone like the doctor they see regularly who pokes and prods and sticks them with needles? This also is not what they sense they need.

The best way for a parent to help their child handle this dilemma is to provide them with accurate information. Suggesting to them that: "It sounds like you have a lot of things going on inside of you and it's important for you to have someone to talk to about them." Once in the office, it is the job of the therapist to establish a relationship with the child and to convince the child of its value.

There is nothing for a child to dislike about therapy. There, they receive the total attention of an adult and can play games or cards, color, do puzzles, or engage in another enjoyment. Before which I tell the children my two basic rules: that they must choose the game we play; and have to laugh at my jokes. Few children believe the second instruction though some are polite enough to go along with it.

Despite this, some children may say that they do not like or need therapy. But this sentiment merely reflects the normal ambivalence about therapy which all patients—adult or child—experience since therapy arouses novel thoughts and feelings which can be temporarily uncomfortable. Having a good relationship between the therapist and the patient, a good *therapeutic alliance*, is essential to bridging this stress.

A child's resistance to therapy may also reflect their sense that their parents do not want them in treatment. So, at the time of their appointment, the child disappears into a friend's house or about the neighborhood. Then, therapy is over.

Psychotherapy for Common Childhood Symptoms

1. **Psychotherapy For Nightmares**

Nightmares scare children and frighten parents who inaccurately believe that this symptom reflects serious psychological problems. Thus some parents ignore them, or comfort themselves with the thought that the child will outgrow it. And usually they do, for nightmares are merely the mind's way of communicating that there are scary things going on inside of it. Which could be a new and healthy experience or opportunity. But persisting nightmares indicate that more than temporary, normal stress is occurring, and the need for therapy to alleviate it.

Severe nightmares are called night or sleep terrors. This is when the child repeatedly awakens from sleep with a panicky scream, feeling intensely fearful and being unresponsive to attempts to comfort them during the episode. Here, no detailed dream is remembered.

Though this event is understandably upsetting to both the child and their parents, even these nightmares are not the problem. They merely indicate that the child is trying to deal with difficulties which they then cannot cope with on their own. When these are mastered, the nightmares will disappear since they no longer serve any function. There is a logic to all mental health symptoms.

2. **Psychotherapy for Continuously Difficult Behavior**

A common diagnostic term used by those who treat children and adolescents is *oppositional-defiant*. This derives from the mental health classification of *oppositional-defiant disorder* which covers eight symptoms including: having temper tantrums; being argumentative and refusing requests by adults; being annoying and annoying others; blaming others for their mistakes; being angry and resentful; or behaving spitefully.

While every youth behaves with some of these symptoms at times, diagnosing this as an emotional difficulty requires that at least four of these problem behaviors are present for at least six months. Being irritating to parents or teachers for a few weeks isn't enough.

Everyone goes through periods when they are difficult to live with. When the stress causing this behavior goes away, so does the symptom. Oppositional-defiant disorder is a frequent diagnosis for children because their first line of defense when they are unhappy is to be difficult. By this behavior they intend to communicate to their parents that they need help. With exactly what they don't know, or the kind of help they need. They rely on their parents to understand these things believing, accurately, that they have far greater knowledge.

It is not easy to live with a child with these symptoms. Therapy will alleviate them but not as quickly as all would wish, including the child whose difficult behavior reflects their pain. And telling the child how they *should* behave is not helpful for lack of knowledge is not their problem. They know what they should do but are unable to control their behavior.

While permanent change of behavior will occur once the child's unhappiness is alleviated, this does take time. But improvement can be made by following the therapist's suggestions about relating to the child when they are acting-up. If the child is reached emotionally, their misbehavior can sometimes be instantly stopped.

An eight year old girl who I treated for several years was, at times, almost impossibly annoying. She was so difficult that shoppers would comment on her behavior in the supermarket. During one incident, when her father felt that he was about to scream, he instead spoke as I had advised. Suggesting to his daughter that he felt there were many unhappy things going on inside of her. The girl's misbehavior suddenly ended and she began crying.

Parents sometimes feel that a therapist doesn't believe how difficult their child is since most children behave courteously in their therapist's office. Children who never clean their room often spontaneously put away toys in my office. And the eight year old girl I who described above, dusted my waiting room bookshelves with tissues and color-coordinated their books. Parents have shown me cell phone videos of their child's tantrums, fearing that they would not otherwise be believed, though this was unnecessary. Therapists who work with children fully understand that, all too often, the stress of parenting is no little business.

3. **Psychotherapy for Attention-deficit Disorder (ADD)**

The most widely used yet misunderstood term by both parents and teachers is ADD (*Attention-deficit Disorder*). For, though appearing to explain problematic behavior, it actually explains nothing and creates unnecessary stress too. The anxious mother of a seven year old boy described her fear to me: "He might have the ADD."

Attention-deficit disorder (ADD) or a*ttention-deficit/hyperactivity disorder* (ADHD) is a group of symptoms. The most noted are restlessness (being fidgety), having difficulty concentrating particularly in school, talking excessively, and impulsiveness. While believed by many to be a modern concept, the origins go back more than two hundred years, it first being described as "mental restlessness" in a book by Sir Alexander Crichton. Fifty years ago these symptoms were considered to reflect "minimal brain dysfunction" (MBD). ADD or AD/HD being just the present terminology for this human condition.

Further muddying the waters are the wide ranging figures for its occurrence throughout the world (between two and fourteen percent); that its incidence is far higher on the East Coast of the United States than the West Coast; and that boys are diagnosed with it more than twice as frequently as girls. There is conflict among clinicians and scientists as to whether this disorder even exists since its symptoms are identical to those for anxiety and depression. Though this disorder seems to present a puzzling situation, it can be understood by considering the facts of mental development, about which there is no dispute.

All people have psychological abilities which include the ability to control their behavior and thinking, to tolerate feelings, to modulate their mood, and others. These are not inborn but develop within the first three years of life.

If too great stress exists during this period, weakness in one or more of these abilities will occur and cause later difficulty in concentration, impulse control, mood modulation, and others. But this is not a black or white affair. Minimal weakness will have no effect on daily functioning while major weakness can severely effect it. It is the weakness of one or more of these basic psychological abilities which ADD and AD/HD describe.

The most effective treatment involves replacing these deficient psychological capacities with more mature ones by providing psychotherapy to the child and guidance to their parents. Can medication help children cope with this disorder? These have been widely prescribed since the nineteen seventies though there is no sound evidence of their effectiveness and increasing concern about their safety. One recent criticism was of how brief these research studies are for many last only four to six weeks!

My general conclusion about medication for this condition is as follows. Some children find it helpful; others find it unhelpful and experience uncomfortable feelings, worrisome medical effects, deteriorated behavior, or several of these. With a third group of children it seems to have no effect.

These drugs are powerful and parents should fully investigate them when considering their use, which must be closely monitored by a physician.

4. Psychotherapy for Enuresis and Encopresis

Though unfamiliar terms for most parents, *enuresis* and *encopresis* are daily battles for some. Enuresis is the professional term for bed-wetting, the urinating of a five year old or older child onto their clothes. Encopresis is the fecal soiling of clothing or fecal discharge onto the floor or in another inappropriate place by a child of at least four years of age. These circumstances must be persistent and unrelated to a medical condition, as it rarely is, though prolonged encopresis can lead to painful bowel movements and associated medical complications.

Though these conditions are often treated with physical methods—wetness signals and medication* for enuresis, and laxatives, enemas, and dietary change with encopresis—their underlying psychological causes are similar, with encopresis indicating the more severe psychological difficulty.

Enuresis reflects both a child's indirect expression of their angry feelings, and their desire to regress to an earlier period of life when fewer demands for greater maturity of behavior, which they have difficulty achieving, were present. Encopresis also reflects the desire to regress but on a more profound level.**

Essentially, the child or adolescent wants to become a baby again and to redo their life. Both symptoms can also occur in reaction to an immediate stress like the birth of a sibling or a significant environmental change. But in these cases it will quickly disappear once the stress is over.

One five year old, who I had treated a year earlier for oppositional-defiant behavior, became encopretic upon beginning a new school. I advised her mother that, since the soiling never previously occurred, it was unlikely to persist and would disappear shortly, which is what happened.

---

*These drugs (Desmopressin, Amitriptyline, Imipramine), though temporarily effective, can have severe side effects.
**Fenichel, Otto. *The Psychoanalytic Theory of Neurosis,* New York: Norton, 1972, pp. 233-234.

But enuresis and encopresis usually reflect powerful unconscious desires. Their change, even with psychotherapy, is slow and unpredictable. The symptoms may last for months or years with both boys and girls*, young children and teenagers, to their shame and embarrassment and the frustration of their parents.

Though learning about the causes of enuresis and encopresis—unconscious anger and maturational difficulty—will not end them, providing this information to the child will place these symptoms within a logical framework, thus removing them from the category of being weird and reducing stress. Because these symptoms are so personal, it is best that parents provide this important explanation to their child and their therapist will explain how best to do so.

Yet, as with all psychotherapy, rigid treatment prescriptions are unwise. A twelve year old boy who changed greatly during his therapy for impulsive behavior, then spontaneously raised the issue of his long-term daily bed-wetting.* Which I explained to him, as had his mother earlier following my instruction. As therapy succeeds, enuresis and encopresis will naturally disappear—just like every symptom which no longer has a function.

*Enuresis is far more common among boys than girls.

Reassurance About the Two Diagnoses Which Parents Most Fear:
Childhood Autism and Bipolar Disorder

1. *Childhood autism*

Childhood autism is a diagnosis which terrifies parents and for good reason. While other childhood emotional problems also affect intellectual and social functioning, the limitations are far more severe with autism. Qualitatively, it is in an entirely different realm.

A child with autism may appear to function normally in the first year of life but, as they approach their second year, their interest in people diminishes (if it was ever present) and they become more greatly involved with objects. They may even have seemed precocious, as if trying to overcome their developmental problems by passing over infancy and, prematurely, becoming an intellectualized adult.

This impossibility causes a breakdown in functioning as they approach their third year, when autism's common features appear: a marked lack of interest in social interaction; individualized odd speech patterns which may be repetitive; limited and abnormal interests as in clocks or vacuum cleaners; repetitive movements like hand flapping or rocking.

When older, some autistic children may try to mutilate themselves by banging their head or picking at their skin. Though it is now many years later, I still remember the horror I felt at seeing a six year old girl who was immobilized in a wheelchair in a hospital's Emergency Room to keep her from harming herself.

The treatment needed for autism is extensive, involving not only daily, long-term individual psychotherapy requiring a high degree of creativity but years of specialized educational services. Yet when a child is provided these, significant change is possible. The wife of my graduate school adviser, a psychologist skilled with children, once treated an autistic child who went on to win a National Science Foundation scholarship.

A recent National Institute of Mental Health funded study at the University of Washington found that when very young autistic children (ranging in age from eighteen to thirty months) were provided intensive treatment, both their language skill and their IQ increased considerably. Almost thirty percent of these children received a less severe diagnosis two years later.*

More good news, if it can be so described, is that much parental worry is unnecessary. Autism is a relatively rare disorder which is often misdiagnosed. Some autistic symptoms (as hand flapping, having obsessive interests) commonly occur with very young children but there is a vast difference between their presence and an accurate diagnosis of autism. These autistic-like features will often disappear after just several months of traditional child play therapy, if it is needed at all.

*Pediatrics (online), November 30, 2009.

There is also a great difference between children who are on the high end of the autistic scale, with their difficulties having a far better prognosis, and those who are more limited. The scarcity of clinicians who can accurately diagnose infant disorders causes many parents to suffer unnecessarily.

2. Bipolar disorder

A common misunderstanding in mental health matters is the belief that to diagnose a symptom is to understand it. An even greater difficulty occurs when the diagnosis makes no conceptual sense. This is the case with using the term *bipolar disorder* to describe troublesome childhood behavior.

Bipolar disorder refers to behavior which tends to vary between depression and mania with the manic behavior being considered a psychological defense against an underlying deep depression. An earlier term, manic-depressive illness or manic-depressive psychosis, was coined in the late nineteenth century by the eminent German psychiatrist, Emil Kraepelin.

Like all psychological difficulties, there is no definitive test for this disorder and symptoms can vary. Some people experience little mania, others more. When depressed, the person may have feelings of sadness, hopelessness, anger, anxiety, fatigue, loneliness, or have difficulty concentrating or sleeping or eating. When manic, a person experiences a heightened or irritable mood, an increase in energy, impaired judgment, and difficulty concentrating.

They may engage in behavior which is unusual for them, as going on spending sprees or indulging in substance abuse. Often, they feel out of control. When extreme, delusions of grandeur may occur.

Mania must be distinguished from hypomania which is a milder version of it. Here delusions do not occur and the person may feel good and deny that anything is wrong. They may even seem competent at work though their judgment may be poor.

While few deny that bipolar disorder exists among adults, there is disagreement as to its frequency, and much controversy as to whether this diagnosis should *ever* be applied to children and adolescents.

The first objection is that many of the symptoms of bipolar disorder (difficulty concentrating, sleeping and eating disturbances, anger, anxiety, sadness) are normal feelings which every child and adolescent experiences throughout their development as they encounter and overcome the stresses of normal development.

The second objection is more basic. Bipolar disorder is an *adult* diagnosis which implies that the person has a fully developed (adult) personality. Children and adolescents by definition do not possess this, which should preclude their ever being so diagnosed. Unfortunately, this is not the case.

Thus potent anti-psychotic drugs, having gravely inadequate or no research with children and documented physical and psychological dangers, continue to be prescribed to youth. Surely they deserve better.

School Practices Which Drive Parents Crazy: Those Puzzling Pupil Classifications

Parents get furious at their treatment by physicians, lawyers, and mental health professionals. But none of these groups seems to create as much consternation and puzzlement as does the behavior of school officials.

Some parents have no complaints. Their children are bright and learning oriented, have always done well in school and would excel in virtually any district no matter its deficiencies. Other parents are less content. Their children may potentially be even brighter but suffer from emotional difficulties. These parents continuously complain about how badly the schools treat them and their children while ignoring their complaints. To which I reply: "It's not just you. They treat all parents like that."

There tends to be a prevailing attitude in school systems: that their staff are the experts and know what is wrong with their pupils, and listening to contrary information from others is a waste of time. Thus, though behaving courteously at parent-teacher conferences, they tend to ignore suggestions which are contrary to what they believe.

Schools view themselves as being factories which produce educated students. Their quality control measure is the standardized tests which they periodically administer, these being increasingly demanded by the government. Thus an unruly or poorly performing child reduces the school's "production" and must be referred to the Committee on Special Education (CSE) for further testing and remediation. This would make perfectly good sense if it were properly carried out.

Instead, two things happen in sequence. First, the child is determined by their teacher to be a problem. Perhaps they talk too much in class, are too aggressive on the playground, prefer to read when the teacher is instructing, or are assertive towards their teacher. One five year old stated loudly that his teacher was no good and should retire.

Another boy protested when a female teacher was appointed as monitor in the boys' locker room. Because he had previously gone through the CSE routine and was then, at sixteen, capable of being expelled, this was immediately done. After which the boy printed business cards and set up a small, successful home repair business with his friend. Ten years later I heard that he was working as a store manager and about to be married. Another CSE success story!

A teenager suffered from panic attacks and didn't want his peers to view him at those times. Still, he was refused permission to speak with the school nurse. When he went anyway, he was given detention: forced to sit alone in a room all day. This enforced isolation exacerbated his problems and caused his refusal to attend school. Though meaning well, there could not have been devised a more destructive intervention for this troubled youth.

Yet some teachers and principals go far beyond what any reasonable person would expect. After treating a very difficult nine year old for a year, I spoke with the principal of his school and was floored by her efforts on his behalf. She even got a wealthy family to donate a violin for this child so he could play in the school orchestra. Alas, the boy then beat up their son. It is unlikely that these parents donated more money to the school.

Why are schools so unable to help their failing students? Certainly not for lack of effort and they spend much taxpayer money in the process. Moreover, some children who require supportive services *are* benefited. But these are usually children with *physical* disorders: vision and hearing limitations, cerebral palsy and others. Something *visible* which school personnel can empathize with, so unlike psychological difficulties which create a child who is simply *difficult*.

In order to gain special services funding, schools must classify children.. Thus if a child has a problem paying attention they are classified as having "attention deficit disorder." If a child has a problem sitting still they are described as being "hyperactive." If a child has a problem learning they are placed in the category of "learning disability." And if a child is generally troublesome they are diagnosed with a "conduct disorder."

While the attempt to define a child's problems should be applauded, schools tend to make the same mistake as do too many mental health professionals: believing that to name something is to understand it. There is further confusion because schools use the identical terms as do mental health professionals, though children who fit into one group's classification may not fit into the other.

Thus a child who is diagnosed by a school as suffering from "conduct disorder" may not fit into the mental health classification with the identical name. But even if they do, because these classifications are behaviorally based and, intentionally, unassociated with any theory, there is no explanation associated with any of these terms. To gain this explanation and provide effective remediation, one needs further knowledge, which too often is lacking.

Though schools must cope with children having all manner of complex psychological difficulties and family issues, their mental health personnel have the least training with most being ineligible for licensing as independent practitioners. Thus they defensively fall back on naming symptoms rather than understanding children. And if their canned solutions don't improve the child's functioning, they throw up their hands, call in the parents, and demand that *they* do something. Thus does the layman come to be considered the expert.

Because many schools lack sophisticated mental health knowledge, they rigidly assert the validity of their advice even as it continually fails.

I advise the parents of my young patients as follows. If a teacher states that their child has some difficulty there usually is, though the reason may be other than what is believed. Thus it is important to gain as accurate a description of their child's difficult behavior as they can, while keeping in mind that the teacher's description may be exaggerated. A child may be depicted as being "completely out of control" for pushing a chair twice during a week. Or called "violent" because they hit a child who took their toy. Which, while unacceptable behavior for a five year old, most often reflects just temporary babyish behavior.

It is also best to have the child's therapist be the intermediary between the parents and the school about the difficulties which the teacher is having. Often after the teacher phones the therapist and gains information about the nature of the child's difficulties and receives child guidance suggestions, the teacher feels less helpless and out of their depth. They become calmer and more capable of interacting helpfully with the child, which improves the situation for all.

Having long treated principals and teachers, I am well aware of the stress which problematic children and anxious parents can cause in the classroom. These situations are made worse by the impossibly difficult task which many teachers face: having to cope with children possessing complex difficulties that have nothing to do with providing basic educational services. Just one severely problematic child can wreck the most conscientious teacher's efforts with the rest of their class.

Teachers and administrators usually welcome a child's involvement in therapy for they realize that as the child improves, their job will become easier. Yet despite this encouragement and the pain experienced by families, some parents resist getting therapy for their child.

What School Bullying Really Involves

When considering school bullying it may seem heartless to consider other than the victim: surely it is only they who suffer. But school bullying—whether conducted with blows, words or online—is a complex phenomenon involving many people: the bully and their family; the victim and their family; the bystanders; and, of course, school personnel.

Simply speaking, bullying is any situation in which (1) a person is repeatedly made to feel uncomfortable by another who gains satisfaction from this, and (2) there is an imbalance in their power such that the victim would have a hard time defending themselves.

Bullying need not be physical: teasing and social isolation can be even more painful. And, though parents often feel that it is only their child who experiences it, being bullied is fairly common: ten percent of all students have been found to be involved,whether as victim or bully or bystander*.

Another study found that about ten percent of teachers bully their students, use their power to punish or deprecate a child unreasonably**, as both principals and parents have long believed.

Another painful truth is that there is a relationship between the bully and their victim, akin to a love relationship which went wrong. Each depends on the other to satisfy their unconscious needs. Their behavior is affected by the bystanders who are also damaged through identification with one or the other. Vicariously enjoying the infliction of pain, or viewing themselves as helpless and dependent. As the bullying persists the victim becomes traumatized and increasingly unable to defend themselves, a situation which, unconsciously, they may feel compelled to repeat throughout their adult life.

*Hazler, R.J., Hoover, J., & Oliver, R. (1993). Student perspectives of victimization by bullies in school. *Journal of Humanistic Education and Development*, 29, 143-150.
**Lane, D.L. (1992) Bullying. In D.L. Lane & A. Miller (Eds.), *Child and adolescent therapy: a handbook*. Buckingham, England: Open University Press.

Both school bullies and their victims are unhappy. All suffer from emotional conflicts and feel compelled to act out their life dramas on the theater of school experience. Though they are usually unpopular, bullies can attract followers from fear. Bullies are often sadistic, depressed, or anxious; and disrupt classes with their impulsiveness, whining, or inability to concentrate. Their behavior meets with frequent suspensions, school failure, and conflicts among teachers as to how best cope with it.

The root cause of these difficulties lies within the bully's family, which is often depressed or violent. The parents may, unconsciously, even identify with their child's behavior and gain satisfaction from it.

The victim's behavior also reflects family's psychodynamics. Their masochism, loneliness, submission, and sometimes irritating behavior, derive from being overly protected or devalued by their parents. They may also unconsciously be repeating a pattern of dominance and submission which they viewed in their home.

These statements do not, however, apply to situations in which the bullying derives solely from a particular demographic characteristic such as race or religion or sexual identity.

The role of the bystander is equally complex. Some students revel in the behavior of the bully and egg them on into increasingly disturbed behavior; while others, who identify with the victim, act out their distress by being increasingly disruptive in the school.

To successfully change these behaviors first requires their identification and then intervention. The earlier this begins, ideally in the pre-school, the less likely that formal treatment will be necessary. Yet because the roots of these behaviors lies in the home, parents, students, and school personnel must all be involved. Which is a demanding requirement since long held patterns of behavior are not easily changed.

Why Some Parents Resist Getting Psychotherapy For Their Child

Growing up is not easy. It involves struggles which most people are happy to forget for few had a lifetime of the fortunate family experiences which are chronicled in "G" rated Hollywood movies. So it is not surprising that adults tend to resist any relationship in which they feel dependent, as they did during their childhood. Even if they must endure this sometimes, like with their employer.

But therapy cannot exist without the acceptance of some dependency. Though it is certainly not complete for no patient, whether child or adult, has problems in all areas of their life. Nor does any parent receive advice from a therapist about how to cope with all their child's requirements. Parents are, whatever the extent of their child's emotional difficulties, responsible for their child's health and physical needs. And when treating a child, the parent's marital relationship need not be treated too, though some parents do seek this intervention.

Many parents resist consulting a therapist about their child. They expect to be criticized and condemned both for what they did and did not do. Like for not having brought them for treatment earlier when they sensed that something was wrong. But these things don't happen.

Living with a troubled child is painful for all and no one knows this better than a therapist who treats children.

There are other unconscious factors aroused when therapy is being considered. When parents confront behaviors in their children which aroused anxiety in their own upbringing, the residue of forgotten conflicts may be raised. How they earlier responded to *their* parents and what then happened.

Even from long past events, anxiety can be generated. An eighty-five year old physician, after a distinguished academic career, regretted that her deceased mother could not learn of the latest award she received for conducting an important public study since her mother always believed that she would be a failure. Early life experiences remain the bedrock of personality.

When an adult is placed in a dependent position they feel themselves to be a child again. Much like when they are in a medical doctor's office. Submissive. Seeking approval. Welcoming praise.

But during the first therapy session, parents learn their essential role in their child's treatment. That, however much their child is engaged in therapy, they still live with their parents who must continue to make crucial decisions for them. And that both the therapist and the parents must work together to heal the child.

Following this insight, the parents' reduced stress and the child's improving behavior, the natural resistance which some parents had towards their child's therapy diminishes, though it may never completely disappear.

Psychotherapy for Toddlers

Parents are the first to notice when something is wrong with their child. Though, frequently, the difficulty is not as serious as they feared, it is important that they pay attention to their instincts for no one knows their child better.

Yet pediatricians, when evaluating infants, often fail to advise a mental health consultation. They erroneously believe, as do most people, that children of two or three years cannot be treated psychologically. Though this is the best age to intervene: with psychological difficulties before they are fully formed.

The basic psychological capacities are created before the age of three. These abilities, which are crucially important, enable a person to deal with their feelings, to control their behavior and thinking, to develop a sense of who they are, and to modulate their mood. Weakness in any of these abilities will have far ranging effects on later adult functioning. These can be avoided through early intervention.

What might take several months of treatment in these early years will require far more therapy later, when these basic psychological abilities are inadequately formed. Just as it is easier to make structural changes while a house is being built than after the construction is completed.

Because a child has limited (but rapidly increasing) verbal ability between the age of two and three years, there are modifications in the techniques for their therapy. Involvement by the therapist with infant play materials is essential, along with speaking to and praising the child both directly ("Wow, you are a really good puzzler!") and using stuffed animals as intermediaries.

Here, the therapist must be even more active than they are with older children, speaking almost continually to the child about their joint activities and those of the stuffed animals all of which, in my office, have names and families and interesting ongoing events in their lives.

Parent involvement, as during all child therapy, is crucial. Parents must be educated so they are better able to reduce their child's stress and promote their healthy development. While such a young child does not understand what therapy is, there is no question that they value it.

One, two year old, who greatly enjoyed therapy and was resistant to leave, punched his mother in the face when she picked him up. A three year old so enjoyed therapy that she insisted on bringing her two year old sister. Who, though she could not participate in the therapy session, later played happily with her sister in the waiting room while I spoke with their mother.

Still, despite the increasingly recognized value of early intervention, it continues to be rare except for children suffering from crippling developmental disorders. I am often told by parents that they did discuss their two, three, or even four year old's mental health symptoms (nightmares, difficult behavior) with their pediatrician. But their concerns were glossed over with the comment that the symptoms would be outgrown. Or the parent was advised by a mental health facility that their child was too young for treatment. Bring them back when they are six or seven, they were told. These attitudes are unfortunate for much present and future family pain could otherwise be avoided.

Why Toddlers Who Bite
Don't Need Psychotherapy

There are few more nightmarish moments for a parent than when their child takes a bite out of the child beside them. Most parents are unsure what to do. Should they apologize to the other parent, punish their child, seek psychotherapy for them, or do all three?

Despite parental anguish, biting by a child only has clinical significance with a preschool child,, one older than three years. For infants under twelve months of age or toddlers between one and three years, biting is a normal developmental event and indicates nothing about their future. No more than does their preference for one color over another.

Statistically, one out of every ten infants and toddlers bite, with boys being about one-third more likely to do so than girls*.

Infants bite as a form of exploration. They use their mouth because it is the most developed part of their body. Infants are impulsive and lack self-control. They bite because they are overstimulated, as by loud music, or to experiment with cause and effect, or to relieve teething pain.

Toddlers bite to communicate. They have not yet developed enough language skills to control situations and biting is a powerful way to control others. It demonstrates independence and is a quick way to get attention or a toy. Biting can also be defensive, a means of self-protection against other children who bite. Toddlers usually bite when they are experiencing stress: their routine has been interrupted or their favorite toy was grabbed by a peer.

These younger children can be helped by encouraging them to identify and to talk about their feelings rather than acting them out. Saying "stop" or "no" or "mine" if another child takes their toy. And by determining why the biting occurred: it might have reflected an overcrowded nursery, over-stimulation, a lack of toys, being hungry or sleepy or teething, and then reducing or eliminating this source of stress.

Above all, do not bite the child to show them that it hurts: this just fosters their belief that violence is OK.

Biting by children over three years is a relatively rare occurrence since by that age most children have developed enough communication skills to deal with the frustrations they encounter. Professional involvement may be required to determine why they have not yet gained these verbal abilities.

But when these children bite they do so for the same reasons as younger children: to gain control over a situation, for attention, or from extreme frustration and anger.

*Garrard, J., Leland, N., & Smith, D.K. (1988) Epidemiology of human bites to children in a day-care center. *American Journal of Diseases in Children*, 142 (6), 643-650.

Chapter Twenty One

Psychotherapy for Borderline Personality Disorder, Posttraumatic Stress Disorder, Substance Abuse, Panic/Anxiety Disorder, Obsessive-Compulsive Disorder, and Phobias

MUCH WIDELY BELIEVED INFORMATION about mental health difficulties is gained through popular articles, novels, or films which have little sophistication. These include borderline personality disorder, posttraumatic stress disorder, substance abuse, and obsessive-compulsive disorder.

Psychotherapy for Borderline Personality Disorder (BPD)

Borderline personality disorder (BPD) is a mental health diagnosis consisting of symptoms which include: being very impulsive (having an emotional hair trigger); feeling empty; feeling insecure about one's identity; using poor judgment; and tending to have intense, unstable relationships which end in an emotional crisis and may trigger suicidal or (rarely) homicidal behavior. This diagnosis creates major distress, as was noted by the United States House of Representatives when it unanimously declared the month of May to be Borderline Personality Disorder Awareness Month.

Unfortunately, the movies which popularized this problem (*Fatal Attraction, Play Misty For Me, Single White Female)* have focused on its most extreme version.

Here, anger is acted out by murder rather than through suicide, which is the far more frequent result. So dramatic have these representations been that the intense suffering which is caused by this problem is often overlooked. Some sufferers are misdiagnosed as being psychotic (schizophrenic) rather than, more accurately, as suffering from a combination of BPD and substance abuse difficulties.

The concept of a borderline personality disorder, an illness which borders between the severest weaknesses of psychological abilities (psychoses) and the less severe disorders, neuroses (disorders which reflect conflict between parts of the personality), has a long history.

The Greek writers Homer and Hippocrates noted that some people were prone to impulsive behavior, sadness, and mania. In the nineteenth century this was termed "borderline insanity" and, beginning fifty years later, it was considered to be a mild form of schizophrenia and described by such terms as "ambulatory schizophrenia" and "pseudoneurotic schizophrenia."

Later thinking turned away from associating BPD with schizophrenia though it was still considered to reflect an immature level of personality organization between the neuroses and the psychoses.

To understand borderline personality disorder one must consider how the human mind develops. That while all people have the same basic psychological capacities, those which enable them to distinguish reality from fantasy, modulate mood, experience feelings and use them to make decisions, and to develop a stable sense of who they are, these are not inborn. Instead, these abilities are created through a complex interplay between the parents and their child. If there is a great difference between what the child needs and what they are provided by their parents, weakness of one or more of these capacities occurs. This results in deficiencies which, if severe, is termed a borderline personality disorder.

The essential distinctions between BPD and a psychotic disorder such as schizophrenia are (1) that the weakness of these psychological abilities is far more severe with a psychotic disturbance than with BPD; and (2) that while the behavior of one who suffers from BPD may, at times, appear psychotic, this will only be during an exceptionally stressful period. Once this passes, the symptoms will quickly diminish and the person will appear normal again. The behavior of a person with BPD will fluctuate widely but return to the apparently normal state; that of a psychotic may not.

The goal of psychotherapy with BPD is to replace the deficient psychological abilities with more mature ones. The symptoms of BPD will disappear once the patient gains a secure sense of who they are, can better tolerate feelings, is able to modulate their mood, and has good control over their thinking and behavior.

Medication may help to alleviate symptoms and forestall behavior which can have damaging consequences, though the best medication is that there be a good working relationship between the patient and their therapist who would be immediately available in time of stress.

Like with those who possess any severe mental health difficulty, BPD patients are challenging to treat and not all therapists like to work with them. Some will reject them out of hand, viewing them as being manipulative (which they are), and resenting the excessive time and attention which successful treatment requires. The tendency of BPD sufferers to drop out of treatment increases their unpopularity as patients.

Still, their healing is possible by a skilled empathic therapist who they trust. But it will not be quick or easy, and when lengthy self-medication using alcohol or drugs is concurrent, treatment becomes even more difficult.

The presence of a supportive non-judgmental family, one which views their extremely difficult member as suffering and lacking self-control rather than being deliberately manipulative, increases the probability that treatment will be successful.

Psychotherapy for Posttraumatic Stress Disorder (PTSD)

Were I writing this book several years ago I would not have included information about *posttraumatic stress disorder*. But today, interest in PTSD has skyrocketed because of the many troubled soldiers returning from repeated combat tours in Iraq and Afghanistan, pain which their families share.

"The most stressful situation would have to be my husband deploying to Iraq...One time we were were talking on the phone (his phone center has 2 phones outside in his small base camp) and I heard mortar rounds hit one after another and my husband told me "I gotta go, I gotta go!" and the phone dropped and was banging and I could hear everything, them returning fire and yelling. It scared the hell out of me. When it was all happening I just sat on the phone and listened in fear and disbelief. Eventually it stopped and he came back to the phone..."*

"During this deployment, I have encountered more stress with my children. My daughter has been having panic attacks and can make things very difficult and stressful. She feels scared all of the time and worried. It's been very difficult to get medical attention due to the amount of people deployed. It took 2 months for me to get an appointment with a family psychologist in the area."**

PTSD is not unique to soldiers or even to adults. Consider an eight year old child, Billy, who is walking down a street near his house. He barely notices the black parked car at the corner, being intent on the basketball he is dribbling and thoughts of his new teacher who is stricter than his last one. Though Billy is an "A" student and his homework is always done perfectly, he still worries. Particularly after his teacher wrinkled her nose when she read another boy's book report to the class, a report which was better than the one written by Billy.

*Erin E. Dimiceli, Mary A. Steinhardt, and Shanna E. Smith, Stressful Experiences, Coping Strategies, and Predictors of Health-related Outcomes among Wives of Deployed Military Servicemen, *Armed Forces & Society*, January, 2010, 36, 2, p. 359.
**ibid., p. 358

When Billy reaches the corner, a dog who escaped from a neighbor's house barks and runs towards him. Becoming startled and unsure what to do, the boy misses his beat and the basketball rolls in the direction of the frightened dog who then bites Billy on his leg. Though the physical injury is not serious, Billy now begins having nightmares of murderers with long knives coming after him. He becomes anxious when he sees a black car and even more nervous when he sees his teacher. Though formerly neat, his room is now disorganized and he forgets to hand in his homework.

A more common situation is the following. Late one evening, Alan's car hits another as he drives from a supermarket's parking lot along a side road. Alan has driven along this road hundreds of times. Though the cars were moving at a low speed, under twenty-five miles per hour, and the physical damage to both would classify them as mere fender benders, the psychological impact is great.

Alan, who drove thirty years without having an accident or even getting a ticket, has now become a jumpy driver. When a car approaches, his hands grip the steering wheel tightly, not relaxing until the auto passes his. He no longer listens to the radio while driving, and has stopped driving at night and to supermarket where he long shopped.

Though Billy and Alan are not soldiers, their symptoms reflect posttraumatic stress disorder (PTSD). These include: experiencing intense fear in which danger or potential harm occurred; its later effect in thoughts, nightmares, flashbacks or hallucinations; and intense distress when cues associated with the traumatic event occur. Other symptoms can include sleeping difficulty, outbursts of anger, having difficulty concentrating, and being excessively vigilant.

Though the experiences of soldiers are far more intense, the basic cause of PTSD for them and civilians is the same. That the human mind has limited endurance and, when this is exceeded, symptoms develop. These differ depending on the type of injury.

Where the traumatic experience was primarily physical, as from a battlefield blast, the depression, difficulty concentrating, and atypical behavior may reflect actual brain damage similar to that which athletes suffer after a concussion. These concussive forces are created by waves of air pressure faster than hurricane winds, causing the brain to crash against the skull and for brain tissue to be damaged. Unfortunately, this damage cannot be detected by MRI's or CAT scans. Though these people may have the same diagnosis of PTSD, the underlying cause and optimal treatment will differ since their trauma is primarily neurological in origin while the other is largely psychological.

What a soldier or another who has experienced a traumatic injury must do is to integrate this experience into their normal life. Which is no different from how people relate to a lesser event such as a relationship breaking up or a job loss or the death of a close relative.

It is important that the trauma be viewed within this context lest the patient become stigmatized, as were many Vietnam veterans. Thoughts of wartime experiences which later occur merely reflect the mind's normal attempt to reintegrate itself following a major stressful event. Much as occurs after divorce, when the initial dating steps are hesitant and fraught with past associations.

The risk of misdiagnosing PTSD is increased by cultural and financial issues. Considering PTSD to be more widespread among veterans than it actually is, enables some to express repugnance towards foreign policy and the Iraq war. There are also monetary incentives to be gained by having this diagnosis.

Yet the number of veterans who accurately suffer from PTSD is significant, a recent (2008) Rand study estimating that twenty-three percent of the veterans of America's modern wars developed it. Veterans of the Iraq and Afghanistan conflicts, in which multiple deployments became the rule rather than the exception, may be developing PTSD at a higher rate. The helpful therapist will relate to PTSD with sensitivity: empathizing with the pain while expressing the belief that the disturbing memories have meaning and are capable of being overcome.

Psychotherapy in the Military

The many differences between psychotherapy in civilian life and in the military is obscured by their common use of terms like "psychotherapy" and "mental health." While there must be similarities, since all clinicians deal with the human mind, these are not great. Two examples come to mind.

In the past, psychologists worked far from the risks of combat, in rear echelon clinics and hospitals, but this has changed. Now they may be embedded in combat units and carry weapons. One military psychologist described her life: conducting therapy in a crowded office and in the field; trying to convince soldiers to rest away from the combat zone though they were loathe to leave their comrades; the difficulty of getting traumatized soldiers discharged for many were considered to be exemplary warriors by their commanders.

An army psychologist who was interviewing a detained terrorist, spoke of the similarities they shared despite their religious differences. Then the officer asked what the prisoner would do if he were released. The prisoner was clear: "I will find out where you live and kill your entire family." The officer was taken aback for he had treated this man kindly. I offered the following explanation.

Through his humane treatment, the psychologist had managed to reach this prisoner emotionally, causing him to question his ideology. To forestall this, by ending the closeness he felt with the interviewer and to reinforce his political faith (which was essential to his identity), he threatened violence towards the officer's family. Because this American soldier had committed the inexcusable: convincing the terrorist that both were simply human.

No civilian therapist confronts situations like these. Yet, often, therapists who join the military expect their treatment activity to remain the same though they now play a different role. Not recognizing these differences, a soldier may consider their military therapist to be unfeeling or even inhuman but this reflects a misconception.

Every clinician, whether civilian or military, is merely carrying out their expected duty. That of civilian therapists is to their patients, whose welfare they are expected to keep foremost in all of their interactions. This is why therapists try to be continually available and patients cannot be arbitrarily dropped without good reason and a treatment alternative being provided.

But the allegiance of military therapists is to their service: to help patients resolve their emotional difficulties to the degree that they will be able to return to duty as effective soldiers. Immediate treatment, close to where the soldier became incapacitated and with the expectation of their rapid return to combat, are the goals of military therapists. Killing the enemy is the basic military mission and all efforts must contribute to this task. Unlike in civilian life where the therapist's goal is to diagnose and treat emotional difficulties and the patient's welfare, not that of the military, is paramount.

These goals may conflict. For example, therapy in the military is geared towards short-term treatment. Because soldiers must be able to be transferred in line with military needs, the dependency which occurs with all long-term treatment must be avoided. Thus those requiring lengthy treatment will be discharged.

Moreover, soldiers may break down when experiencing the stress of combat, which is a situation where no normal person wants to be. Seeking mental health treatment as a way of avoiding combat provides a significant personal advantage, what is termed professionally a *secondary gain*. While this can exist during therapy with civilians too, it is much less common since civilians enter therapy at the cost of their time and money.

In civilian psychotherapy, confidentiality is a bedrock of treatment. Even before the changes in federal regulations in 2003 which increased the privacy of medical records, therapists were the most cautious of all health practitioners in handling them. To reveal what was learned during therapy was considered not only unprofessional but abhorrent.

Confidentiality in the military is a different matter. Because the primary allegiance of military therapists is to their service and not to their patients, there is no confidentiality of what is learned. Unlike in civilian life, records do not belong to the therapists and their patients but to the military organization. Such matters as homosexual behavior, adultery, or dating a colleague, can have severe consequences in the military.

While the military has become more sophisticated about mental health matters in recent years, even the presence of what civilian clinicians consider relatively benign symptoms can affect career advancement. Another basic difference between treatment in the military and civilian life is that whereas the civilian therapist makes the final decision about what is best for their patient, the military therapist can only offer suggestions for the final decision remains with the soldier's commanding officer.

Though these distinctions appear to disparage therapy in the military they do not. What is best in one environment can be disastrous in another. This was found during World War Two when using civilian practices in the military, which included failing to recognize the role of secondary gain, resulted in huge numbers of soldiers being considered mentally incapacitated: at one point the number of soldiers evacuated exceeded those being inducted.*

To summarize, psychotherapy in the military and civilian spheres operate by fundamentally different guidelines and have dissimilar goals: one is not better than the other. They are simply different, and the inappropriate use of either practice will result in disaster.

Psychotherapy for Substance Abuse Difficulties

People hold many conclusions about alcohol and drug abuse difficulties. That they are genetically derived, run in families, and virtually untreatable. The latter belief gains credence from the dismal statistics which follow the typical fourteen to twenty-eight day in-patient treatment regimen. An alternate belief is that the major problem with substance abuse is legislative: that there would be no societal problem if drugs were available legally rather than forcing people to obtain them through criminal activity. There is some truth to all of these beliefs.

*O'Neill, F.J., The Public Mental Health Hospital in Modern Psychiatry: What Everyone Knows or Ought To. In *The Psychiatric Forum*, New York: Brunner/Mazel, 1972, pp. 163-170.

To understand substance abuse difficulties we must first recall that basic psychological capacities develop in the earliest years and that weaknesses of them may then occur. These can affect a person's ability to distinguish reality from fantasy, to control their behavior, to deal with feelings, and others; and make it difficult for them to succeed socially, in school, and on the job.

An adolescent is expected to achieve certain goals: to separate appropriately from their parents; to explore intimacy through dating which requires the ability to tolerate powerful feelings; and to make decisions about their educational and vocational future which demands having a sturdy sense of who one is (*sense of self*). If the teenager lacks sturdy psychological abilities they will have difficulty negotiating these goals and become depressed, this feeling indicating their sense of the depth of their problems.

Then, psychological symptoms become evident: deteriorated school grades, sleeping or eating problems, talk of suicide—or the adolescent tries to self-medicate their distress through drug or alcohol use. This is why substance abuse difficulties most often begin in adolescence though they can start earlier or later.

How this substance abuse should be treated depends on the degree of control which the person has over their drug or alcohol use. If there is no control and the abuser's life revolves about drinking or using drugs, hospitalization is needed to wean the person from their dependency. But if the alcohol or drug use is secondary to their emotional problems, successfully treating these will cause the alcohol or drug use to greatly diminish or to disappear.

Substance abuse problems are difficult to treat and particularly when a patient is beyond their adolescence. Therapy takes time, whereas the illusory satisfaction gained by alcohol or drugs is nearly instantaneous, to say nothing of their addictive qualities. Because these substances are so effective in temporarily eliminating distress, stopping their use doesn't eliminate the craving. Thus it is wisest, after recovery occurs, not to tempt fate by using these substances again. Theoretically, after emotional healing occurs through psychotherapy, the patient is so changed that they will no longer be in danger of again becoming addicted. Still, I would be wary.

Those suffering from substance abuse difficulties, whether with alcohol or drugs, are often shunned by therapists who reason as follows: why bother treating a person who tends to miss appointments, drop out of treatment, and causes such enormous stress to their family that out-of-office interventions may be required. In addition to which, these patients often don't pay their bills. Let another clinician treat them!

Successful psychotherapy with these people requires a therapist with great empathy and sophistication about their problems. One who views therapy in terms of years, not months or even weeks, which is the length of the typical inpatient substance abuse program today.

Another difficulty in treating substance abusers are the varying, popularly held views about them. Does their behavior reflect a disease like tuberculosis, a moral deficiency, or is it simply a bad habit? Prescriptions will vary depending on whether the body, the culture, or the devil is blamed. And if we consider it a disease, what then?

While alcoholism can certainly have severe physical consequences, is the illness medical or emotional?

To avoid these unhelpful distinctions it would be most useful to describe an alcoholic or a drug addict as being a person who is using more of the substance than is good for them. One who cannot control their use of the substance, some of which (like cocaine and heroin) have had long, well-accepted medical use. Even if the person also suffers from emotional problems, a substance abuser must no longer use alcohol or illicit drugs before their mental health disturbance can be successfully treated. Thus, substance abuse must be considered their primary disorder, one which gravely affects both the person and their environment.

I am not moralistic about using substances to feel better for this quest has always existed. Americans consume huge quantities of prescribed psychotropic drugs for this purpose, though with dubious outcome. The widespread use of illicit drugs damages societies and destabilizes nations by funding international terrorism. But a morally vigorous attitude does not cure. Substance abusers have addictions which reflect their inability to stop using a product (alcohol or drugs) because it fulfills their understandable need to function.

Having been healthy throughout my life, I didn't require any pain killing medication. Until one weekend when the pain from an abscessed tooth was so severe that I became incapacitated and had to continually hold ice to my face to reduce the pain. Which had already disappeared by Monday, when my dentist again became available.

Years later, when another tooth became abscessed and its location could not be precisely determined, I was prescribed Percodan and was amazed at its pain relieving effectiveness. The pain disappeared completely! Had I experienced continual pain to the degree caused by my earlier diseased tooth, I might well have become a Percodan addict..

Thus, people become addicted to alcohol, drugs, or cigarettes, because of pain. They remain addicted because of the physical and psychological pain from withdrawal and the psychological discomfort from no longer using a substance to relieve their distress.

All addiction reflects an attempt to gain externally what is missing psychologically, the attempt to fine-tune emotions with a preferred drug. That, and the fear of how they might become were they to end its use, which enables them to operate even if inadequately. How would they function without their daily-fed addiction? Who would they be?

With these huge unanswered questions, even the potential deadly side effects of drug use do not inhibit them: convulsions and drug induced psychoses from cocaine; agitation, sleeplessness and anti-social behavior from amphetamine use; the emotional impoverishment of morphine and heroin users; psychotic episodes and possible brain damage from psychedelic drugs like LSD and angel dust. But these describe theoretical problems while their daily pain is real. What should be done?

When treating addiction, the choice of drug tells us little about the person since this depends on their knowledge of drugs which is gained through friends, its availability, and social and cultural factors. But, generally, those who feel empty tend to use the "up" drugs (cocaine, amphetamine); those who feel anxious tend to use the "down" drugs (alcohol and tranquilizers); while the opiates (morphine, heroin) appeal to both groups.

The essential element in all addictions is that the substance used grants the person the sense of power over their mood and feelings. This enables them to temporarily forget their self-hatred, and alleviate their abysmally low self-esteem which is caused by their unconscious sense of the depth of their problems. And, for the socially insecure, it gains them a like-minded community of equals, and a stable if fragile sense of who they are to replace their absent one.

But, being unrealistic, the addictive solution must fail. Things get worse as the addict becomes enmeshed in their cycle of pain, relief, and decreasing functioning. Though the psychological limitations of both alcohol and drug addicts is similar, their problems differ because drugs are illegal and the consequences of their use lend even greater complexity to their life. Were alcohol use illegal, alcoholics would likely behave as criminally as does the typical drug addict today.

Diagnosing the addict is easy. Their behavior, though often successfully hidden, eventually becomes evident through: their absence from school or work and deteriorating performance; their drastic personality change and emotional outbursts; and their social withdrawal and paranoia.

While addiction is serious, recreational drug use or adolescent drug experimentation should not be confused with it. These do not necessarily lead to addiction unless the associated underlying psychological difficulties are present.

Psychotherapy alone can be successful when drugs are used for recreation since this usually diminishes over the course of treatment. But psychotherapy alone is not effective for the active addict. Here, hospitalization, therapeutic communities, and self-help groups are necessary to deal with the medical and psychological problems of those who are unable to stop drug use on their own. Thereafter, therapy can begin.

Therapy is difficult for the recent ex-addict regardless of whether it is alcohol or drugs they have stopped using. At this point they are in crisis, having lost their powerful defense against distress and its associated social network. They have ambivalent feelings: depression and hope; and hunger for their magical solution against despair but rejecting this. Most of all, they feel vulnerable.

During this initial stage the successful therapist must: build the therapeutic relationship; identify and help the patient to cope with those of his feelings which have long been submerged; and help them re-establish and create, perhaps for the first time, a healthy relationship with their family. The therapist must also be supportive as they cope with employment and other issues in their life. But, as has long been said in the substance abuse field, one step at a time.

First comes the practical issues of housing and employment and family. The great emotional change which is required for permanent sobriety will begin later. Now is the time for simple interventions, support, and education though, since psychotherapy requires an individual prescription, no rigid instruction can be made.

Once the ex-addict's life is stable, treatment of their basic personality deficits can begin: their inability to control their anxiety and to soothe themselves, abilities which develop in the early years of life. Healing is difficult for it is precisely this void which the addict has been attempting to fill, unsuccessfully, throughout their life. It produces the immature personality characteristics which addicts are noted for: poor judgment, being self-centered, creating unrealistic goals.

The ideal therapist for the ex-addict will have practices akin to those of the late Victor Borge as he carried out his celebrated performances: playing the piano and telling jokes in no particular order, depending on what he sensed his audience would best respond to. Which is what this therapist must do.

Their tasks include explaining how the new, painful feelings which the patient is experiencing is good for they reflect his increasing sobriety. Allowing this issue to remain unexplored will risk the patient falling back onto their long-familiar, quickly comforting defense of alcohol or drug use.

While listening is also a form of activity and is an essential element of all therapy, successfully treating an ex-addict requires an active therapist. The therapist must move back and forth, from interpretation to support to suggestions, perhaps on how the ex-addict might best relate to their spouse or children or employer. It is this ability to sense, on a moment-to-moment basis, the most effective way to relate to an addicted patient, that distinguishes the successful therapist.

Psychotherapy for Panic/Anxiety Disorder (PAD)

When You Think That You're Dying:

Few disorders are more immediately frightening than panic/anxiety disorder (PAD). Try to imagine it. Your heart races, stomach feels bloated, hands become cold and clammy and you notice a tingling sensation moving down your arm. These symptoms increase as you rush to hospital's Emergency Room and declare that you are having a heart attack. Until medical tests reveal that you are physically healthy: another of the 40% to 60% of patients who are evaluated at Emergency Rooms and found to suffer not from the heart attack they feared but from Panic/Anxiety Disorder (PAD).

Here are guidelines to help you cope with the terrifying symptoms of PAD, and what most therapists will suggest.

1. After the symptoms occur for the first time, be medically evaluated so you can, in the immediate future, safely reject the belief that your distress reflects an underlying illness.

2. You must then repeatedly insist to yourself that your symptoms reflect anxiety, which is your friend. Yes, the anxiety is your friend even if it is an experience which causes you to believe that you are about to die. Because the purpose of anxiety is a good one and is similar to that of fever: to inform you that your existence is in danger. But with PAD the danger is not to your body but to your mind, the insistent, unavoidable message being that you must

make changes in your life, perhaps in your work or social activities, in order to continue to live healthfully.

When you experience the symptoms of PAD you must continually tell yourself that what you are experiencing is not a heart attack but anxiety, which can mimic virtually any physical symptom. And that anxiety cannot kill you and will go away. Meanwhile, try to figure out when the anxiety symptoms began and what thought or feeling might have triggered them.

Psychotropic medication helps some to get through these anxious periods, and psychotherapy can aid virtually all people in eliminating or greatly reducing them. Though painful, anxiety is always beneficial for it enables you to become the better person that, unconsciously, you sense you should be.

Psychotherapy for Obsessive-Compulsive Disorder (OCD), and Phobias

Though the symptoms of panic/anxiety disorder (PAD) and obsessive-compulsive disorder (OCD) differ, they result from an identical cause: the human mind's normal and continuous attempt to reduce anxiety so that a person will function without pain and be at their very best.

If a person experiences too great stress from any of many possible causes (employment, home, social, or school problems), two things will happen: a symptom (the sign that something is wrong) develops, and the mind attempts to reduce the stress, or anxiety, using one of its natural built-in mechanisms. Prominent among these are the psychological or *ego defenses*, one of which is the *obsessive-compulsive ego defense*. This sounds complicated but it is really very simple.

An obsession is a *thought* which is repeated over and over, like a tune which you can't get out of your mind. A compulsion is a *behavior* which is repeated, like continually cleaning or being what is called a "neatness freak." None of these mental operations reflects "being crazy" and some of the most successful people in our society behave similarly.

When a person becomes mildly obsessed or compulsive, they feel more relaxed and their obsession or compulsion is not ordinarily visible to others. When it can be seen, this is because the anxiety level is so high that though the ego defense is operating in overdrive, it is still unable to reduce the anxiety to a tolerable level. It is these people who are diagnosed as having an "obsessive-compulsive disorder."

Psychotherapy for this condition involves reducing the patient's anxiety level by eliminating the stress which is causing it. After which the obsession or compulsion naturally goes away since its operation is no longer needed. But this is harder than it sounds. Some symptoms have existed for many years and become ingrained into the personality, which is always slow to change. Or there may be a benefit, a secondary gain, to the symptom, as by allowing the person to avoid an activity in which they don't want to engage.

An obsession may be something as ordinary as repeatedly checking to see that the door is locked upon leaving the house, or bizarre, like the recurring fear or *obsessive phobia*, which Victoria developed.

Why Victoria "Freaked Out"

For as long as twenty-eight year old Victoria could remember, she had "a thing" about dirt and germs. Because of which her clothes were always spotless and she would be used as an example by neighborhood mothers for their daughters. Victoria's first menstrual period was difficult, but she adjusted.

As she grew older, her fear of germs expanded and, after sitting on a chair in a restaurant, she would immediately change her clothes after returning home. But her parents never questioned this for they considered it her idiosyncrasy, something which everyone has.

Victoria graduated from college with a degree in math. She accepted a job teaching in a high school, being unable to find a job in industry like her mother who had a degree in statistics. In graduate school, while fulfilling the requirement for her teaching certification and tenure, Victoria met Billy, a biology teacher. They married and, three years later, she became pregnant.

Since her adolescence, Victoria's fear of germs had remained about the same. She was still reluctant to eat in restaurants, fearing to sit on a chair on which another person had sat. But her husband, being frugal, didn't object and they shared the cooking chores at home. One day at school, Victoria felt a twang in her stomach and began worrying about the health of her unborn daughter. Would she be deformed, retarded, stillborn?

These thoughts continued as Victoria taught geometry to her tenth grade class. She asked a girl, Laurie, to come to the blackboard and solve a problem. Laurie reluctantly approached and then leaned on her teacher's desk as she spoke. Seeing this, Victoria suddenly "freaked out" and became unable to speak. Thankfully, it was the day's last class, the bell rang, and the students left the room quickly. Victoria called in sick the rest of the week for she now couldn't bear to sit at her desk which a student had touched.

What caused Victoria's suddenly increased fear of germs? Possibly the normal anxieties of pregnancy, difficulties in her marriage, a problem with the school principal, another issue, or some combination of these. Whatever generated enough anxiety to push the operation of her phobic and obsessive ego defense mechanisms into overdrive.

Chapter Twenty Two

Psychotherapy for Medical Problems and Grief

THAT STRESS AND PSYCHOLOGICAL PROBLEMS can have a major effect on medical illness is no longer questioned. Experiencing a highly stressful childhood has been linked with heart disease, liver disease, lung disease, and other medical conditions in adulthood, and can slash decades from life expectancy.* Today, scientists are trying to harness the body's immune system to fight disease, and to provide medication based on an individual's biology.

Even when the cause of an illness is believed to be known the question remains: why did *that* person develop *that* illness at *that* particular moment in their life? Why not a day before or later? And why, for example, though we all possess cancer cells, do only *some* people develop cancer?

Biological structures are unique but so are the stresses which people endure, how they react to them, and the different effects this has on their bodies.

*Interview with Dr. Robert Anda, Center for Disease Control and Prevention, reported by Reuters Health, October 9, 2009.

Some adults, when they are anxious, develop a sinking feeling in their stomach or diarrhea. Others may vomit or feel a lump in their throat or hot or cold sensations. Anxiety, which the mind produces when it senses approaching danger, is automatically aroused by the body. Just as it was with our stone age ancestors when a hungry animal approached. The body goes into overdrive with some functions being reduced while others, those which are essential to fight or flight reactions, being heightened. When fear of the expected danger disappears, so does the body's physiological stress reactions, and the levels of the hormones involved become normal again.

These profoundly affecting reactions occur continually throughout a chronic, life threatening illness, or when one first learns that they have it or a bodily injury. Which is to be expected for this confrontation means having to totally reorient one's life. The person feels as if they were hit on the head, being stunned and dazed, paralyzed and numb.

Yet after gaining emotional support, some people endure and even thrive. They learn new coping mechanisms while maintaining their sense of who they are. During these extreme crises, or periods of disequilibrium, these people become more open to outside influences which enable them to better cope with the new tasks they face: dealing with pain, incapacitation, and treatment procedures; developing working relationships with medical staff; and coping with the reality of their uncertain future. None of which are simple matters.

They must decide whether it is permissible to express anger towards their doctor for not seeing them;

when to request additional pain medication; and learn how to deal with such distressing symptoms as weakness, dizziness, or paralysis. These are particularly difficult tasks for people who are cut off from their feelings, or are unable to gain the emotional support which is needed to perform them effectively.

Eighteen Year Old Jack Faces Death and Finds Love

Calling eighteen year old Jack "a jock" would have done him a disservice. For though he ran many miles each day while trying to win a place on the freshman track team, he kept his "A" average by studying on the train during his daily three hour commute to and from college.

Both his parents worked so it wasn't until the weekend that his mother noticed the large sores on Jack's legs. Her worry and insistence that he see a physician resulted in blood tests and a bone marrow biopsy which brought devastating news: their only son had acute lymphocytic leukemia with a life span ranging from months to several years. At first, Jack's parents lied. They were unable to tell him the truth about his condition and explained it as being anemia. Two months later, after his first successful round of chemotherapy, they told him.

Further chemotherapy followed with stronger drugs being required each time. These produced remissions but also more severe side effects like vomiting and bleeding gums. Despite this, Jack returned to college, becoming captain of the track team and an award winning runner until his illness resumed its course.

Periodically, Jack required hospitalization; once he realized that all his friends on his ward had died. Jack survived one infection following days of fever but died a year later, nearly two years after his predicted death.

During his final year he fell in love with a healthy young woman who he met in the hospital. She accepted that their time together would be brief. Their relationship and the unflagging support of his family throughout his medical crises enabled him to accept his fate.

Finding a psychotherapist who is skilled in dealing with physical illness is more difficult than seeking one for help with emotional difficulties. Psychotherapists have chosen this field because they are comfortable dealing with emotional issues. Helping another to cope with the stresses of physical illness is a far different task, though not because specialized medical knowledge is required. Needed information about a medical condition and symptoms can ordinarily be gained from the patient who has been forced to become knowledgeable, or through quick study.

But counseling those who suffer from a life threatening illness can raise serious stress in the therapist. It forces them to confront issues about their own aging and health and mortality, and can even cause illness.

A Psychologist Becomes Ill After Confronting a Dying Child

A seven year old girl was dying from leukemia. She had been discharged from a noted medical facility in another city and returned home. Her insurance company pleaded that I see her.

During our initial session I spoke first with her parents. They were greatly distressed. Then I spoke with the child as we played games which children are familiar with: Chutes and Ladders and Connect Four. While playing, the girl held a pan in case she became nauseous. She did not look well and over the following week I found myself thinking of her continually, more than about all of my other patients combined.

At the next session the girl seemed happier. She was animated and I told her fictional stories about the activities of the stuffed animals in the room, their names and family events. During later weeks I told myself that maybe the girl was getting better and not really dying, for she seemed so much better than at her first session. But this reflected my denial of the truth, which is a coping mechanism often used when one first confronts a serious crisis.

Her mother called me before her next scheduled appointment. Her daughter was now too weak to come to the office: could I see her at home? I did, and we spoke briefly as she lay in bed. Because of her sleepiness, I spent most of the time speaking with her parents and older brothers, helping them to cope with what was inevitable. The girl died two days later, at home.

Despite our brief involvement and my having many other patients, I was strongly affected by this experience. I suddenly developed diarrhea which would occur unexpectedly though blood tests revealed nothing physically wrong with me. This symptom was so disturbing that I was unable to engage in one of my usual, greatly enjoyed tasks: serving as a government expert witness in court cases. After three months the diarrhea disappeared as quickly as it began and never returned.

Two months later I was asked by a physician to treat another dying child. I refused, having learned from this experience that it affected me too strongly.

Not every therapist can deal with every situation and comforting the dying demands a special breed of practitioner. I cherish those, like hospice workers and some physicians, who can repeatedly endure this crucial, final task.

Helping a person to cope with the crisis of dying when their life increasingly lacks self-control and direction. The feeling of helplessness as they consider unrealized plans and dreams. The assaults on their self-esteem as they become less productive and independent and endure increasing personal discomfort. Having to come to terms with these, and their fear.

But helping a person with emotional problems to cope with their medical condition is an easier task. A mother brought her eight year old son to see me. Several months before, he had learned that he had diabetes and would have to inject himself daily with insulin. While in the hospital he did this but after his discharge he claimed that he was unable to do so.

During his first therapy sessions the boy spoke little: he was emotionally constricted and had great difficulty relating words to feelings and experiences. So, during our play with board games and puzzles, I told him stories about our stuffed animal friends. Gradually, I asked him about about his experiences in school, at home, and in the hospital.

After five months of therapy, during which he became increasingly capable of speaking about his feelings, he again became able to inject himself with insulin. The boy had been unconsciously interpreting the insulin injection as an assault upon himself, like stabbing himself with a knife. A fantasy which disappeared as he became able to speak of his angry feelings, after which he could again carry out his required medical task.

Outcomes are not always so fortunate. Some, like the death of an infant or the birth of a seriously ill or deformed child, creates life-long stress and chronic sadness. Parents may create fantasies to help them deny the truth in order to enable them to continue their parenting tasks. Like the hope that, someday, their child will be able to function more independently.

While the grief experienced after the death of a child is intense but lessens over time, chronic grief is unresolved, as when parents confront the fatal illness of a young child. Here the therapist must help the parents to cope with their doubts and their feelings of guilt and mourning; and to communicate more effectively with medical professionals and family members. Such a therapist will need the best professional qualities which have been described in this book—and more.

Are Children Too Young To Mourn the Death of Their Parent?

While a graduate student I met a psychologist who everyone agreed was brilliant: he had won an award for his research. But one clinical opinion which he forcefully held, and proved logically in a professional paper, I regarded as nonsense. Thankfully, even then I was tactful and politically smart enough not to express my opinion.

This doctor believed that children could not mourn the death of their parent for they lacked the life experience to do so, not yet having an accurate sense of what death is. Today, one might say that he adopted his clinical belief by doing what a driver does who ends up in a river: blindly trusting their GPS system and ignoring their observations.

In fairness, there has long been professional dispute as to whether children are capable of mourning before they reach adolescence though not by me for I have seen their reaction after a parent or pet died.

But for a young child to be able to mourn, they need a parent with whom they can discuss their feelings, one who is emotionally available to answer their questions. Understandably, this does not always happen after the death of a spouse for the mourning parent may not be able to supply what their child most needs. Without this outlet the child may develop problems: school or sleep difficulties or another mental health symptom. A child's attempt to "parent their parent" can also put their emotional responses on hold.

The important question is not whether children—even those as young as three or four years—are able to mourn, but the factors which keep them from expressing their feelings. So that they might resolve their fantasy of restoring their dead parent to life, and become capable of loving once again.

Chapter Twenty Three

Psychotherapy for Family Violence

Grace: From Beatings to Bombs To Freedom

"I loved him, and the money helped too," was how Grace explained her disastrous marriage. Grace was the youngest of four children. Her father was an alcoholic tractor mechanic who earned a good living when he worked. Her mother's drinking increased as her husband demanded greater companionship, and over the years her alcohol use came to match his.

There was a sixteen year age difference between Grace and her oldest sister, who behaved as her real mother. All of the children fled from the family as soon as they could and settled in different parts of the country. Grace managed to graduate from high school before leaving home but attending college was, financially, out of the question. Her parents gave her two hundred dollars, wished her well, and she took a bus to the nearest large city.

Her first jobs were menial: packing in a perfume factory, and doing housekeeper in a motel. She attended the local community college without any career plan in mind. After graduating, Grace found a job as assistant buyer at a department store. She didn't date and had never done so, feeling uneasy with men and rejecting their regularly arriving advances. Two years later, while passing the jewelry counter, she met Tim.

He said that he was buying a present for his mother and asked her advice. A pickup, she realized, but a polite one. She was twenty-five and it was time for her to lose her virginity, or surrender it as she preferred to think.

Tim was fourteen years older and divorced. He had a daughter he rarely saw and, she learned after their marriage, parents he visited as infrequently. He was a salesman though of exactly what she wasn't sure since Tim didn't encourage questions. But she gave him what he wanted: two boys and a girl, sex whenever he wanted it, meals he usually liked, and a clean home. Whether she was happy she never asked herself though she did love her children.

The beatings began soon after their first child was born. Tim was careful: instead of hitting her where it would leave marks, he used a belt on the soles of her feet. His reason for the first beating was a dish she cooked or that the meal was late. Or maybe the cleaning wasn't up to his standards. She no longer remembered.

After awhile the cause for her beatings didn't matter and they became a normal part of her marriage. Like cleaning up after the children and doing the wash. All became a blur. Caring for her children. Cooking. Cleaning. Sex. A beating. Grace became like those soldiers who have endured too much and operate by rote. And, she told herself, the beatings didn't last that long: only until she began crying. Then he would put away the belt and go on as if nothing happened. Paradoxically, Tim never hit their children and condemned parents who did.

Grace didn't want to live in Kuwait but this, like other family decisions, wasn't hers to make. Tim's job transferred him and his family was going along.

Apart from being beaten on the soles of the feet, Grace's story wasn't new: many women have similar experiences. But the rest of her story jolted me. While sitting in my quiet suburban office, I began feeling as if I were involved in a thriller movie. What this small, thin, soft-spoken woman had experienced and accomplished stunned me.

What most surprised Grace was that she liked living in Kuwait. It was a far more liberal country than she expected, and most of the people spoke at least some English. Even the road signs were bi-lingual.

The rented apartment which the company provided was large and, of course, frigidly air-conditioned. They had a live-in maid and the children attended an English speaking school with these costs being picked up by Tim's employer. American foods and fast-food restaurants were available, and the streets were generally safe.

So, apart from having to adjust to the Kuwaiti's terrible driving habits and the flatness of the country, Grace expected their nine month stay to occasion little change in her family's life. The beatings were now less frequent for Tim worked longer hours and arrived home late most evenings. Sometimes he would be gone on week long business trips.

Grace's life again became routine. With the children in school and Tim temporarily away, her only companion was the live-in maid, an English speaking Indian girl barely out of her teens who cleaned and helped with the cooking.

Grace's peaceful world was shattered one morning in August, 1990 when she awoke to the sounds of bursting explosions and gunfire. Looking down from her balcony, she saw soldiers and buildings wreathed with black smoke. All—she, her children, and the maid—huddled in the apartment. That night they heard on the radio that Kuwait was now part of Iraq. With Tim gone, she felt helpless, like a child. During her childhood she had sisters to reach out to. Here, far from America, she was alone.

There were other western families in her apartment complex. They had occasionally met in passing and greeted each other courteously but had no further contact. Now, fear brought them together as the initial disbelief turned to despair. The looting of empty houses, malls, and shops was widespread, but the Iraqis were mostly harassing Kuwaitis, many of whom had fled abroad.

During the seven month occupation, Grace kept her family calm and spent her days searching through deserted apartments for food, dressed in a hooded over-garment (abaya), full face veil (niqab), and long black gloves which she was given by a Muslim neighbor. She moved her family into an abandoned apartment in a less affluent area of the city after hearing rumors that foreigners were being taken hostage.

After Kuwait's liberation, Grace and her children returned to America. She found work, enrolled them in school, and began a new life. Months later, Tim returned to America, contacted her, and wanted to join them. She refused, filed for divorce, and began therapy.

While the statistics reported for family violence differ widely depending on how it is defined, when it does occur it damages everyone in the family, adult and child alike. And while an equal percentage of women and men assault their spouses, women are far more likely to be stalked, seriously injured, or murdered. Yet even if one is not touched, fear can cripple an adult's life and a child's psychological development.

A relationship is abusive when there is physical, sexual, or psychological abuse, the latter sometimes leading to the former. A common example is the attempt to control the spouse's life by demanding to know where they are at all times and insisting that they dress in a certain way and have only "approved" friends.

This is often accompanied by rages when the loss of control is threatened. Humiliation (criticizing another as being stupid or inadequate), with hitting, shoving, restraining, kicking, or the implicit threat of other physical harm being present. One man, after realizing that his wife became frightened when he picked up a knife, thereafter played with it while he criticized her.

It is popularly thought that domestic violence occurs mostly within impoverished, poorly educated families but this is untrue. It occurs in all racial, ethnic, and socioeconomic groups. Twenty- five years ago the chairman of the United States Security and Exchange Commission resigned after his wife described her eighteen years of beatings.

Recently a woman sought a protective order against her paramour stating that he had "stripped her...smashed her against a mirrored dresser and taken two telephones from her to prevent her from calling for help." The man alleged to have done this was a high ranking New York State government official.* That next day in Washington D.C. a forty-three year old lawyer "said her husband tried to kill her, first with his hands, then with a metal flashlight." His last job was as deputy counsel to the president of the United States.**

A well-educated friend of mine who married a European, fled back to the United States along with their children after her husband's abuse escalated to the point where he broke her nose. A patient's husband would use choke holds on her which he learned in the Marines. His hobby of collecting guns increased her fear.

Living under these conditions can lead to depression, eating disorders, and attempts at suicide. There is usually a cycle of violence in these families. Following the abuse there is affection, apology, and a vow of ending violence. After which, because of poor communication and tension, the victim will try—but fail—to calm the batterer and avoid further violence.

---

*"Questions of Influence in Abuse Case of Paterson Aide."*The New York Times,* 10 February 2010,
** "Case of John Michael Farren seen as refresher course on domestic violence."*The Washington Post*, 25 February 2010.

There are varying theories why violence occurs in families. Psychologists emphasize the existence of poor impulse control leading to outbursts of anger because of an inability to talk about feelings and relieve them in a mature fashion; and the presence of low self-esteem. Or, in line with the psychoanalytic concept of the *repetition compulsion*, a person who was abused in childhood may thereafter seek abusive relationships and attempt to master their earlier trauma.

Increased stress caused by financial or employment problems, or having an infant in the family, are sometimes factors; as is the dependence of a woman on her husband for financial support.

When therapy is begun in families where violence exists, therapists have one overriding concern: to assure safety. Thus regardless of their clinical orientation, all therapists insist that the violence must stop or the couple must separate for the risk of harm is too great.

When advising this, I sometimes joke that if the couple think therapy is expensive they should consider what a lawyer will charge following their arrest. To say nothing of the lifelong guilt after injury. Only after this agreement, that threats and violence will cease, can therapy begin, with the goals of improving communication and relieving stress.

When there has been abuse of a child, the situation is different. While all therapy by a licensed clinician is confidential, there are major exceptions: when a court order (not merely a subpoena) is received; when the president is threatened; or when child abuse or child endangerment exists.

A court order must be adhered to (or be legally appealed); a threat against the president must be reported to the Secret Service; and the state's Child Protective Services must be notified of the abuse of a child.

Paradoxically, the rarest of these events, a serious presidential threat, is the easiest for a therapist to cope with. They need only telephone the Secret Service which will immediately take charge of the case. The patient is then hospitalized or prosecuted, and the therapist becomes removed from future involvement.

But when child abuse is reported, the therapist remains involved. Which is good, for this is a stressful time for all. The child fears the consequences of having revealed the truth and the parents fear the wrath of the court and its potential serious effect on their future: being formally classified as an abuser bars one from working with children. An event which could end the teaching career of a parent who, in a moment of exasperation, slapped their child.

The need to make a Child Protective Service (CPS) report occurs infrequently in a therapist's practice. Once the report is received, CPS will interview the child and parents separately at least once, to try to determine the truth. They will also seek information from the therapist, who can usually calm the situation. Thereafter, CPS must decide whether legal prosecution is warranted. Generally, prosecution is not recommended, except when there has been injury or sexual abuse, or child endangerment (inadequate medical or other care) exists.

Sometimes it is not easy for CPS workers to make the right decision. Partly because they differ in knowledge and skill; also because, as any lawyer will tell you, people lie.

One fourteen year girl's situation was reported by her therapist to CPS after the mother's boyfriend introduced the child to cocaine before having sex with her. The mother was furious—until the boyfriend promised to take her and her daughter on a European vacation. The CPS worker went to the home and spoke with the child and her mother together, for she would not allow her daughter to be interviewed separately. Both denied that anything improper had occurred and the mother added that she was breaking up with her boyfriend. But this CPS worker was sharp and asked, "If nothing happened, why are you breaking up with him?" Still, because both mother and daughter stuck to their stories, no CPS action could be taken.

Psychotherapy for stalking involves the therapist supporting the victim in gaining the intervention of the legal system and is beyond the scope of this book. The best advice regarding stalking and personal protection that I have found is in a book by Gavin de Becker, *The Gift of Fear*. I strongly recommend it.

Chapter Twenty Four

Psychotherapy for Childhood and Adolescent Suicidal Behavior

AN INCORRECT BUT POPULAR BELIEF holds that psychotherapy can only benefit youth with mild problems. Those who function well but just have difficulty organizing their lives or getting along with their peers. Children who are anxious or depressed but still able to attend school. Those who are unable to accomplish these ordinary tasks are believed to require medication or hospitalization, with both being marketed in some quarters as being optimal.

This is true—but only for the comparatively rare youth who have serious suicidal or homicidal intent or are completely unable to function. All such situations require careful evaluation for were everyone with occasional suicidal or homicidal thoughts to be hospitalized there would be few people walking the street. These expressions are common. What wife has not said,"I was so mad that I wanted to kill my husband last night." Or angry child has not responded to their mother, "I wish I was dead."

What concerns clinicians are what what lies beneath these statements. Before the extreme step of hospitalization should be recommended, four crucial factors must be evaluated. Does the person truly intend to harm themselves or another? Do they have a realistic plan for doing so? Do they have the means to carry out their plan? And, finally, does the individual have adequate control over their behavior?

If the answer to all of these questions is "yes," then immediate hospitalization is the safest and only action to be taken. But the answers to these questions must be gained by a licensed mental health professional, not a relative or job supervisor. Though well-intentioned, these individuals lack clinical training and sophistication and are unable to assess the situation accurately.

Unfortunately, another factor must be considered: that hospitals are businesses like any other. A car repair shop needs cars to repair and a hospital requires patients. So, like all retail establishments, hospitals market their services widely: in schools, government agencies, and businesses. This is one reason why many people are hospitalized unnecessarily.

Hospitalized Charlotte's Changing Diagnoses

Fourteen year old Charlotte had problems. No one denied it though many were typical of adolescents. Like her alternating crushes and fluctuating math grades, though the latter seemed caused by a personality conflict with the teacher. And, though personally clean, her room was often a disaster area with soiled clothes and discarded granola bar wrappers left on the floor. Still, her parents tolerated her idiosyncrasies and she accepted theirs, until the family's world caved in.

Her father was arrested for bank fraud, her parents separated and she, her two sisters and their mother, moved from their spacious home into a small apartment. Then her boyfriend dropped her for a girl whose mother let him sleep over, and she failed a math test. That afternoon a classmate informed the school nurse of Charlotte's statement: "I want to die." The school's staff, which had recently received a presentation from a nearby psychiatric hospital, sprang into action. They called Charlotte's mother and advised immediate hospitalization.

Being unconvinced, Charlotte's mother brought Charlotte to her pediatrician who advised that a one week evaluation at the hospital could do no harm. Five months later, Charlotte's mother contacted me. She was feeling stressed and wanted to make changes in her life, but first she wanted to get her daughter home. Yet whenever she raised this issue with the hospital they accused her of being a bad mother. Once they even threatened to report her to the state Child Protective Services.

And whenever the insurance company, which was paying the cost of hospitalization, raised the issue of Charlotte's discharge, her diagnosis would suddenly be changed and she would then require a new course of treatment. A fifteen hundred dollars a day charge can arouse much professional creativity.

I advised the mother as follows: she should inform the hospital that unless her daughter was immediately released her lawyer would be contacting them and a lawsuit would follow. Upon hearing this, Charlotte was diagnosed as "improved" and sent home.

I treated Charlotte for five weeks: she was my healthiest adolescent patient. Her major worry was the reaction of her peers to her having been in "a mental hospital." I predicted this would soon become old news and that was what happened. "Glad you're back," was what they said, before turning to current matters.

Charlotte never intended to kill herself when she said that she wanted to be dead. She was upset, spoke carelessly, and needed a mental health evaluation by a therapist. But not hospitalization which leaves lingering psychological scars no matter how comfortable the setting. Previously, Charlotte was an unremarkable teenager, before becoming an "ex-mental patient."

Despite the widespread fear of going crazy and being hospitalized, this is a comparatively rare event: virtually all mental health difficulties can be handled in a therapist's out-patient office. But children who present a real danger do require hospital services, though it can sometimes be difficult to obtain.

A Suicidal Teenager is Rejected by a Hospital

Joan was a nineteen year old college freshman who was living away from home for the first time, in a college dorm room with three other girls. Her mother became upset by the increasingly depressed tone of her daughter's daily phone calls and brought her to me for an evaluation.

All of Joan's roommates dated and were involved in campus activities. One had her boyfriend sleep over occasionally. When Joan wasn't in class or the cafeteria, she studied in her room. A few days before her appointment with me she thought of throwing herself from her dormitory room's window. "What floor is it on?" I asked. "The fifth," she replied, adding that her bed was next to the window.

I advised Joan as follows. I said that I felt she was very unhappy and had been for a long time. It might be that she would benefit from hospitalization but I wasn't yet sure. Was she willing to see me twice a week? Did she feel that she could control her behavior and keep from hurting herself? Would she call me immediately if the thought of killing herself returned? Joan answered "yes" to my questions.

Over the following weeks, Joan became more talkative, began exploring activities on campus, and seemed happier. Her thought of suicide disappeared. Until it returned, along with a nightmare: that she was driving in a car which was increasingly out of control.

I told Joan and her parents that she now needed the safety of a hospital. Her parents objected, and offered to take her home and watch her closely. I understood their feelings for the popular view of psychiatric hospitals, derived from countless melodramatic movies, is not good: electric shock treatments, strait-jackets, screams, and the like.

I advised Joan's parents that there was no alternative. They could not provide the daily continuous supervision which she now needed. Recognizing this, they agreed, and drove to the nearby state hospital. But the staff refused to admit Joan, saying that she wasn't disturbed enough. This hospital didn't ordinarily see courteous, well-dressed people like Joan for their usual patient was violent and disheveled and threatening.

Joan's mother called me and I advised that they go to a private hospital five miles away. There, she was hospitalized for two weeks and Joan found my description of a hospital to be accurate: that though the food was generally good, it was a very boring place to be. She spent her free time writing overdue letters to members of her large extended family.

Psychiatric hospitals, though expensive and overused, *are* occasionally needed to save lives and to preserve the stability of families. Even the most loving parents cannot provide for all of their child's needs and the stress from trying to do so when severe mental health problems exist can be destructive to all. Yet while psychiatric hospitals can defuse emergencies, they are a short-term measure. It has been decades since they treated people more than briefly. Earlier, children might be institutionalized for years and attend school at the facility but, largely, those settings are long gone..

Recognizing the psychological damage and cost of long-term hospitalization, many government institutions were closed. It was promised that less expensive, comprehensive out-patient services and supportive living facilities would be created in the community. But the money saved by closing these hospitals went into the state general budgets and they were never built. Thus, by default, in a move which should shock everyone's conscience, the prison system has now become the mental health facility for far too many youth and adults.

There are other facilities in which psychotherapy may be received. Because immediately after their release from hospitals, some youth are not yet ready to return to school, *day hospital* programs have been created. Here, former hospital patients receive, essentially, the same program they did while in the hospital. Group and individual therapy and often lunch—but out in the community. These are beneficial for they provide the structure which all people need to function. They are so helpful that they are sometimes opened to people who were never hospitalized.

At one day hospital setting, where I ran a therapy group and consulted for many years, a women in her early seventies became very depressed following the lingering dying process of her husband. Though not meeting the day hospital's admission requirements, she was permitted to attend upon her psychiatrist's recommendation.

The program helped her to recover quickly and her involvement and warmth encouraged other, far younger patients to get better too. Eventually we did have to discharge her though many of the staff objected. She had become an important asset to the program.

What Should I Do When My Child Speaks of Suicide?

Every parent becomes frightened when they think that their child might kill themselves. And, being fearful that a wrong word would precipitate what is apparently just a possibility, they say nothing. Or pretend that their child was joking. And, usually, suicide does not occur though their child's pain continues.

Suicide is not motivated by just a poor school grade, or the failure to gain admission to a desired college, or a break-up with a boyfriend or girlfriend. What it or the suicide gesture reflects is long term unhappiness, the depth of our horror at a youth's potentially premature death being as great as their despair.

When a child considers suicide, the most immediate goal is to safeguard their life. Thus a crucial decision must be made as to whether real risk exists or that their words reflected the temporary frustration and occasional silly statement which everyone makes. This conclusion, deriving from knowledge of child development and psychopathology and supported by clinical experience and intuition, must be made by a mental health professional. Unlike other parenting matters, it cannot be a parental decision.

Most children who make a suicidal statement or gesture do not intend to harm themselves or require hospitalization. But they would benefit from counseling, for maybe just a few sessions, to enable them to clarify their goals and how they would be most likely to achieve them.

A suicidal gesture is often designed to *force* that counseling which the child long sensed that they needed but feared. Even when a child's act was potentially lethal, hospitalization may not be necessary: if they have a continuous relationship with a psychotherapist who is certain that the child has control over their behavior and will not again attempt harm; if their parents will reliably monitor their behavior; and if the clinician will be telephoned immediately if suicidal thoughts re-occur.

Though horrifying in its potential, a suicidal gesture contains an element of hope for it indicates the child, though despairing, still believes help is available and, through this aid, that their life can improve.

Chapter Twenty Five

Psychotherapy for Juvenile Criminal Behavior
"Nobody thinks their kids are going to do these kinds of things but it does happen."
—John Waters, Public Broadcasting System Radio, August 10, 2009
"Jails and juvenile justice facilities are the new asylums"
—Joseph Penn, M.D., Texas Youth Commission

WHILE ON COURTTV, I discussed the painful case of a teenager who had shot up his high school. Thankfully, no one died but there were several serious injuries and the boy was sentenced to forty years in prison. Our discussion concerned the fairness of this very long sentence.

The lawyers said the judge felt that he had no choice: he was not given good enough reasons to justify a lesser sentence. The diagnoses of ADD and depression did not clarify why this boy behaved as he did, unlike many other youth who are similarly described. Simply put, the explanations made no sense.

For this boy to avoid imprisonment, he would have to be declared unable to tell right from wrong at the time of the attack. But before the attack, the boy knew that what he was about to do was wrong. Still, he did it. Why had he behaved so irrationally and destructively?

After reading the many pages of court transcript and news reports which the CourtTV staff faxed to me, I understood the boy's motives. Though appearing normal, this boy was unhappy for a long time and had never received the mental health treatment he needed. From his despair, a murderous thought arose: how to reveal his anger and assert himself even if it ended his life and that of others.

Once this plan was adopted, he could not fail to act for doing so would make him even more of a failure and lower his self-esteem to an intolerable level.

This boy finally did get the mental health treatment he needed—two weeks after beginning his forty year prison sentence when he tried to kill himself.

I considered not writing this chapter for this book is intended to help consumers choose their therapist and in prisons and jails there is no choice. Even for the therapists who work there for they must accept the decisions of the wardens and sheriffs who run these institutions. But then I remembered another experience and decided that this information would be useful to many as they try to safeguard family members.

An eighteen year old was arrested for attempted rape and his parents wanted to be sure that he was OK. The prosecutor, his attorney, and the court welcomed my evaluating him, as they usually did. The more complete and accurate pre-sentencing information which is available, the more appropriate will be the court decision which follows.

I never liked to evaluate people in jail. Not because of the task which, like all initial clinical contacts, is as interesting as solving any complex puzzle. But jails have institutionally painted walls and rigid procedures; and needing permission to enter and leave through multiple locked doors is unpleasant. But the prisoners were always glad to see me. I was a change to their drab routine and one of the few people who really listened to them.

Local jails have bad reputations. While many are deserved, their major discomfort is usually boredom. They hold prisoners serving short sentences (less than a year) or who are awaiting trial. Here, despite the occasional unexpected amenity like evening donuts, there often isn't much to do. No vocational education classes or work exist, though substance abuse groups (Alcoholic Anonymous and Narcotics Anonymous) take up some slack. Visits by attorneys and clinicians are welcome indeed.

Colin, a Young Clean-cut Rapist

I evaluated Colin in early August. Before entering the jail, I witnessed an interesting sight. An attractive blond woman in her twenties wearing an amazingly short skirt stood outside the main door. She had apparently just been released and was unsure where to go. I recognized her as being a frequent patient at the local mental health clinic. Guards and visitors passed her but she stood fixedly, staring at cars which first slowed and then passed.

Finally, the driver of a convertible stopped. He was a local attorney I occasionally sparred with in court when I testified as expert witness for the government. He apparently asked the woman if she wanted a ride, she accepted, and they drove a short distance down the street. The car then stopped and the woman got out. It seemed that one or the other had quickly concluded that further contact was unwise. I smiled, and entered the jail.

Mental health evaluations are usually conducted in the same rooms which lawyers use to speak with their clients. They are small and hold only a small table and two chairs, all bolted to the floor. The clinician or lawyer signs in, states who they wish to interview, and the prisoner is brought to the room.

I wondered what Colin looked like for his crime was bizarre. According to reports, he had tried to rape a woman in a store which he entered half-naked, about noon on a sunny weekday. After his arrest, his girl-friend broke off their relationship but he already had a new one. When he arrived at the room I understood why.

Colin was clean-cut with good looks which belied the criminal stereotype of bulging muscles and tattoos. Because few would resist opening a door or riding in an elevator with such an attractive man, he was a dangerous person.

Before testing Colin with intelligence and personality tests, I questioned him about his life but not about his arrest for his conviction might be appealed. He answered my questions willingly with a friendly smile, until I would press him. Then he became angry very quickly.

Only one of his responses was odd: that he was never angry with his mother, not even after she slapped him. Which, he felt, she had the right to do when he made a mistake. Clearly, the unconscious, rage which Colin felt towards his mother and he couldn't allow himself to express were being acted out towards other women.

Colin was looking forward to his transfer to state prison. There, he would build-up his muscles on the weight lifting equipment and take whatever college level courses they had. While writing my report on Colin, I thought of other handsome, psychologically twisted youth and the horrors they inflicted.

The infamous Ted Bundy, who committed many sexual assaults and murders; and an earlier crime couple. Carl Austin Hall and his paramour, Bonnie Brown Heady. Both grew up with financially comfortable but unloving parents. After squandering their money and following years of alcoholism, they kidnapped a child for a $600,000 ransom. But murder, not money, was their real intention.

"I hate little people," Hall explained, after his arrest. Six year old Bobby Greanlease, with his school medal pinned to his shirt, was shot dead soon after he was taken from school by Heady, allegedly to see his sick mother. The kidnappers were captured and, like Bundy, were executed.

When families think of those who are incarcerated, images of criminals like Bundy and Hall and Heady pass through their mind. But they are the exceptions. More than four million American families have had a member in jail. Some, just briefly, following their arrest for a first DWI or on a minor drug charge, while others spend years being locked away.

Several generalizations can be made: most prisoners are male but the number of females is increasing as is the number of violent offenders; and many prisoners have drug related charges.

There is a constitutional mandate to provide basic services to all prisoners, including food, clothing, shelter, and medical (which includes mental health) care. With the closing of juvenile mental health institutions, the prison system has, unfortunately, become the residence of last resort for many adolescents who are mentally ill. Suicide is a major cause of death in prisons, and particularly in local jails where new, young offenders may become overwhelmed by shame.

Many prisoners who are not mentally ill suffer from alcoholism or drug abuse; and all experience the initial shock of incarceration. Becoming part of a community which is separate from the outside world. A place without personal freedom where doors are automatically locked behind you, behavior is monitored, and inspection is continuous.

For therapy in prison to be effective, it would have to differ depending on the nature of the prisoner. For those who were not mentally ill before their incarceration and will return to society shortly, it would involve providing support and coping skills to enable them to psychologically survive their transformed life. For those who were long emotionally disturbed, the mental health treatment required would be little different from that provided in the community.

But prisons were basically constructed to hold another type of inmate: for punishment and because they are too dangerous to live in society. Their treatment must be very different, for their personalities are unique.

These people live not in our world but in an environment shaped by their values and rules. They do not trust others though demand that they be trusted. They request honesty and safety but feel free to lie, break promises, and harm. They insist that they are independent but rely on others to satisfy their needs. They seek not friendship but to control and use others for their own ends, then to discard them. They like people only when these people agree with them, help them with their plans, or idolize them and thus support their fragile self-esteem.

These people profess love but are incapable of it. They pretend to be tough and deny their many fears, considering these to be weaknesses. Among their fears are: appearing afraid; being caught; and being putdown, which occurs whenever someone does not meet their needs.

Unconsciously, they view themselves in black or white terms ranging from being extremely inferior to possessing grandiose power. When feeling worthless, they may assert themselves by engaging in criminal activity to end this pain. Their continuous but often invisible anger reflects their inability to satisfy their unrealistic exaggerated goals for the notion of hard work is foreign to them. Their inability to behave realistically, to make sound decisions, and to view their own faults rather than to blame others, make them unfit for civil society.

Despite which, these criminals consider themselves to be good and not evil people, for whatever they want to do they believe to be "right." Even their crime, which they view as their job. The criminal sees things so differently from other people that honest conversation is impossible for them since it would force them to cope with their personality inadequacies and the intense pain which would follow this acknowledgment.

When a mentally ill person holds unrealistic views it is because they are not in touch with reality. But the criminal knows what is real, though only in matters apart from themselves. So when they are apparently paranoid, it is because people *are* actually after them.

The therapy required for the criminal differs greatly from that of traditional therapy and is beyond the scope of this book. In fact, because criminals do not consider themselves to be mentally ill, they see therapy as a way to avoid punishment and prison. They will study the therapist while they are being studied, and say only what they believe is valuable: that which is helpful in achieving their goals—which does not involve personal change.

Families who are involved with such relatives must be aware of their gravely distorted personalities. A criminal can change but it is not easy. Yet the difference between major and minor criminal acts and personalities is very great so except for those who have proven to be violent, the possibility of change must always be considered. Still, the prison experience brands all with the same emotional scars.

One hundred and fifty years ago the American Correctional Association established principles to be followed in managing prisons. Among these were: to foster behavior change, not suffering; to preserve the prisoner's self-respect; and to produce free men rather than obedient prisoners.*

Few prisons attempt to model these suggestions. Today's prisons cause more negative than positive change in prisoner behavior, with more people being incarcerated in America each year. Educational and vocational programs in prisons, which might improve the behavior of released felons, range from nonexistent to inadequate**, and many are now being closed because of state financial problems. Even those which occupy a tiny fraction of the corrections budget and lower the recidivism rate drastically..

Separating prisoners with different offenses from each other would be productive but is rarely done because of overcrowding and security concerns. The prison environment, pervaded by distrust, fear, and violence, fosters coercion and reduces a prisoner's dignity. They feel helpless, having little privacy or power to behave independently, thus losing their identity and becoming "a number." A person who must, in the interest of safety, be separated from the majority of society.

The shame which prisoners feel upon their release is maintained by the responses they receive from others when they learn of this event, this adding an additional burden in their attempt to change their lives.

*Menninger, Karl. 1968. *The Crime of Punishment*. New York: Viking Press.
**Wicks, R.J., 1974. *Correctional Psychology: Themes and Problems in Correcting the Offender*. San Francisco: Canfield Press.

Why Children Steal

Children and adolescents steal for a number of reasons and only rarely does this act reflect the criminal reasoning and motives which are described above. Very young children take things because the concept of ownership has no meaning to their immature mind. In their thinking, everything belongs to everybody and if they want something they have a right to it. Only through education do they learn the nature of personal property and come to accept it.

Children also steal to test the boundaries of acceptable behavior and from anger. One angry three year old stole his mother's wedding ring and threw it into the trash. Teenagers may steal from anger too, as part of a group "adventure," or to put things over on adults: shoplifting without getting caught.

Two very pretty teenagers approached a mall's exit, carrying shopping bags filled with stolen clothes. They panicked when a young guard suddenly ran passed and then turned to face them—until he courteously held the door open and, with a big smile, said, "Good afternoon, ladies."

Though this is a funny story and these girls laughed hysterically once reaching their car, they didn't realize that it is far easier to become involved with the legal system than to remove it from their lives. Because of the potentially serious consequences for teenagers who are arrested, stealing behavior should be investigated by a therapist who is experienced with youth.

Chapter Twenty Six

Psychotherapy and Psychological Testing

Although the insights gained from psychological testing have sometimes been described as being "magical," this type of evaluation reflects nothing like magic. It merely uses samples of behavior to make conclusions about an individual. The precursors of today's psychological testing industry reach back two hundred years, to English and German astronomers who wondered about the "personal equation": the individual differences between scientists which caused their measured observations to vary.

Later, Charles Darwin's cousin, Francis Galton, questioned whether the inheritance of genius could be measured and investigated this mathematically, leading to the development of the science of statistics.

A few years later the foremost figure in the history of psychological testing, Alfred Binet, noted the changes in children's intellectual abilities as they develop. He attempted to devise a group of tasks, or a test, to distinguish normal children from those who were unable to benefit from traditional French education and would require special schooling. Based on his work the first intelligence test was devised in 1905. A much revised edition, the Stanford-Binet, is used today and considered among the best of all psychological tests.

In contrast to such complex psychological entities as intelligence and personality, beginning during World War

One measurements began to be made of distinct functions like mechanical aptitudes and particular behaviors. Woodworth's Personal Data Sheet measured the adjustment of soldiers to life in the American army.

Today, psychological testing is widely used in schools, the government, personnel departments, marketing and political research agencies, and private clinical practice to answer important questions. Is this person suitable for the job? Should they be promoted? Is this person emotionally stable or likely to collapse under the stress of their government duties? Why is this child performing so poorly in school? What type of person is more likely to buy a product or vote for a candidate holding a particular position? Is this person legally insane or are they capable of standing trial? All of this information can be gained, most accurately and rapidly, by using psychological tests.

A psychological test is a group of highly structured tasks or questions which are presented to the subject in a rigidly prescribed manner. The value of any test is determined by the extent to which it produces adequate, accurate results. Tests must have a high *validity* and *reliability* to be useful.

The validity of a test is the degree to which a test measures what it intends to measure. Thus if the military wants to identify recruits who would become good fighter pilot from those who would wash out of aviation training, will this test distinguish between these groups more quickly and economically than actually training them and seeing what happened. While no test is perfect, it must be better than the alternative, more expensive and lengthier method of selection.

Using this example, the value or *predictive validity* of a test can be statistically determined by correlating ("co-relating" or contrasting) the scores on this test which were made by successful and unsuccessful flight trainees. Similarly, to determine the usefulness of tests intended to measure academic performance, the Scholastic Achievement Test (SAT) or Graduate Record Exam (GRE) student test scores are compared with their later academic records.

While no test has perfect validity, each being a work in progress, it must enable better (more economical, easier) prediction than not using it. Thus a test with a low validity might sometimes be used but only if it would be better than trying to predict performance without it.

This is not true of a test's *reliability* which indicates the degree to which, when repeated, the test will provide similar results. An unreliable test, one which provides results subject to random influences, is, by its nature, too inadequate to be useful for these scores apparently have little to do with what is intended to be measured.

So not every test is good, and because it is printed, published, or even widely used means nothing. An early inadequate example is the Szondi test which consists of six sets for a total of forty eight photographs of people in European psychiatric hospitals. The task is to choose which two photographs in each set is most liked and disliked, the theory being that there will be a similarity between those chosen and the subject's genes or hereditary tendency.

Two broad categories of psychological tests are *objective tests,* in which answers are restricted such as having to be true or false; and *projective tests,* which allow for a freer response. Objective tests, which include the widely used Minnesota Multiphasic Personality Inventory (MMPI) and the Strong Vocational Interest Test, consist of conventional appearing questions. Projective tests like the Rorschach Psychodiagnostics and the Thematic Apperception Test have unfamiliar tasks and require subjects to relate to ambiguous colored forms or drawings of people.

Both types of tests require much training to be interpreted accurately. Like with all assessment instruments, a poor interpretation results in inaccurate conclusions being made. While the findings from psychological testing can be invaluable, those from invalid tests or unskilled examiners can destroy a person's future.

The quality and results of psychological testing varies as widely as that of psychotherapy. Once, at a major medical school, the new Director of Psychiatry downplayed the usefulness of psychological testing until he began reading the reports. Thereafter, the psychological test results were considered to be *the* diagnostic conclusion, and psychiatrists in training were not permitted access to them until after they presented *their* reports.

The results of an intelligence test should contain both the actual test scores and the estimated *intellectual potential* of the subject. All psychological testing involves basic assumptions: that the person taking the test is emotionally and physically healthy, has shared the common culture, and is motivated to do their best. If any of these is absent, the results do not indicate the person's true potential. A person who is emotionally conflicted or sleepy or ill or has a hearing or visual limitation will not be performing in line with their ability, and a report giving only the achieved score will be inaccurate.

For example, consider a test with ten questions, each of increasing difficulty so that question ten is more difficult than question nine and the first question is the easiest. A person can gain a score of five by correctly answering questions six through ten or questions one through five though the abilities or knowledge reflected by the identical score of five are vastly different in the two situations.

Thus whenever an intelligence test is administered both the person's present level of intellectual functioning and their intellectual potential should be declared.

The intellectual potential can be determined by treating the test as a clinical measure. Looking at each failed question and deciding whether it reflected emotional conflict, a neurological limitation, a cultural or physical factor, or if it was an accurate measure of the person's intellectual capacity. Doing this requires a level of clinical sophistication which is rarely found in schools, and why this critical estimate is so often absent from their reports, which are increasingly being produced by computer software.

Apart from business and the government, psychological testing is most useful in four clinical circumstances: when it is considered that a person might be intellectually limited; when it is believed that neurological impairment may exist; during a court proceeding when crucial decisions are made and the most extensive information about a person is required; and when an adequate diagnosis cannot be made through the clinical interview alone (for example, of one who is unable to speak).

Nowadays, psychological testing is uncommon during outpatient therapy. Partly because managed care companies reimburse this lengthy process poorly, but mostly because enough information can ordinarily be gained through the interview process.

When psychological testing is recommended, it is important to ask why. If the situation does not fall within the above four categories, and the therapist still insists on its necessity, gaining a second clinical opinion should be considered. And, at the risk of belaboring the obvious, the skill of the psychologist performing the testing is crucially important.

Chapter Twenty Seven

Psychotherapy and Religious Belief

THE CONFLICT BETWEEN RELIGION and psychology is relatively recent, perhaps because psychology is so new. Traditionally, religion battled astronomers in the seventeenth century, physicists in the eighteenth century, and biologists for the next hundred years. Thereafter, despite such exceptions as the eminent early twentieth century psychiatrist, Adolph Meyer, most mental health workers were hostile towards religion.

Religious ritual was termed pagan and believers were described as neurotic. The concept of heaven was considered a disguised sex dream; and the notion of religion to have originated in "the general laziness of mankind."

The interests of religion and psychology merged gradually as both became concerned with alienation and anxiety, and Christianity turned from studying the Bible to the inner life of Jesus and how people might share it on a personal level.

The later rise of the existential psychology movement in the nineteen fifties brought increased attention to anxiety, courage, and freedom, ideas which many religions could embrace. This led to the current reconciliation between clerics and mental health practitioners, who see themselves as viewing identical critical topics but from different perspectives.

There is no inherent conflict between religion and psychotherapy for they deal with dissimilar issues. Religion, with morality and the meaning of life; psychotherapy, with psychological healing leading to increased self-control, which is needed to thoughtfully follow any religious teaching.

Over the years I have treated mainstream Protestant ministers and their children, a rabbi's teenage daughter and, as part of Catholic Church requirement, once evaluated an older man seeking the annulment of his marriage. I have treated Evangelical Christian and Muslim children; and did marital counseling with an Irish Catholic couple whose presenting conflict was the wife's religious conversion. Only once was a patient's religious belief significant: during an adolescent therapy group when a seventeen year's old desire to begin dating like the other group members conflicted with her Jehovah Witness affiliation.

Religion, which traditionally has been concerned with the healing of bodies and souls, allied itself to psychotherapy early in its development. The Emmanuel movement began in Boston in 1906, spread widely, and trained clergy in psychotherapy to heal their troubled parishioners.

As psychoanalytic and behavioral psychology ideas influenced seminaries, the field of pastoral psychology arose and became more professional. H. Flanders Dunbar, a physician and influential founder of the field of psychosomatic medicine which views some medical difficulties as being intertwined with emotions, arose from the pastoral counseling tradition.

Pastoral counseling changed over the years. At first it was hostile towards psychotherapy though using some of its insights on human behavior in its traditional pastorate role. Later, it fully accepted the validity and value of psychoanalytic tenets and a cooperative spirit arose between clinicians and clerics.

Both now spoke of aloneness and isolation, with pastoral counselors viewing their role as enabling people to gain enough freedom from their emotional problems to be able to choose a healthier lifestyle. For clerics this included gaining a stronger, more mature faith; for traditional psychotherapists, the element of faith was absent.

Despite this conflict, both professions share important goals and beliefs though to different degrees: the possibility of experiencing a profoundly meaningful conversion; how to confront such human dilemmas as guilt and illness and death; and the desirability of expanding the human potential. Moreover, both fields of practice will forever be allied in the ongoing human struggle against irrationality and the occult, for all share the elements of mystery and transcendence.

The capacity to relate to these specifically human experiences are ingrained into the human psyche and enable them to deal with experiences which are on the fringe of their capacities and sometimes beyond: birth and death; conversion; and the encounter with extraordinary goodness or evil. When forced to recognize these human limitations, people feel weak and inadequate and look beyond themselves, no longer feeling as the center of the universe. With this shift they may experience a power greater than themselves and a sense of self-affirmation during which they experience awe and bliss. They may even, possibly, sense the Holy.

Considering these experiences to be illusions is doing them a disservice for, as Freud has written, they fulfill the "oldest, strongest and most urgent wishes of mankind," adding that illusions need not be false or unachievable.*

The most important function of the concept of God has been considered to make man feel finite.**

There are other important differences between pastoral counseling and traditional psychotherapy. Pastoral counseling tends to be supportive and short-term, reality oriented and focusing on real life concerns in the present using the patient's existing psychological capacities. Psychotherapy deals with deeper, longer lasting, primarily unconscious difficulties, and seeks to change basic psychological structures through support, questioning, and interpretation.

Moreover, while psychotherapy is a unique profession, pastoral counseling is part of something else. For example, with alcohol counseling, the primary focus is the abuse of alcohol with the treatment of other issues being additional to this.

*Freud, Sigmund, *The Future of An Illusion*, 1927.
**Mead, S.E., In Quest of America's Religion, *The Christian Century*, 87, 752-756.

Similarly, intrinsic to all pastoral counseling is the concern with religion and morality, the need to gain meaning and a fixed star in life even if, often, this goes unspoken and religious terms are absent. And the views of pastoral counselors are public, unlike traditional psychotherapists who keep theirs private.

People seeking pastoral counseling often wish to apply their religious convictions to the dilemma and pain they face: whether to end an affair; or how to simultaneously love and relinquish a dying child. Though, because of the separateness between the cleric's priestly and counseling functions, prayers and sacraments are only rarely conducted during their counseling duties.

The most basic difference between the pastoral counselor and the psychotherapist was perhaps best described by the psychiatrist Victor Frankl, a survivor of the Holocaust: "The religious man differs from the apparently irreligious man only by experiencing his existence not only as a task, but as a mission. This means that he is also aware of the taskmaster, the source of his mission. For thousands of years that source has been called God."*

*Frankl, Victor, 1973, *The Doctor and the Soul: From Psychotherapy to Logotherapy*. New York: Vintage, p.xiv.

Chapter Twenty Eight

Brief Psychotherapy

ONE CRITICISM OF PSYCHOTHERAPY is that it lasts too long. For most medical illnesses, physicians will be consulted once or twice and then not seen again for a year or two. This is why the patient roster of medical doctors is hundreds of times larger than that of psychotherapists. Yet the most frequent number of psychotherapy sessions for all patients is just one and some medical patients are seen weekly or more often.

So the crucial questions are: which mental health difficulties are emergencies and require immediate treatment; which can sensibly be treated by personal, watchful waiting; and which require only brief treatment. But about even these there is dispute. Not the definition of true emergencies but that of brief treatment which, for the purposes of this chapter, will be defined as one session per week of psychotherapy for less than six months.

When Behavior Requires Immediate Evaluation

The behaviors which demand immediate evaluation are thoughts and behaviors which greatly impair normal functioning or those which contain a significant health risk. Suicidal or homicidal behavior, eating disorders such as anorexia nervosa or bulimia, alcohol or drug abuse, potentially dangerous social behavior such as teenagers going off with strangers they met on the Internet. In short, any persisting thought or behavior which can have life threatening consequences.

Other symptoms can be puzzled over alone or through discussion with friends. These include frightening dreams, feeling anxious or depressed, obsessive thoughts, or such compulsive behavior as sorting things or compulsively cleaning. Any seemingly odd behavior which is temporary and does not involve a health risk. These symptoms arise in times of heightened stress and will naturally disappear when the stress diminishes. If desired, the scheduling of one session with a therapist to learn about the healthy role of these symptoms may be comforting, but it is not necessary. Particularly since in doing so, by following the procedure required to become "a patient," the stress will initially be increased and it will soon go away on its own. Just like most people get over the ordinary cold without medical attention.

But if the symptom lasts longer than a month then, just as with persisting cold symptoms, professional advice should be sought.

When Is Brief Psychotherapy Enough?

What distinguishes small from greater mental health difficulties, and thus the need for brief as contrasted with longer therapy, is the state of the person's life. Do they function well in their daily tasks but have one specific problem: communication difficulty with their boss or spouse or child; being unable to choose their vocation even after consulting a school counselor; having difficulty balancing their work and personal lives. Some problems which initially appear to require lengthy treatment can be helped in just a few sessions.

Anita First Attempts Suicide, Then Calls Me

I had just entered my office and turned on the auxiliary electric heaters. Keeping the office warm was a constant problem which neither I or the other tenants had been able to resolve in our small commercial complex. The buildings were constructed in stages and on cold windy days the heat seemed to evaporate. So, to supplement the propane heat which was supplied by the landlord, I placed heaters in every room. For twenty-two years, every month before it came time to renew my lease, I vowed to find another office but had remained. Apart from the heating issue, the office met my professional needs.

It was very quiet, and repairs were done quickly by the landlord, who lived nearby. And it was convenient, being on a major road, and liked by my patients who preferred its apartment like structure to the sterility of medical offices. But the office was still cold when Anita phoned and spoke her chilling words: "I tried to kill myself yesterday. I need to make an appointment."

Anita had overdosed on Xanax following an argument with Ross, her husband. Their fights were now frequent for there were financial issues, child-rearing disagreements, and problems with relatives. They began dating in high school and married soon after graduation.

Ross owned an auto repair shop and made good money. Anita intended to attend college until she became pregnant with her first son and three more soon followed. At twenty-six, Anita found herself the mother of four young boys, which is not easy. Most mothers consider girls easier to parent. This is generally but now always true. Over the years I had treated several girls who would give any boy a run for their money. Still, boys are more active and more likely to get into trouble.

So Anita had her hands full, having to spend all day with her sons and provide them the continual attention they demanded, just like all young children do. She shopped to relax. Not purchasing extravagances for she typically dressed in jeans and shirts and had no interest in jewelry. And what she bought was *sometimes* needed, though Ross never could understand her need to collect frog figurines.

As the balances on their credit cards increased, the family's finances deteriorated. Anita and Ross argued more frequently and, late one evening, he screamed: "You're a worthless mother. Why don't you kill yourself. I'd take care of the kids alone better than you!" Whereupon Anita fled to the bathroom and swallowed the remaining Xanax in the bottle. Then, horrified by what she did, she told Ross.

Both rushed to the local hospital's Emergency Room where the staff knew what might happen: sleepiness and confusion, followed by the slowing of reflexes and coordination problems. After which came difficulty breathing, coma, and death. But the doctor and nurse did their job well. They pumped Anita's stomach, added fluid through an intravenous line, and agreed to release her, but only after she promised to call a therapist the next day.

The embarrassment and discomfort of the medical treatment aroused Anita's vow that she would never again attempt suicide. Her symptoms—depression and suicide attempt, low self-esteem, impulsive behavior—are usually considered to require far longer treatment than the seven therapy sessions she needed.

During our meetings I first spoke alone with Anita and then with she and Ross together. We discussed her long-term unhappiness and impulsiveness, the stress of parenting, and the communication problems in their marriage—which was unlikely to end despite what Ross had said. Neither had ever dated another person and both loved each other and wanted to stay together, though their sex life had diminished greatly since their communication problems began. Moreover, their children were developing well and were simply healthy and boisterous.

By the seventh session, Anita had made plans to begin college part-time, Ross was helping more with household chores, and a three day family vacation went well. Once, when Anita refused to have sex, he now understood why she was angry.

Anita's therapy was successful and her symptoms disappeared. What enabled her to change so quickly? How do the techniques used in brief psychotherapy differ from those found in longer treatment?

The length of treatment required depends on three factors: the nature of the presenting problems; the psychological strengths of the patient; and practical issues such as whether there is a supportive environment. Financial stability too is important, for a person who has lost their job or may soon lose their home has little energy to devote to personal change.

Anita had good psychological strengths. Despite the impulsive streak which was revealed by her suicidal act, she was a good, reliable mother and her four children were well cared for. She also had a good sense of who she was, and possessed the capacity for love and intimacy. The sexual problem in her marriage, which began two years earlier, reflected the couple's communication difficulty and not deeper issues. Moreover, her husband strongly supported her therapy, and attended all of the sessions.

Ross participated fully and was receptive to his wife's criticism and my comments. These caused him to view their interaction differently and to change his behavior. With this marital improvement, the couple quickly stabilized their financial situation. Anita again began paying their bills as she had done earlier in their marriage; and Ross learned where their income was going rather than just complaining about it. Both took pride in the successful raising of their children.

Two factors distinguish the techniques used in brief treatment: the activity of the therapist, and whether specific conflicts can be rapidly identified and quickly resolved. During short-term therapy the therapist quickly identifies treatment goals from all that the patient says, and provides continual interpretations and emotional support consistent with the patient's strengths.

This "active attention" is in contrast with the "evenly suspended attention" which prevails in the longest mental health treatment of psychoanalysis. Moreover, the short-term therapist chooses several conflicts to work on and focuses attention on these, following the philosophy that change in the central difficulties will positively influence spontaneous change in the patient's entire personality. And while psychoanalysis depends on the therapist's interpretations to effect personality change, short-term therapy relies far more on confronting, clarifying, and reflecting back to the patient for study, their thoughts, behavior, and feelings. One feature of short-term therapy is the giving of direct suggestions to support the patient's judgment, a technique which is virtually never used in psychoanalysis.

Optimism too is an important factor. That the therapist continually communicate to the patient their positive outlook, their view that the therapy is timely but not timeless.

The therapist's role is to be a temporary helper, not a lifelong parent to be adopted by the patient. With each success in overcoming difficulties, the patient becomes readier to end therapy. They have become more optimistic about their capacity to make future changes on their own, and developed the process to do so which will persist long after therapy is over.

Short and long term treatment techniques are not opposites but lay on a continuum. More complex difficulties, those existing for many years and consisting of significant psychological weaknesses, are not amenable to short-term therapy. Misdiagnosing one for the other situation can do harm by causing the therapist to fail to offer that treatment which the patient requires when they are most receptive to it.

Chapter Twenty Nine

Getting Your Psychotherapy Over the Internet or by Telephone

TRAVELING TO A THERAPIST'S OFFICE is often not easy. Particularly for those with physical limitations or who live in suburban or rural areas where travel time and cost are important factors. There, specialized treatment may not even be available. With the increased availability of high speed communication, offering psychotherapy over the Internet and by phone has been considered. Because of staff shortage, the Texas Youth Commission allows video conferences between mental health personnel and youth in their prison system.*

Why would anyone object to a practice which frees them from the need for travel. How is this different from working at home, which many people already do? But conducting psychotherapy by phone or computer has significant drawbacks.

*"Mentally Ill Offenders Strain Juvenile System," *The New York Times*, August 10, 2009.

A seriously disturbed teenager, who was receiving high dosages of several psychotropic medications, was graduating from high school. She was very talented and wanted to attend one of the few American colleges offering a major in her field. Because this school was thousands of miles away, I didn't think it was a good choice. I suggested to her parents that she continue living at home, receive therapy, and attend a fine nearby college for two years. She could then transfer to the other school. But their daughter was adamant and my suggestion was rejected. Her parents asked that I continue to treat her by phone while she was away. I refused and gave some of the reasons which I describe in this chapter.

While providing emotional support for current therapy patients over the phone or by mail has long existed, treating new patients similarly is controversial and of dubious legality. I tell all patients to feel free to phone me whenever they feel the need. Despite this offer, most of the calls which I receive are merely to make or change appointments. Knowing that you can get immediate help reduces the need to do so.

Sometimes a rapid telephone response is important even if the situation is not a true emergency. A child has a temper tantrum lasting an hour. A couple's loud argument has brought the police to their home who wonder if their child is safe being with them. A man feels distraught following the latest argument with his wife. A father reports that his teenage son is standing on the balcony and threatening suicide. A mother is upset about her five year old's puzzling behavior.

Of these calls, only that involving the suicidal teenager and the police required immediate advice, though the information and reassurance which I provided to the others was certainly valued. But in all these calls I knew the patient and, if they were a child, had already spoken with one or both of their parents.

Yet, sound advice can be provided without prior contact. I have given free, general advice over the Internet to strangers and treatment suggestions to worried psychologists on several professional Internet sites.

Experienced therapists, after just telephone contact with a prospective patient and particularly when the issue concerns a child, can usually diagnose the problem and treatment which will be needed with some degree of certainty. But without further information from the patient in-person, the therapist cannot be certain of the patient's psychological strengths and limitations and this information is crucial to providing adequate, safe treatment.

Providing mental health services online is as old as the Internet itself. Nearly twenty-five years ago psychologists at several universities began a mailing list to share information about mental health issues. With the development of the World Wide Web browser in 1993 the availability of online mental health information and support groups greatly increased.

Some sites offer the opportunity to ask personal questions anonymously, to be answered online like on radio call-in shows. While the commercialization of Internet therapy with payment by credit card has been offered, this practice usually distinguishes itself from "real" therapy. Despite which it has drawn criticism, and for the same reasons that online therapy by traditional clinicians has failed to expand: because of privacy and licensing issues, and from ethical concerns.

Few use encryption for E-mail since doing so is not easy. Yet without it, E-mail has less confidentiality than sending information on a postcard since copies of E-mail remain on Internet servers, available to anyone with a valid subpoena or password cracking skills. Internet corporate employees may read personal E-mails under broadly interpretable conditions, this consent being given automatically when a person signed up for the E-mail service.

Few would feel comfortable having their most personal information, in E-mail and video formats, residing in perpetuity on corporate servers. All being available for instant access by—just exactly who?

Scandals involving political and business figures have already occurred. Recently, an American governor's E-mail communication with his Argentinian lover was leaked to newspapers and gained international readership. While movingly written, the notes caused significant personal and political repercussions.

During conventional in-person therapy there is only one copy of notes and these are kept locked. Information cannot be provided without the patient's written consent. So unless a patient speaks of their therapy, no one else will know of it. While there are circumstances under which a therapist can break confidentiality (broadly speaking, when another person is endangered), in actual practice this rarely happens. A therapist who violates a patient's privacy can lose their license whereas an Internet company behaving similarly receives, at worst, brief and usually unnoticed bad publicity.

Moreover, if an Internet company changes ownership then all that they possess, including server copies of your E-mail or video communication and your personal information, is suddenly transferred, and to a company you may never have heard of.

The professional licensing issues which need to be resolved before therapy can be offered over the Internet are even more complex. At present there is no federal licensing of health care workers. All regulation is done by the states, creating fifty different sets of regulations. Which makes little difference to most therapists who usually practice in only one state and are licensed there, though some therapists do become licensed in several states. If working near a state border, it is entirely proper to see the residents of that state for treatment. The patient accepts that the licensing laws of the therapist's state will govern their transaction.

But a therapist cannot legally provide services in another state without first being licensed there, though there are exceptions. Some states permit a therapist who is licensed in another state to practice to a limited degree in their state, perhaps for several hours a month. But this depends on state regulations, which vary widely.

Providing psychotherapy is a legally regulated health service, no different from performing a dental extraction or a gall bladder removal. While these cannot be done online, psychotherapy can. Yet which state's laws governs the practice? That state where the therapist works or where the patient lives? Which state should the patient complain to if they are dissatisfied with their treatment? At present, there is no clear answer.

Because the legal and regulatory issues remain unresolved, providing psychological services over the Internet, apart from the offering of free, general mental health information, has not taken off.

Even what seems a simple requirement—how an Internet therapist should behave when they confront a homicidal threat—remains murky. While rarely encountered, this situation can have great consequences. Yet the state court rulings which govern it differ. Responding to a patient's online suicidal threat is an equally complex matter.

Therapists would try to screen out patients who present a suicidal or homicidal risk but this is not always successful. And while the stress on a therapist who confronts one of these situations in their office is great, it would be far worse when this crisis must be dealt with online. Within a fluid, rapidly changing situation where the therapist may lack such critical information as the patient's home address, and where the continuous in-person contact with a suicidal or homicidal patient, which is required professionally, cannot exist.

Once, in a psychiatric day hospital program, a patient telephoned and threatened suicide. Only then did the staff discover that while they had this patient's post office box mailing address, they lacked his home address to which they could send the police. After frantic minutes, the address was obtained from the patient's employer. If such an event could occur at this highly regulated major hospital setting, consider the consequences of what might occur online where therapy transactions are unregulated. For these reasons, at present, it is safest that therapy be sought not over a telephone line or on the Internet but in a therapist's office.

Chapter Thirty

The Cost and Value of Therapy

No ONE WILL ARGUE that psychotherapy is not costly though it is far less expensive than other life changing interventions such as heart surgery. The cost of psychotherapy derives from two factors: that the training required to become a therapist is extensive, and because the field was developed by a physician, Sigmund Freud, and medical fees have always been high. Had Freud been a store clerk, therapy fees might be lower.

The usual manner of payment, fee for service, can also lead to problems. Therapists, like most people, value a stable income and some keep patients longer than is necessary. But this is no different from physicians who prescribe unnecessary MRIs because they own the machine. In a perfect world these unethical tendencies would not exist or could be managed through means similar to when one buys a car.

Before entering a dealership, most purchasers become fully informed about the car they are interested in: its good points and limitations, available options and price; and suitable models of competing brands. Many buyers are better informed than the auto salesperson. But when purchasing psychotherapy, the situation is different. Here, the typical patient knows little or nothing about what they are buying with few even knowing the difference between a psychologist and a psychiatrist.

But even if the prospective therapy patient has done their research and is informed, they are usually unsure of the nature of their difficulties except in general terms: "I'm not happy." "My marriage is rocky." "My son is driving me crazy." Moreover, anxiety may prevent them from thinking clearly and trusting their perceptions which, because of their distress, may be temporarily awry.

Thus whatever a therapist advises will tend to be accepted, and the patient will usually be provided the kind of treatment which the therapist offers or until its failure becomes evident. Though this may reflect not the clinician's lack of ethics but their ignorance of other treatments and what is really needed.

A therapist who is trained to provide a particular type of treatment values it, has had teachers they idealized who also valued it, and so naturally believes that *their* method of treatment is best. Which it likely is, for particular problems and patients. The therapist's self-interest may also prejudice their belief in the greater benefit of longer or more frequent treatment. A recommendation which is not always selfish for more intensive treatment is sometimes needed;

Another confusing factor in choosing a therapist is when therapists present themselves as being expert on many conditions regardless of their training or experience. This would cause only the most supremely confident patient, who lacks similar knowledge, to question them.

Were the job of psychotherapist just highly paid and status laden, many more people would enter the field. Instead, relatively few do, perhaps sensing the difficulties of the work. There is a high rate of suicide among mid-life psychiatrists,* higher than the general population.**

Therapists work alone for long hours, and the anguish of their patients often accompanies them home for none can really relax while a patient's crisis remains unresolved. Because therapists are isolated from healthy people, their view of the world may become distorted and increase their distress.

After working in a private hospital for six months, spending my days with very disturbed adolescents and fellow clinicians, I found that my perception of acceptable behavior had become distorted. What I would earlier have regarded as bizarre (as, a social worker flipping a light switch on and off upon entering a meeting), I still viewed critically, but now with disinterest.

Even with healthier patients, and most adult patients do function well in the world, the role of the therapist is a peculiarly difficult one. They must be warm and concerned, yet remain distant and apart. Freely and continually discussing their patient's most personal concerns but never revealing their own, being forbidden greater intimacy by law and ethics.

*Rosen, D.H., Suicide Rates Among Psychiatrists, *JAMA*, 224 (2), 246-7, 1973.
**Ross, Matthew: Suicide Among Physicians: A Psychological Study, *Disorders of the Nervous System.*, 34 (3); 145-50, 1973.

This special relationship, one which is unnatural yet healing for the patient, demands continuous separation and frustration for the therapist. A difficult task indeed, but there are compensations.*

Effective therapists view themselves as functioning in accord with the best in their nature: being warm and accepting, non-judgmental and ever-available by phone. The ideal parent which, like all people, they never had.

Their therapy office becomes a microcosm of how a truly good world could be. One in which distinctions like race and religion and ethnic background are immaterial A place where people are provided the opportunity to change and become the better person they would like to be. A place of refuge which is apart from the world but of it; and where a special type of caring, one which is non-intimate but healing, can be gained.

Life After Therapy

Erik: A Soldier Returns To His War At Home

Erik came to believe that to function best in combat he had to accept that he was already dead, and to operate without compassion or remorse. Several years after leaving the military he was still struggling. Not against the bullets or hidden bombs which became a familiar experience, but from attempting to separate from his desperately unhappy marriage. Now in its twenty first year, their relationship had been rocky from its start.

---

*An excellent treatment of this issue is in the book by Sheldon Heath, M.D., *Dealing With the Therapist's Vulnerability to Depression*, 1991, Jason Aronson: Northvale, New Jersey.

He and his wife, Andrea, hated each other when they first met in kindergarten. But it was hard to avoid her since they lived three houses apart and their parents were friends. In the fourth grade he hit her with a snowball and lost TV privileges for a week.

Four years later, while their parents socialized upstairs, Erik and Andrea watched Indiana Jones on the basement TV and explored sex on the couch. After which they became inseparable: doing homework together; attending family dinners; even going to church though neither was a believer.

Unaware that their children were sexually active, the parents approved of their friendship. The teenagers encouraged each other academically and with their future plans. Erik, after ROTC in college, wanted to become a career Army officer while Andrea planned to be a nurse.

They married the week after college graduation and had three children over the next four years. Two were girls, the youngest was a boy, and it was he who always seemed to be in trouble.

At first the parents blamed their marital problems on him; later they cursed the separations caused by Erik's Army career. Finally they realized the truth: that, over the years, they had grown apart and become more friends than lovers, as was evidenced by their non-existent sex life.

After twenty years, Erik left the army and began working for a military contractor. There was much he had to learn about civilian life, and dating too. Erik had never learned to date, having grown up both socially and sexually with Andrea. Though affairs do exist in the military, they are a bad career risk and one he never tried.

Erik learned to date by attending Parents Without Partners meetings and local dances. Soon he found himself being pursued by several women. Once, while in the hospital, he was visited by two of them simultaneously. Each was attentive to him and glared at the other.

Separating from his marriage wasn't as easy. It rarely is. Erik and Andrea fought over the usual issues: alimony, visitation, and child support. Previously they lived in army housing, shopped at the PX, and had their children attend the military's excellent schools. Now they had to pay two high rents, and battle with school personnel who are sometimes less than supportive of struggling families. Despite which Erik, who was my patient, did his best by Andrea. He paid child support on time, tried not to argue with her, and even gave her money for her advanced nursing certification education.

Still, Andrea became increasingly angry with Erik. She was unwilling to accept that the man she grew up with was now leading a separate life—and with other women too. So Andrea interfered with Erik's visits with their children.

I treated Erik for several years. When it ended, he said that he felt something dramatic should happen at his last therapy session. It seemed too ordinary. After he left my office, I decided what to do. Two days later, Erik received a FedEx delivery from me: a huge chocolate cookie with icing which read, "Happy Graduation."

Erik's feelings are not unusual. Therapy, particularly that which lasts more than several months, is an intense experience. Leaving it is emotionally like experiencing a divorce for only with one's spouse, and less often with a friend or parent or sibling, has a person risked speaking so openly about their true feelings. This is possible because of the neutrality and professionalism of the therapist. Meetings which, ideally, will end only when they are no longer productive and further personal growth is impossible.

What happens in therapy is analogous to what occurs in the best friendships and marriages. If a therapist is accurately attuned to their patient, their relationship acts as a catalyst and fosters healthy personality change. But when communication difficulty exists, barriers are created. Growth stops, frustration and anger build, and the relationship ends. Or not, if explanation and understanding follow.

"You thought that I was putting you down like your parents did when you were a child." "You went on vacation when I needed you and I felt that you didn't care." Simple words and elementary interpretations like these can have great effect within a warm, trusting relationship. Because, ideally, this always occurs in psychotherapy, it is through this special relationship that change is most likely to occur.

Both Erik and Andrea remarried and, as their children grew, eventually became the good friends that they had once been. Which is what can happen after therapy ends too. Not the common attributes of friendship such as sharing meals, for such are forbidden to therapists by their professional code. Instead, that more rare and valuable experience: realizing the accurate nature of the other and what really happened in their relationship. Misunderstood communications which were resolved, or not. Frailties and fears being spoken of, or remaining hidden.

Interpretations during therapy must occur within a relationship during which a deep understanding of feelings and longings exist. For only through this can a person's sense of self, their personality, be transformed, and their openness to new, healthier, and more fulfilling experiences occur.*

This is particularly important for those who experienced severe emotional derailments in childhood. Thereafter, they will be prone to anxiety and depression, and tend to be easily led by others. Their inaccurate perceptions and poorly articulated feelings may even result in medical problems: headaches, skin conditions, an immune disorder, or worse.

Through therapy, the tapestry of life becomes rewoven: nightmares disappear, and trauma linger as only faint memories. But therapy is not magic. Each person solves their problems as best they can, each process of life remains individual.

Freud advised that therapy can grant not happiness but only the gift of experiencing ordinary misery as life becomes simpler, unhindered by powerful, unconscious motives. By gaining better control over these, a person becomes more open to experiences and more likely to fulfill their needs.

*Atwood, G.E., & Stolorow, R.D., 1984, *Structures of Subjectivity: Explorations in psychoanalytic phenomenology.* Hillsdale, NJ: Analytic Press.

Ingrid, as Child and Woman

I first treated Ingrid for several years, after the death of her twin brother when she was five years old. Later, as an adolescent, she returned to therapy when she dropped out of high school. Ingrid was a highly intelligent girl who struggled with an abusive alcoholic father but had a dedicated mother for support.

Ingrid returned to school, battled her problems, and was days from graduating—until a teacher insisted that she had failed to hand in an assignment and could not graduate. Ingrid and her mother pleaded with the teacher, and her mother appealed to the principal and the school superintendent. But they held firm and the teacher wouldn't budge. Ingrid became very depressed, went home, and cried.

But her mother had not given up. That next day, Friday, she returned to the school and again argued with the principal and school superintendent, losing her voice in the process. Finally, they relented: Ingrid could graduate with her class if she handed in the missing report on Monday.

Ingrid worked all weekend and handed in the assignment. Then she ran to the stadium where her class was practicing the graduation ceremony. When they saw her, knowing of her suffering, practice stopped while all three hundred students spontaneously chanted "Ingrid Ingrid Ingrid" and teachers began crying. When Ingrid's mother told me this story, my eyes were wet too.

Ingrid got a part-time job at which she worked faithfully; and attended college with increasing commitment while going from bad boyfriends to better ones. Just before her twenty-third birthday I heard that she had given birth to a girl, an event which pleased both she and her husband who earlier seemed not to have been a good choice. But, Ingrid's mother reflected, he loved her deeply and had been driven nearly crazy by her daughter's difficult behavior. Which we struggled with too.

Ingrid's ambition, she once told me, was to use up her body by the time she was old. Or, in the words of Dylan Thomas, "Do not go gentle into that good night. Rage, rage against the dying of the light."

Therapists deal with the "real dark night of the soul...(when)...it is always three o'clock in the morning."* They explore issues of shame and guilt, innocence and awareness, failure and triumph, pain and loss. Including the great questions: Why has my life become as it is? How much can it change? Or, more simply, why me?

Answers which can only come in time, for they first need to be lived. Through life the answers may come, or not, and a crucial task of the psychotherapist is to encourage hope. The conviction that, despite despair and disappointment, strength exists and can prevail. "Tho' much is taken, much abides...heroic hearts, Made weak by time and fate, but strong in will."**

*F. Scott Fitzgerald
**Tennyson, *Ulysses*

Thus, above all, the psychotherapist must foster the patient's expectation that they will achieve a brighter dawn: that "the darkness shall be the light, and the stillness the dancing."*

*T.S. Eliot, *East Coker*

Appendix: Dictionary of Common Mental Health Terms
(Explained in Greater Detail in the Text)

Anorexia Nervosa: the psychological disturbance with the highest death rate, characterized by restricted eating leading to a body weight less than eighty-five percent of normal, caused by severely distorted body and self-images.

Anxiety: The uncomfortable sensations which the mind creates when it senses danger. Ideally, anxiety would be analyzed and not feared for it is analogous to another normal physical signal, bodily fever which occurs when infection exists.

Attention Deficit Disorder (ADD): a description of behavior which, contrary to popular belief, explains nothing, it only indicating that a person has difficulty paying attention. This diagnosis is often accompanied by a pseudo explanation which exhibits circular reasoning: the statement that a person has a problem concentrating because they have Attention Deficit Disorder which is evidenced by their problem concentrating.

Bipolar Disorder: behavior which varies between depression and euphoria, the inappropriate feeling of happiness being a defense against the painful underlying depression. An *adult* diagnosis which has been incorrectly applied to children and teenagers..

Bulimia Nervosa: a psychological disturbance often associated with stress, characterized by binge eating followed by exercise or vomiting or the taking of laxatives to compensate for the increase in calories.

Conduct Disorder: persistent, severe oppositional or defiant behavior which may include criminal activity.

Depression: A feeling which the mind creates when: (1) conflict over a course of action exists, the person then giving up and *depressing* their feelings; (2) the conclusion that one has major problems, this causing a person to *depress* their feelings; (3) the memory of having repeatedly failed as a child which causes a person to give up and *depress* their feelings. One or any combination of these factors arouses depression. This, like anxiety, is a common though painful experience and best studied not feared.

Diagnosis: the shorthand professional description of what is clinically wrong.

DSM: the Diagnostic and Statistical Manual, a widely used mental health classification which, to gain reliability, is behaviorally based and *atheoretical*, or non-explanatory, in nature. The ICD, International Classification of Diseases, contains both psychological and physical disorders and is also used in diagnosis.

Encopresis: fecal soiling, reflecting the unconscious desire to return to an earlier period of life when fewer demands for mature behavior were made. Essentially, the child wants to begin life anew.

Enuresis: "bed-wetting," which reflects both an indirect expression of angry feelings and, like encopresis though to a lesser degree, the desire to return to an earlier period of life when fewer demands for greater maturity of behavior were made.

Homicidal Ideation: the thought of wanting to kill another person. Here, as when evaluating suicidal thoughts, the important factors as to whether hospitalization is required are whether the homicidal intent, plan, and means are serious, and adequate self-control exists

Hysterical: a personality disorder in which the predominant psychological defense is repression and there is difficulty tolerating strong feelings, these tending to be expressed in physical disorders or exaggerated ("hysterical") emotional outbursts.

Narcissistic: a personality disorder characterized by grandiosity, envy, and the feeling of being special and entitled to favorable treatment.

Nervous Tic: a symptom of anxiety which spontaneously disappears when the anxiety lessens.

Neurosis: a conflict between parts of the personality, as when a person both wants and fears intimacy.

Nightmare: a frightening dream which we create to tell ourselves that there are emotional matters troubling us. All dreams, even when painful, are intended to be helpful for they are only attempting to tell us what we are worrying about though in disguised form, like a mystery movie or a puzzle which we can solve to learn our conflict.

Obsessive-Compulsive Disorder: the use of obsessive-compulsive psychological defenses to lower the level of anxiety by using an obsession (a recurring worry, as whether one has locked the door) or compulsion (a recurring behavior, as continually cleaning). The use of these defenses is not usually noticed unless the anxiety is great. Some very successful people are highly obsessive.

Oppositional Defiant Disorder: one of the most common childhood mental health diagnoses. Refusing parent or teacher directives as an indirect way of expressing angry feelings and communicating unhappiness, with the hope and expectation of gaining help.

Panic Attack: a severe anxiety experience during which the symptoms are misinterpreted as reflecting physical and not psychological distress

Phobia: an unrealistic fear caused by a frightening experience, or one which the mind creates to symbolize an emotional conflict which the person fears to confront.

Personality Disorder: a persisting pattern of self-defeating behavior which is not easily changed.

Play Therapy: a treatment technique which is used with children who are most comfortable communicating during and through play.

Posttraumatic Stress Disorder: lingering symptoms which the mind tries to integrate after experiencing overwhelming stress.

Psychiatrist: a medical doctor who treats mental health difficulties.

Psychoanalyst: a psychotherapist who treats mental health difficulties using such psychoanalytic concepts as the unconscious, resistance, transference, ego structure and ego defense.

Psychologist: a psychotherapist with a doctorate (Ph. D. or Psy. D.) degree.

Psychosis: a severe weakness of those basic ego capacities which govern the ability to distinguish reality from fantasy, to control thinking and behavior, to modulate mood, and to develop an adequate sense of who one is ("sense of self").

Psychotherapist: a general term for one who treats mental health problems. This term is not legally protected so anyone may call themselves a psychotherapist.

Psychotherapy: the treatment of mental health difficulties.

Psychotropic Medication: medication which is used to treat mental health disorders.

Social Worker: a psychotherapist who holds an M.S.W. or D.S.W. degree.

Suicidal Ideation: the thought of wanting to kill oneself, its seriousness being determined by the strength of the suicidal intent, whether the suicidal plan is realistic, if the means of causing suicide exist, and the degree of self-control which the person possesses.

Symptom (mental health): a statement or behavior which indicates unhappiness or emotional conflict.

www.ingramcontent.com/pod-product-compliance
Lightning Source LLC
Chambersburg PA
CBHW030003290326
41934CB00005B/201